DEMOCRACY AND THE POLITICS OF SILENCE

RHETORIC AND DEMOCRATIC DELIBERATION
VOLUME 35

EDITED BY CHERYL GLENN AND STEPHEN BROWNE
THE PENNSYLVANIA STATE UNIVERSITY

Co-founding Editor: J. Michael Hogan

EDITORIAL BOARD:

Robert Asen (University of Wisconsin–Madison)
Debra Hawhee (The Pennsylvania State University)
J. Michael Hogan (The Pennsylvania State University)
Peter Levine (Tufts University)
Steven J. Mailloux (Loyola Marymount University)
Krista Ratcliffe (Marquette University)
Karen Tracy (University of Colorado, Boulder)
Kirt Wilson (The Pennsylvania State University)
David Zarefsky (Northwestern University)

Rhetoric and Democratic Deliberation focuses on the interplay of public discourse, politics, and democratic action. Engaging with diverse theoretical, cultural, and critical perspectives, books published in this series offer fresh perspectives on rhetoric as it relates to education, social movements, and governments throughout the world.

A complete list of books in this series is located at the back of this volume.

# DEMOCRACY AND THE POLITICS OF SILENCE

MÓNICA BRITO VIEIRA

The Pennsylvania State University Press | University Park, Pennsylvania

This volume is published with the generous support of the Center for Democratic Deliberation at the Pennsylvania State University.

Library of Congress Cataloging-in-Publication Data

Names: Brito Vieira, Mónica, author.
Title: Democracy and the politics of silence / Mónica Brito Vieira.
Other titles: Rhetoric and democratic deliberation ; v. 35.
Description: University Park, Pennsylvania : The Pennsylvania State University Press, [2025] | Series: Rhetoric and democratic deliberation ; volume 35 | Includes bibliographical references and index.
Summary: "Investigates the largely overlooked role of silence in democratic politics to argue that silence can help support fundamental democratic goods and produce democratic subjectivities bearing a promise of new beginnings"—Provided by publisher.
Identifiers: LCCN 2024039649 | ISBN 9780271098883 (hardback)
Subjects: LCSH: Democracy. | Silence—Political aspects.
Classification: LCC JC423 .B7847 2025 | DDC 321.8—dc23/eng/20240904
LC record available at https://lccn.loc.gov/2024039649

Copyright © 2025 Mónica Brito Vieira
All rights reserved
Printed in the United States of America
Published by The Pennsylvania State University Press, University Park, PA 16802–1003

The Pennsylvania State University Press is a member of the Association of University Presses.

It is the policy of The Pennsylvania State University Press to use acid-free paper. Publications on uncoated stock satisfy the minimum requirements of American National Standard for Information Sciences—Permanence of Paper for Printed Library Material, ANSI Z39.48–1992.

*Each day I pray into the silence. I pray to all of them. All of them who are not here. Into this emptiness, I pour all my desire and want and need, and in time this absence becomes potent and alive and activated with a promise.*
—Nick Cave

CONTENTS

Acknowledgments | ix

Introduction | 1

1  Unsaying | 23

2  Silence's Freedoms | 38

3  Self-Silencing and Social Silences | 61

4  Silent Sisterhood | 86

5  The Silences of Constitutions | 118

6  Representing Silence | 137

7  The Silence of Nature | 165

Conclusion | 187

Notes | 195

References | 201

Index | 217

## ACKNOWLEDGMENTS

While researching and writing this book, I had some of the hardest and most turbulent years of my life. The book was a place of refuge when things got too tough or out of control. Several interruptions occurred during its writing, and this has meant that it has taken longer than originally planned. During those years, I have acquired quite a few debts of gratitude, which I can never repay. The least I can do is to acknowledge and show my appreciation for the people who have supported and believed in me.

First, I would like to acknowledge the British Academy for its funding of the research. Funding is the lifeblood of thinking that takes risks and tests unlikely ideas. The British Academy dares to do, and for this reason alone it remains an invaluable institution.

Special thanks, too, are owed to the Department of Politics of the University of York, for its support of the project when I needed it most, and in particular to Martin Smith, its previous head of department, and Nina Caspersen, its current one. My department has provided a wonderful place in which to work, and I am grateful for its collegiality and its generous sabbatical policy, which allowed me to see the book project through to completion. I am lucky to be surrounded by a group of very talented political theorists at York, who are a constant source of inspiration and who offered critical suggestions on some of the chapters. Special thanks are owed to Matthew Festenstein and Alfred Moore for reading through the whole manuscript and providing valuable comments. Despite all its struggles, academia—as that metaphorical grove of trees where ideas and arguments are shared—is alive and well. Thanks in particular to the group of scholars working on silence who joined me at York for a workshop in the early stages of the book: Sean Gray, Theo Jung, Karsten Lichau, Mihaela Mihai, and Toby Rollo. Conversations with them helped clarify my ideas and open up some new areas of research. Their insights and their work have fed deeply into this project. My students are a constant source of learning and motivation for doing the work I do. A thank you to them. I am grateful to the people at Penn State University Press, especially Patrick Alexander, Ryan Peterson, Kendra Boileau, Archna Patel, Josie DiNovo, Laura Reed-Morrisson, and Regina Ann Starace.

They have offered unfailing support, enthusiasm, and forbearance throughout the writing of this book. To Joe Davidson, a big thank you for editing the manuscript in an insightful and helpful fashion.

I would also like to express my deepest thanks to Filipe Carreira da Silva for his friendship, encouragement, and intellectual companionship. Without him, I could not have gotten this far, or perhaps even started. Few projects are ever completed alone, and he, alongside my father and my brother—perhaps without knowing it—is the bedrock of this one.

A final thank you to Culturgest for allowing me to reproduce on the cover of the book *Ouve-me* (Listen to me; 1979), a photo panel by the Portuguese artist Helena Almeida (1934–2018). The striking sequence of images shows a detail of a face, with a woman's mouth adopting different positions, and the word *ouve* (listen) drawn on the lips like a suture. While in some images the lips look as if they were sewn together, in others, the mouth and tongue adopt playful positions. Lip-sewing has in recent years become associated with protest enacted through self-harm. But in Almeida's artwork, the mouth's repetition with a difference dispels such readings. The photo sequence is serious and humorous at the same time. It evokes silencing but it also performs silence to operate the former's ironic inversion.

As this project is brought to a close, it seems only fitting to make special mention of those who were there at the beginning but did not live to see it finished: my uncle, my grandmother, my mother. They made me who I am, but I am afraid I always managed to fall short of their delicacy, lovingkindness, and strength. It is sometimes difficult to see the absence they left behind as something activated with promise. But I keep trying—and my son, who, in his instinctive humanity and gentleness, reminds me of them every day, is beauty enough. I like to think that the three of you are watching over us and know that we will be okay. This book is for you.

An earlier version of chapter 6 appeared as "Representing Silence in Politics" in *American Political Science Review* 114 (2020): 976–88. Reprinted with permission from Cambridge University Press. © Cambridge University Press. I am grateful to the editors and publisher for permission to reprint that article here.

# INTRODUCTION

Silence is nothing merely negative; it is not the mere absence of speech.
It is a positive, a complete world in itself.
—Max Picard, *The World of Silence*

This is a book about silence as a fundamental dimension of democratic life. As simple as the statement may sound, it is also wrapped in paradox. The constitutive coincidence between politics and speech is one of the—if not *the*—most firmly established principles of politics. Hannah Arendt makes the point most poignantly: "Wherever the relevance of speech is at stake, matters become political by definition, for speech is what makes man a political being" (1958, 9).

Arendt's words have a long pedigree. Aristotle was the first to deem humans political: they had speech on their side and used speech to figure out how to live together. For Aristotle, speech underpins a distinctively human form of sociality based on reasoned and communicative judgments about "the advantageous and the harmful and hence also the just and the unjust" (1996, 1253a8). With Aristotle, speech developed into more than just a feature defining the human species. It became synonymous with the polis itself, now understood as an association in speech for the pursuit of the good and the just.

The Aristotelian view of speech as that which constitutes and has the power to endow political existence with normative value is not just a descriptive claim. It is an evaluative claim about what politics is and what it is about. As such, it is an instance of politics itself, responsible for shaping how we have come to see politics and what it is that we see—and do not see—when we look at it.

With speech elevated to the reason proper to politics, what lies outside speech has been exiled from politics. Athena Athanasiou writes, "Silent or vocal articulations that do not conform to the disciplinary semantics of proper language" have been "excluded from the lexicon of politics" and "relegated to the pre-political or anti-political, [deemed] either irrelevant or subversive" (2017, 260).

This is how silence has figured until recently, when it has figured at all, in the study of politics: as a dangerous outside or a negligible spare. Practically associated with negativity—failure, absence, lack—silence has found itself marginalized as the kind of *no-*thing that naturally and unproblematically might escape the field of political perception.

The route taking us to this point is clear. In politics, one studies political *things*. Speech has been cast as *the* thing of politics, the way it is done, the way we partake in it. Silence, its opposite. The established asymmetry between speech and silence as the figure and ground of politics is explained not just by our understanding of what counts as politics but also by methodological limitations that determine, and ensue from, the conceptualization of silence as *no-*thing. For how might one recognize, let alone study, a *no-*thing, a *non-*occurrence, something that is *absent*? How might one study that which leaves no trail, of which there is no evidence? The conventional answer is that silence is unfit for study (Zerubavel 2006, 13; Schröter 2013, 42). Figured as a cognitive threshold, it is a barrier that cannot be crossed.

What I have said about politics in general applies with special force to democratic politics. Democracy is founded on equality with regard to speech. This comprises the equality of every speaking citizen with every other speaking citizen and their equal right to address each other in public deliberation. With vocal citizenship the norm, both in the sense of being considered desirable and "the norm," vocal processes of activism and decision-making—however rare they might be in citizens' everyday experience—have set the ideal of democracy (J. Green 2010, 11). Accordingly, democratic theorists have mapped out the distinction between political participation and political nonparticipation to speech and silence, respectively (Barry 1974, 91). "If speech is action," they have surmised, "then silence is failure to act" (Langton 1993, 314).

Within vocal models of citizen empowerment, speech does all the work of democracy while providing its legitimating ground. It is through involvement in discursive exchanges, where they discuss issues affecting them in their daily lives, that citizens make their needs, interests, and concerns heard; clarify differences and preferences; construct commonalities; and raise their voices. Citizens then secure the translation of those needs, interests, and concerns—via the formation of public opinion and the choice of representatives who speak on their behalf—from the public sphere to the political system and from this to political decision. Against such an understanding of citizenship as participation and influence in processes of verbal communication, silent citizenship emerges as a troubling anomaly, even an oxymoron. As the absence of speech, silence cuts democracy off from its life and blood. In the words of Robert Dahl, "Silent citizens may be perfect subjects for an authoritarian ruler; they would be a disaster for democracy" (1998, 97).

And thus the idea advanced in this book, that citizens may practice and mobilize silence to advance key democratic desiderata, finds itself discounted upfront in the theoretical and empirical literature. Instead, scholars have come to view silence as a threat to the workings of democracy—or at best a form of rational indifference. Where silence has been indulged, this has been for doubtful democratic reasons: namely, as a quiescence protecting the democratic political system from democratic excess, an "overload" of popular mobilization (Huntington 1975, 114).

The pursuant belief that silence is the site where democracy comes to die has been, if anything, reinforced by well-rehearsed topoi of silence as a domain of illegitimate "secrecy (arcanum), shielding the machinations of the powerful from public scrutiny and the need for justification" (T. Jung 2019, 426); as oppressive, or something we suffer that deprives us of political voice; as unthinking, apathetic, quiescent, or something that we just let happen; as self-serving, or free-riding on others' political participation; or as blameworthy, because complicit in others' political wrongdoing. Each and every one of these claims, while not necessarily dismissed, is critically interrogated in this book. Together they present a one-dimensional view of political silence that has emptied it of any positive normative force.

By turning my focus to political silence, I have no intention of denying that democratic life presupposes that we engage one another, and key aspects of our world, with speech. Nor do I wish to disclaim the possibility that citizen silence can, on many occasions, undercut the possibility of that engagement. The democratic life of silence—just like that of speech—is complex, something that will hopefully be clear from my parallel discussions of democracy-promoting and democracy-hindering silences, world-making and violent speech. But behind my shift in focus from speech to silence is my desire to demonstrate that silence is not just the condition for all our speech but also a practice and mode of relating that is vital to democratic subjectivities and the good workings of democracy.

In claiming this much, I will also be critically engaging with some of the democratically limiting effects of speech-centrism and the single-minded view of the democratic public as "normatively locutionary" (K. Ferguson 2003, 54). One such effect is the exclusion of non-locutionary citizens (and non-locutionary entities, more generally) from the politics of the *polis*, an exclusion that is not confined to, but reaches its extreme in, the case of those affected by loss or impairment of speech (Rollo 2017, 2019). Think, for instance, of how the expression "deaf-mute" continues to be used to imply that the Deaf, Deafblind, Deafdisabled, hard of hearing, and late-deafened people are silent, without voice, without capacity for communication, perhaps even without capacity for reasoned thinking. This comes across most emphatically in the common use of "dumb" to mean both lacking the power of speech and dull-witted. Where spoken language is favored and posited as the way to overcome their current exclusion, the agency of Deaf people is once again bypassed, and they are excluded from shaping new beginnings. Their recognition and inclusion as political actors in their own right, who may actively participate in changing the very political reality that excludes them, must thus start from the recognition of the possibility of political action outside of speech rather than the insistence on political subjectivation and mobilization through speech alone. The silencing of the Deaf is a pathology of ableism. As Ukrainian-born Deaf poet Ilya Kaminsky reminds us: "The deaf don't believe in silence. Silence is the invention of the hearing" (Kaminsky 2019, 79). It is also a pathology of a speech-centric politics. Although this book does not delve into the politics of deafness, it intersects with it in its call for an acknowledgment of the richness of the ways in which people may act politically without speech despite, or even because of, their lack of engagement in speech-action.

Distilling the main purpose of *Democracy and the Politics of Silence* into a few words, I would say that it seeks to raise silence next to speech as a fundamental yet still largely overlooked dimension of democratic life and to force the admission of political silence into the "repertoire of good democratic practice" (MacKenzie and Moore 2020, 432). I am not entirely alone in this effort. In recent years, it has taken on some importance within political theory (see K. Ferguson 2003; Acheson 2008; Jungkunz 2011, 2012, 2013; Gray 2015, 2019, 2021, 2023; Khatchadourian 2015; Guillaume 2018; T. Jung 2019; Rollo 2019; Freeden 2022). While I am indebted to the work of these political theorists, my work differs from theirs in important aspects (Brito Vieira et al. 2019; Brito Vieira 2020b). Given my focus on silence's democratic potential, I study its relationship with voice, agency, participation, representation—all main components of democracy. The book seeks to distinguish between good and bad, desirable and undesirable silences from a democratic point of view, and its chapters look into different hallmarks of democracy that silence can help promote: empowerment, non-domination, inclusion, equality, reciprocity, and connection across difference. As I shall show, besides assisting in the realization of these goods, democracy-promoting silences help us embrace and productively engage democracy more generally as a politics of openness, freedom, and questioning.

There have been few, if any, comprehensive, book-length attempts by political theorists to examine silence and evaluate its significance for politics. The most recent exception is Michael Freeden's *Concealed Silences and Inaudible Voices in Political Thinking* (2022), which shows an expansive, panoramic interest in "the intertwinement of silence with political thinking" (8) and a more specific focus on "hidden—*silenced, concealed silences*" (17). Distinguishing itself by its examination of the nexus between silence and democracy, my book also sets itself apart by its emphasis on the political meaning of agentic silences, both individual and collective (chapters 1 through 5), and the politics of assigning silence to others, both human and nonhuman (chapters 6 and 7).

Some theorists whose interest has turned, like mine, to the silence-democracy nexus have either focused on institutional settings (Gray 2021) or "insubordinate silences" (Jungkunz 2012). While this book devotes some of its chapters to constitutions and representative institutions (chapters 5, 6, and 7), it takes a broader view of democracy as involving not just institutions but distinctive identities and subjectivities, understandings and practices of power, and a characteristic ethics and practice of mutual engagement. Similarly, while I address insubordinate silences that resist power, my analysis deliberately departs from what I find to be a restrictive silence-resistance framing, which limits the political significance of silence to non-domination (W. Brown 1996; Gray 2023; for the traditional view of silence as "the weapon of the weak" and its conflation with resistance, see J. Scott 1985, 1990). To assimilate silence to resistance is impoverishing because, first, it suggests that silent political agency is exclusive to some groups (namely, the powerless) and to some settings (notably, those where the costs of exercising voice are particularly high); second, it induces a reading of silent political agency as necessary in the struggle for democracy but not as integral to its good functioning; and third, it configures silence as reactive rather than productive, a freedom from but never a freedom *to* construct oneself and the world otherwise. By contrast, it is this book's aim to foreground silence's performative and generative dimensions, seeking to make true Kennan Ferguson's call for a silence that "does not merely reinforce or resist power, but can be used to constitute selves and even communities" (2003, 49).

To bring political silence back into focus, I need to render its theoretical contours and conceptual content more clearly. However, I intend to offer a theorization of silence that avoids the detailed typologies and taxonomies that have become common in studies of political silence. It has been rightly observed that "if there is no exit from the political world, then political silence must be as active and colorful as a bright summer shadow" (Eliasoph 1998, 6), where multiple layers of silence interact and coexist. Any attempt to classify all of political silences' color gradients and to keep them separate, in their classificatory boxes, is therefore condemned to failure. It "risks limiting itself to the purely additive: finding and filling in ever more minute 'blank spots' on the periphery of the map of political research" (T. Jung 2021, 296).

New to political theory, theorizations of silence have traditionally been constructed outside it, in other disciplines, and fall into four main categories: the ontological approach (Picard 1952; Dauenhauer 1980); the epistemological approach (Polanyi 1969, 2009; Kalamaras 1994; Ratcliffe 2005); the linguistic approach (Jaworski 1993; Kurzon 1998), and the rhetorical approach (Glenn 2004; Brummett 1980). In the ontological approach, the emphasis is on the essential characteristics of silence and silence's fundamental significance. The epistemological approach focuses instead on silence as a tacit mode of knowing or, alternatively, as a mode of promoting understanding. Linguistic approaches to silence are the most dominant. They flourish within communication studies and typically focus on the functions performed by silence in communication. Rhetorical approaches concentrate instead on the rhetorical forms, strategies, and effects of silence as a mode of symbolic expression.

The body of research developed in other disciplines is rich and robust, but my understanding of silence departs from it in significant ways. While I embrace the ontological approach's treatment of silence as not merely a negative or derivative phenomenon, I reject its essentialism. I do not take silence to have an essence, a set of invariable characteristics that give it an ultimate ontological significance or a specific valence, whether positive or negative. I am also far less concerned with the question of what silence *is* than with what silence *does*—or, more specifically, the political roles and functions it might perform, what one might politically do with and through it (for the notion of silence-as-doing, see Guillaume 2018). Despite my primary interest in silences that performatively do non-speech, I, like the proponents of the epistemic view, take a keen interest in those silences we make about things we know or care about but collaborate, consciously or unconsciously, in unrecognizing or (seemingly) ignoring. But it is not their epistemic qualities that interest me the most. Michael Polanyi, from whom the epistemic view of silence is commonly derived, understood tacit knowledge as consisting of forms of expertise and ways of conducting oneself that cannot be taught through a verbal formal exchange. In this book, my interest turns instead to processes of collaboration that "may include (but are not limited) to [tacitly] shared knowledge" and the ways in which they may "structure and sustain sociality" (Decena 2011, 20). The silences of the unsaid, of the tacit, of things known, understood, or implied but left unstated, contrast with the silences of the deliberately unspoken privileged by communicative approaches. While I embrace their view that the relationship between silence and speech is hardly one of uncomplicated opposition or necessary alternative, and while I take on their view of silence as articulating speech in more than one way, I see the notion of silence-as-signal they broadly embrace as reductive. Its merit lies in emphasizing the communicative features of withholding speech. Rather than the Other of speech, silence understood as signal is an instance of it: a kind of speech act and thus "part of [our] communicative system" (Jaworski 1993, xii). But to reduce silence to a signal of something else is to perpetuate its subordination to that other and to mask the ways in which silence—as a form of communicating *without* speaking—is and acts unlike speech. From the study of silence within rhetoric, I am most drawn to its attention to forms of inter-natural, creaturely communication (Menely 2015; Hawhee 2017); silence and listening as rhetorical devices integral to effective communication (Glenn and Ratcliffe 2011); and to the constitutive power dynamics of silence and the complex institutional relations determining "who speaks, who remains silent, who listens, and what those listeners can do" (Glenn 2004, 23). Similarly, I am interested in the *politics* of silence and in resisting the facile equation of speech with empowerment and silence with disempowerment. But I find the treatment of silence as the deliberately unspoken, or a mode of symbolic expression that may be used tactically and strategically, restrictive: it tends to recognize silence only insofar as it *acts* like a mode of symbolic expression and a means to specified ends (Glenn 2004). Also, as a work of political theory whose purpose is to examine ways in which silence may be mobilized and practiced to further (or hamper) democratic desiderata, this book takes democracy to be neither exhausted, nor always best achieved, by political talk or, indeed, by the confinement of silence to "an integral component in the making and delivery of rhetoric, as persuasion, understanding, invitation, or something else" (Glenn 2004, 153).

It is common to distinguish between two different strands of silence: silence as an acoustic phenomenon and silence as a human practice. The focus of this book is the latter, and that is what I will be calling "silence" proper (as contrasted with "quietude"). But the acoustic dimensions of silence as practice, which often involves keeping quiet, will remain relevant to my study. To understand silence as an embodied practice, that is, as a practice involving the body as both "subject—as the basis from which we experience the world—and the body as object—that can be actively manipulated, silenced" (Hardon and Posel 2012, S1), I contend, requires an understanding of how we experiment—or fail to experiment—with the senses and of democracy as a realm of not just signification but also sensation. The sense of hearing and a haptic sensibility cannot be left behind in making sense of how silence acts politically.

Here I want to return briefly to something I mentioned earlier, citing Kaminsky's *Deaf Republic* (2019): that silence is the invention of the hearing. As Kaminsky stresses, for the non-hearing there is no such thing as silence. Unlike the hearing, the non-hearing perceive the world unhindered by the dualisms that are ubiquitous in hearing people's accounts of silence. The hearing, who perceive by the ear, invent the idea of sound as well as its opposite, the idea of silence. For the non-hearing, by contrast, there is no such thing as sound and therefore no such thing as silence. As such, where deafness is taken on its own terms rather than as the opposite of hearing, it takes us past the hearing's "invention" of silence to reveal itself as anything but "silent." The Deaf experience sound as sight-signal—"I do not hear gunshots, / but watch birds splash over the backyards of the suburbs" (Kaminsky 2019, 76)—and as touch-signal through feeling the vibrations of sound. The Deaf also have their own sign languages, through which they articulate and express "sentiments, thoughts and wishes, the most diverse and opposed" (Sciacca 1957, 250). Yet from the perspective of the hearing, the phrase "mute silence" is regarded as a tautology. Kaminsky underscores this in the last page of "Deaf Republic" by presenting his readers with what they might take for "silence": a page with no words, lines, or verse, just four illustrations of hands making signs without captions. Readers who took notice of the captions accompanying the hand signs graphically depicted throughout the book will be able to decode the four signs, to allow them to speak, to provide uptake. Other readers will encounter them as "silence"—that invention of the hearing. Dualism, the hearing's contracted disability, is brought into full relief against the contrasting background of deafness as ability.

The power of "Deaf Republic" lies in its opening up to a world unconstrained by the antinomies in which silence finds itself trapped. Although this book engages a similar project, it does not pursue it by dissolving the category of silence altogether.[1] Silence as practice, I submit, is something that presupposes and must be understood with reference to particular capacities or faculties. Just as quiet presupposes and must be understood with reference to one's hearing ability or capacity to perceive sound otherwise, so silence presupposes and asks to be understood with reference to the capacity to act through speech or language more generally. Muteness—either as a form of apraxia or as a medical condition impacting the physical structures involved in spoken speech—implies incapacity and may thus seem incompatible with silence as I understand it. But insofar as muteness does not preclude capacity for language or communication, the mute can practice silence. This much is acknowledged by Kaminsky, who does not abandon the notion of silence in the poem.[2]

"Deaf Republic" tells the story of an imaginary town, Vasenka, that fell under violent occupation. After a young deaf boy gets brutally killed by the occupying forces, the population chooses deafness over hearing, silence over speaking. Whether their silence and their deafness result from an actual physical change that happens to them remains somewhat unclear. What is clear is that both are—at least at first—meant as acts of resistance.[3] As resistance, their deafness is not an inability to hear but the act of withholding hearing as a refusal to acknowledge the occupying forces.[4] Similarly, their silence reflects not an inability for language use or comprehension but their withholding of communication from the new authorities. In effect, the inhabitants of Vasenka keep developing their own sign language out of a mix of different sign languages and made-up signs. Occupiers encounter this unknown language as silence. Its users form community through it while also preventing soldiers from prying. To underscore my point: silence as practice implies ability, the existence of actual or potential hearers or speakers, with (at least) the potentiality to hear or engage in verbal or nonverbal communication. It is only where such potentiality is present that one can speak of silence proper as the (conscious or unconscious) suspension of the actualization of the potentiality to not-hear or indeed to not-speak, not-say, not-share, not-make-common.

Taking silence as practice for its object, this book approaches silence as a historical, sociocultural, and political phenomenon. We know political concepts are contested by nature. While there are disagreements regarding silence's meaning and application, silence appears strangely decontested, naturalized, shaped in ways that might lead one to believe that it has no politics or history. Like dimensions of space and time, silence can appear to be an entity in itself rather than a social and political construction. It is the purpose of this book to show otherwise: to reveal silence to have a social and political history (as something highly politically contested) and to illuminate the ways in which it is regularly mobilized to perform political functions and purposes (Freeden 2022, 46).

There is a depth to the history and politics of silence that cannot be captured by definition. I must begin with a working definition of silence, however. Ideally, to break away from the speech/silence binary one would define silence not in relation to speech but on its own terms. But if I am correct that "silence" is the invention of the speaking, then "silence" cannot be cut off conceptually from its relation to the capacity to act through speech or language more generally. It is rather the case that this relation needs probing and questioning. Hence, my working definition of silence emphasizes the nonperformance of speech and the modes of social and political interaction structured by it. I must make three immediate observations, however. First, by "nonperformance" I do not mean literally not speaking—that is, that speech is not being used. Although silence might imply abstention from speech or verbal language, I take "nonperformance of speech" to include the following: selective abstinence from speech, that is, silence about something, "because a specific [expected] message or theme is absent [ . . . ] or because a particular group or individual fails to be addressed" (T. Jung 2019, 428); speech being used so as not-to-say, to speak away, to unsay; and instances where speech is used but deemed incomprehensible or refused uptake. Second, although my definition may seem close to conventional definitions of silence as a form of "abstention," "withholding," or "forbearing," I reject their common implication that silence is a negative rather than a positive phenomenon, that the nonperformance of speech may not constitute a substantive action or set of actions. On the contrary, as will become apparent, I take silence as a means of communication, expression, action, and interaction in its own right. Third, when distinguishing between democratic and nondemocratic silences, the key question I will be asking is whether the practice of silence may be justified on normative democratic grounds, with the democratic intentions of silence producers—as well as the relational and systemic effects of their practice of silence—taken into consideration.

Starting from my understanding of silence as a practice, I want to establish a relatively simple distinction between commissive and omissive silences. These refer to agentic silences of "doing/being a non-something" and broadly non-agentic silences of "not doing/not being something," respectively (S. Scott 2018, 3, 15). It would be tempting, but incorrect, to equate this distinction with silences that imply or exclude action. That commissive silences imply action is relatively straightforward, though not something necessarily acknowledged in the theoretical and empirical literature on democracy, given its assumption that political action entails speech and speech entails political action, both in the sense of being a form of action itself and the form that political action takes. Yet the potential to do, which we normally take as power, "implies and complies with the power not to do" or the *"positive* action of nonperformance" (Connor 2019, 4; my emphasis). Commissive silence is agentic in this way: we have discursive potential, but we may choose not to act through speech. That is, we may consider and reject the normatively expected action—speech— "through conscious disengagement or disidentification" (S. Scott 2018, 5). Critically, in the case of commissive silence, we choose to act through silence instead. Here silence constitutes one's elective form of action—a positive action of nonperformance. Rather than a barrier to action, it is a substantive action itself, a performative doing of "non-speech." Commissive or elective silence thus constitutes a conscious, reflexive "doing" in a double sense: it involves *doing* or *being* a non-something (not-speaking, non-speaker) out of a *positive* decision not to do, but it also involves doing something *in* and *through* electing silence (this includes positive actions of avoidance, abstention, withdrawal, yielding, giving way, listening, and deferring to as well as a vast array of more affirmative actions of protesting, questioning, performing identity, being-with, and being-present differently). Critically, as I show in the book, this means that commissive silence is a doing/being a non-something that can be powerfully affirmative of democratic agency even where (and sometimes *because*) it acts by deliberately attenuating speech-agency—and that rather than denying political presence, participation, identity, or community, it can form the basis of all of these. Democratic theory has led us to exclude this possibility because in taking speech for political action and silence for speech's opposite, it has cast the latter as inactive. However, the conclusion that to do silence is to do nothing says more about democratic theory's blind spots than about silence: democratic theory's logocentrism entails an insensibility to the *act* of performing silence and the many nonverbal, embodied actions enacted *in* and *through* it.

Surprisingly, perhaps, given the dominant equation of speech with action, omissive forms of silence are modes of "not-doing/not-being something [speech and a speaker] (through *acts* of omission)" (S. Scott 2018, 15). That is, omissive silences can and do involve action, too, sometimes even of a strenuous type. Failure to appreciate this, as has been rightly noted, results from the common exclusion of "unconscious or unintentional practices from the category of acts" (Freeden 2022, 20). This is a mistake, and it explains much of political science's discounting of silence from study and from the realm of relevant political phenomena. Take, for instance, what some have called the "social organization of silence and denial" (Zerubavel 2006, x). This refers to uncomfortable knowledge we hold but also, albeit mostly unconsciously, collaborate in suppressing or not speaking about. A case in point is the looming environmental crisis and how it may fail to break through into citizens' political conversations (Norgaard 2011). Another instance of this is so-called political apathy. Normally taken for a form of inaction or private withdrawal, in-depth qualitative studies show that citizens work hard at producing it, that is, at avoiding the expression of political concern in public (Eliasoph 1998). "Not speaking" in these cases is omissive, a not-doing, a way of avoiding political engagement. But it is also a not-doing that takes considerable individual effort and cooperative work to sustain, including complex processes of social interaction underpinning the creation, reproduction, and management of the silences of denial or avoidance over time.

Commissive and omissive silences are ideal types and thus not necessarily discrete entities in practice. They often work on a spectrum of unfolding co-extensivity. At the outer extreme of the scale of omissive silences, however, we find silences that not only constitute a failure to act but verge on an acquired dis-ability. Take, for instance, anticipatory exclusion, or a citizen's decision not to take part in political discussions owing to the anticipation of being excluded (Fung 2004, 49). What might start as a silent act of refusal can easily slide into a condition or state of being. Repeated failure of uptake creates such social pathologies of misrecognition—including a sense of purposelessness and lack of political efficacy—that individuals may find themselves not just unwilling to take part but thrown into a resigned, speechless condition "by default rather than conscious intention" (S. Scott 2018, 5).

Silence, therefore, runs all the way from a positive action of nonperformance presupposing an intentional or conscious aiming at ends (and a relative mastery of the operations necessary to attain them) to a largely intentionless and unconscious disposition, "the effect of the incorporation of structural violence into the body which is then lived in the euphemised form of a habitus of acceptance or resignation," or what I will be referring to as "silencing" in chapter 3 (McNay 2012, 236). Much *practice* of silence, we will see, lies between these two poles. In shedding light on this in-between, the study of citizen silent agency offers a welcome counterbalance to sovereigntist views of agency often associated with vocal models of popular empowerment, constructing the autonomous subject as self-speaking and self-transparent and will-formation as sovereign, purposive action.

As happens with other political actions, silence as a nonperformance of speech or a simultaneous nonperformance of speech and performance of other (nonverbal) actions may require considerable skill. As a practice and a mode of interaction, silence assumes different forms in different contexts, with different motivations and effects. Given this diversity and given that silence implies a "non-element" (either "doing or being a non-something" or "not-doing/being something"), it requires careful identification and interpretation. In my analysis of practices of silence, I will be looking into silence-makers' intentions and motivations where they are retrievable, and, even where they aren't, interrogating the positionality, location, and context (discursive and otherwise) of the silences they make. But intentions and motivations, even where silences are consciously agential, are only partially determinant. Equally, if not more, determinant are audiences and contexts of reception and what happens between the two. My analysis will not assume, then, that performed silences are "signs whose meanings are fixed, obvious, and in conformity with the exact intentions of the subjects who carry them out," and instead I will turn my attention to what those silences "do, with effects that are ultimately undecidable in advance" (Bargu 2022, 298).

Understood as the nonperformance of speech, silence is inherently relational as "nonperformance" and will only be registerable against audience expectations, namely, negated "specific *expectations* of 'voice'" or verbal expression (T. Jung 2021, 297). That is, it is against context and a structure of mutual expectations that someone (an individual or group) may (or may not) be experienced, recognized, or interpreted as performing an act of silence or as being silent. The relevant horizons of expectations here are the audience's, and they shape how audiences respond to silences. Audiences are not monolithic, however. This means that some audience members may perceive silence where others do not; that some may believe the silence perceived to be commissive or bear meaning where others do not; that silence that is not a sign, or effectively produced so as not to be a sign, can be taken for a signal of omitted speech and engaged as such (Block de Behar 1995, 7; T. Jung 2019, 429); and that different meanings may be attributed to silence even by those concurring in its perception as meaningful. What this means, ultimately, is that except in strongly coded or institutional contexts, there is no non-perspectival way of drawing the distinction between commissive and omissive silences, between silences that are doings and silences that are not, between silences that constitute the sign of something and those that signal nothing at all. In chapter 5, I explore this perspectival feature by reference to things we would expect to see in constitutions: a striking example is secession, whose absence from constitutional texts looks like an omission but can be seen—by seceders or interpreters taking the constitution as setting the ground rules of a liberal democratic order—as a commission. An important implication of the evolving experiences and expectations of silence is that its meaning is likely to be plural and shifting over time.

Accumulated experience and changing horizons of expectations—including the discursive, conceptual, and epistemological frameworks comprised therein—may widen an audience's capacity for the cognition and engagement of silence and make silence's "evidentiary trail" apparent, so to speak. Such frameworks can sometimes make silences (un)recognizable, even to their own producers. Let me provide two examples of silences rendered unrecognizable to audiences and to their producers, respectively. The first example has been famously discussed by Spivak: the story of the suicide of unmarried teenager Bhubaneswari Bhaduri in 1926. Spivak reads Bhaduri's suicide against *sati*-suicide, the practice of Hindu women killing themselves upon their husband's death. Because Bhaduri killed herself while menstruating and because menstruating widows were prohibited from committing suicide, Spivak interprets her suicide as commissive, as a political act rewriting "the social text of *sati*-suicide in an interventionist way" (Spivak 1988, 307). My concern is not whether Spivak's interpretation is correct (I leave that to others) but the broader question she raises, namely, that though Bhaduri might have intended her suicide to be a communicative act affirming her subjective existence and agency, hegemonic discourses deafened it; they could not reckon with her silence's "speakerly" nature and thus silenced her in death as they did in life. Within hegemonic discourse, Bhaduri could not be heard, understood, taken seriously, engaged as the source of valid claims. One is never fully in control of how one's actions will impact the world, as this depends on how others interpret and respond to them, be these speech- or silence-actions. In a context of social domination, social interpretation of an act is very unlikely to affirm the agent's understanding of it, and silence, however commissive, may be particularly vulnerable to distortion. If meaningful silence can remain unrecognizable to audiences, it can also go unrecognized by its own producers. For instance, in a society where intercourse taking place between husband and wife is conceived as a matter of a man's right and a woman's submission to an obligation, the lack of rape complaints by married women will not be perceived as "silence." It will not be perceived at all.

Interpretation is important not simply as a way for us to get at what producers were up to when making silence (if they were up to anything at all) or at whether and how audiences perceived, interpreted, and otherwise engaged silences. Besides being implicated in the quest for silence's meanings and doings, the interpretation—and prior to it, the assignment—of silence is itself a political act (Freeden 2022, 28). As chapters 6 and 7 in particular will show, assigning speechlessness to constituencies as well as claiming for oneself their silence's interpretation are consequential political acts, bearing risks of domination, erased agency, and displaced involvement, and they oftentimes eschew responsibility and accountability for one's own speech *for*, *about*, even "*instead of*" the (purportedly) silent (Freeden 2022, 98). A potential underside of political representation as the act of conferring voice to allegedly silent/silenced subjects, I will argue, is that representative claims can silence a constituency's silence, ventriloquize its imagined absent voice, or further undermine (where it exists, as it does in potentiality if not necessarily in actuality) its own ability to speak and be heard.

Now that I have introduced my working definition of silence, it is perhaps not too late to offer a cautionary gloss. Like a photograph that reveals itself against a photographic developer—the chemical(s) responsible for transforming a latent image into a visible one—silence is developed against specific expectations of voice or speech. But this does not mean that silence cannot be a form of voice, a modality of communication, or a site of meaning and expression in its own right. Nor does it mean that people don't "do things *with* [and *in*] silence" other than communicating (Rollo 2019, 437; see also Guillaume 2018; Guillaume and Schweiger 2019; Austin 1976). Let me take these in turn.

Silence has traditionally been rendered as the absence of speech, a result of abstaining from, forbearing, or forgoing it.[5] Part of the popular appeal of the notions of silence-as-abstention or silence-as-absence is their simple, reassuring, dualistic logic: speech is action/doing where silence is inaction/not-doing; speech is presence where silence is absence. The truth, however, is more complex and more interesting: silence is integral to speech and "never ceases to accompany it" (Merleau-Ponty 1973, 46). As one cannot be without the other, the hierarchical relation between speech and silence inevitably breaks down (Derrida 1978, 54). As Wendy Brown rightly put it, "silence and speech are not only constitutive of but also modalities of one another" (2005, 83–85). Both permutations—speaking silence and silencing speech—are possible, indicating that silence and speech live in what is "a continual, becoming, dialectical process" (Glennon 1983, 271; see also Clair 1998, 5).

The realization that meaningful silence and meaningful speech are realities, and coexisting ones at that, has led to the conceptualization of silence-as-signal. In this conceptualization, which has become dominant, silence is no longer just the omission of verbal signals but "what that omission signals in the context of communicative interaction" (Rollo 2019, 437). Accordingly, political silence can now be rendered as a meaningful absence of speech, which can "send signals and therefore be understood as a kind of voice" (Dovi 2020, 565). The turn away from silence-as-absence to embrace silence-as-signal represents a positive development, especially for someone who, like me, is interested in how silence may be democratically mobilized. It puts flesh to Max Picard's claim that "silence is not simply what happens when we stop talking. It is more than the mere negative renunciation of language" (1952, xix). Under silence-as-signal, silence is its own silent language and thus "not a gap in structure, but structure itself in the organization of interaction" (Philips 1985, 210).

The clarification introduced by silence-as-signal is helpful, but only as far as it goes. To start with, since the value of silence-as-signal—or communicative silence, as it is also sometimes called—is taken to lie in its ability to be or act like speech, speech action remains the exemplary form of political action, with the "speech value" of silence or nonpropositional speech being normally negatively assessed when compared to speech (see, for instance, Gray 2023, 824). As I have already hinted, although the concept of silence gains definition against the potentiality to speak, silence is not the absence of speech, nor is communication without speaking just another type of speech act. Silence-as-signal, however, is still trapped in defining silence exclusively in relation to speech and, what is more, on speech's terms. Second, and relatedly, even though silence may have a "speakerly" or "speechly" substance, and even though "silence only becomes a sign if one makes it speak" by following it "with a caption that gives it meaning" (Barthes 2005, 24, 26), silence does not always work as a sign, and much of its power—or doings—implies a capacity to resist speech determination. Let me take these in turn. While silence can constitute a sign with a meaning or determinable signified, as implied by the notion of silence-as-signal, it is important to note that silence can also be used to sidestep the demand for meaning, as in a "not-saying" or "non-reply" when one is being forced to speak, identify with (or as), or take a side. Also, as we shall see, to empty silence of signification may be necessary for it to become a bearer of potentiality, for instance, for it to restructure and reopen a discursive space that has been closed. Turning now to the view of silence acts as speech acts whose meaning is more or less fixed or can be determined against context, it is important to bear in mind that it is typical of silence to carry meaning that exceeds word captioning, to be open to more than one interpretation or not have one obvious meaning, to convey expression that exceeds and defies the speakable. There is, for instance, a physical and haptic quality to silence that makes us experience it as having a weight and a density, as filling a room or creating a tangible tension in the air. Accordingly, silence holds a power of "direct emotional expression" that bypasses the word and would be diminished by being translated into it (Dewey 1934, 238; see also Huxley 1931).

I am here slipping into the territory of silence as something experienced and made by the body, of silence as enactment rather than enunciation, of silence-as-gesture (Acheson 2008, 537), with gesture being no mere sign of some signification lying behind it but the embodiment of meaning (Merleau-Ponty 1962, 164; see also Bindeman 2017, 57–65). An illustration is in order, perhaps. Take, for instance, Big Mijo's impromptu Krump sequence before Los Angeles police at a 2020 Black Lives Matter protest.[6] Big Mijo is one of the creators of Krump, an African-diasporic street dance style characterized by its aggressive execution. "Aggressively abstract" (Batiste 2014, 201), Krump challenges violent stereotypes with its "ethos of restraint" (Butler 2015b, 41) and constitutes a way of "remembering in the flesh" a history of racial violence and repression (Ohmer 2019, 14). Krump is normally performed to heavy, dramatic bass beats. But Big Mijo's improvisation eschewed musical accompaniment or words of power to embody a near inaudibility, exercising a claustrophobic and catastrophic violence. To use the words of Jean-Luc Nancy, his body "lets itself be touched as meaning right there where it becomes absent as discourse" (1997, 79). Linguistic performative accounts of the body, focusing on what might be spoken or vocalized through it, fail to consider the ways in which bodies act and interact, as Judith Butler poignantly put it, "in excess of what is said" (2015a, 11). Violently embodied silence such as Big Mijo's "open[s] the senses so that our critique of existing power is not merely abstract, but embodied, dynamic, and living" (Butler 2014). This has led some to characterize performed embodied silence "as a modality of parrhesiastic practice" with a consequent "moving from a conception of parrhesia as the enunciation of the truth to parrhesia as the enactment of the truth" (Bargu 2022, 308). This is possible because the gesture communicates itself directly and is read without representation; it manifests, and the audience simply "gets it" and takes it up. The notion of silence-as-gesture will be integral to my analysis of silence as a practice involving the body as both subject and object and using the "nonlinguistic materiality of the body to communicate without speaking" (Bargu 2022, 296). Thus understood, silence probes and transgresses a series of dualisms that continue to blight our understanding of the political and democratic agency of citizens: body and speech, reason and affect, doing and being, domination and emancipation, victimhood and agency (Bargu 2022, 296).

A third, and associated, limitation of silence-as-signal is that it espouses a too-stringent model of agency premised on rational, intentional, purposive control. It reduces communicative silence to the deliberately unspoken, or the "choosing [of] silence to send a message" (Gray 2023, 823). Yet silence can be communicative and carry a significant amount of information in a communicative exchange over and beyond the silence-maker's control (see also Freeden 2022, 43). Silence is communicative if a prime minister leaves a room as a journalist yells "Any comment?" at her, but it is also communicative if she is reduced to silence by someone's powerful testimony of the devastating impact of her policies on mental health provision. To be thus reduced to silence by someone's testimony is a manifestation of affectedness through "unintentional gestures and expressions," and it may even be seen as indirectly agentic in that it affirms "the subjective existence of the agent" (Krause 2011, 307). Importantly, there is here no difference between silence as the outward sign of shock and shock itself. Silence-as-signal cannot grasp this; silence-as-gesture can. I will need both as I examine the practice of silence in different dimensions of democratic life.

Finally, integral to my view of silence as a practice and a mode of interaction is the notion that subjectivities and interaction structured and organized by speech differ from subjectivities and interaction structured and organized by silence. For one, the embodied performance of silence presupposes that a person is present and constitutes a distinctive way of being present and being-with-others, which I will explore in more depth in chapter 4.

A last word is necessary on silence and power. Democratic culture sees power in speaking, disempowerment in silence. Recent attempts to challenge this view and theorize democratic silences have distinguished between disempowered and empowered forms of silence, equating the latter with communicative silence and defining empowering silence as silence that does not just constitute a "free choice" but achieves a "desired outcome consistent with democratic norms" (Gray 2023, 819, 820). This work follows a common trend among students of politics, which is to take political power for power-over, or the power to get someone to do what they would not otherwise have done (Gray 2023, 221).

Power-over is undoubtedly important, as it is the kind of power that enables one to exercise a degree of control over the content and direction of what gets done in situations of actual or potential conflict. But while silence can exercise this kind of power, the added value of silence in thinking through questions of power and agency is that it pushes us to think beyond political power as simply power-over. As we will see, especially in chapter 5, silence is at least equally likely to exercise a "non-decision-making power" (Lukes 1974; Bachrach and Baratz 1962) or to constitute a mode of attenuating assertion, which affirms democratic agency by limiting one's power of voice, influence, or decision. As mentioned above, the potential to do "implies and complies with the *power not to do*" (Connor 2019, 4; my emphasis). Understood in this light, silence is not just a way of *not doing* things, much less a form of impotence or lack of power. It is rather the *action* of not acting (through speech), which exercises a *power not to*, the power to withhold (Agamben 1999, 182). We are also drawn together by this power, which, I will show, is a power integral to the enactment of norms of democratic equality and reciprocity (Connor 2019, 95).

Luce Irigaray brings out the democratic importance of this power to hold back and give way, writing that "the first word we have to speak to each other is our capacity or acceptance of being silent [ . . . ] silence is the word, or the speaking, of the threshold—a space of possible meeting, of possible hospitality to one another" (2011, 114). As such, it will not come as a surprise that giving way is part of democratic procedures and institutions, namely, the "speaking" institutions at the heart of democracy: parliaments. In British politics, members of parliament use the terms "give way" or "giving way" when speaking in the House of Commons. An MP cannot interrupt when another MP is speaking to the House unless that MP gives way, which involves ceasing to speak and relinquishing their standing position to another MP, who may then interject by, for example, addressing a clarificatory question to the member speaking. "Giving way" is a form of self-silencing, which enacts norms of mutual cooperation ("positive reciprocity"), shows good parliamentary citizenship, and enhances the quality and robustness of parliamentary debate. Exercising power over one's own power to speak establishes the conditions of shared cooperative activity: mutual responsiveness, commitment to joint action, commitment to mutual support (Batman 1992). The exercise of control over one's own voice can also be a form of changing the distribution of voice and power within a given community (MacKenzie and Moore 2020, 448). Consider a country holding a referendum to liberalize its strict abortion regime. Polls show a sharp generational divide, with a clear majority of older voters opposed. Given that voters of a reproductive age, and especially women, stand to win or lose more from the result of the referendum, and given that they might be outvoted even if they vote *en masse*, older voters who might have voted against could refrain from participating for democratic reasons: namely, to give priority voice to those most affected by the decision.

Focusing on how well silence may exercise power-over or control will necessarily miss such democratically beneficial uses of silence. It also reduces silence to a resource to be deployed instrumentally, for the advancement of preset purposes, or to a "power to do or accomplish this or that particular thing" (Markell 2014, 129). However, the performance of silence as a political stance and practice, we will see, can enact modalities of power that are far less instrumental and far more open and cooperative—and democratically productive for that. This book foregrounds silences that create space for a future politics which those silences refrain from controlling (chapter 5) as well as silences that are sites of a counter-subjectivation that does not know its destination in advance (chapter 4): creating new subjects, new forms of political subjectivity, new counter-publics, all of which involve "challeng[ing] the contours of the political as they are conventionally imagined" and seeking to bring in audiences as active partners in the process of imagining otherwise (Bargu 2022, 294).

It is now time to lay out a roadmap for the book. Each chapter of the book focuses on a different sphere of politics: personal identity (chapter 1), the legal right to silence (chapter 2), self-silencing and social silencing (chapter 3), silent protest (chapter 4), constitution-making (chapter 5), and representation (chapters 6 and 7).

I first turn to the relationship between silence and identity and to silence as a practice of freedom to be and become. The notion of "breaking silence" and "coming out"—the speech act articulating one's sexuality—as personally and politically emancipatory has been integral to the feminist, gay, and lesbian movements from the late 1970s onward. By contrast, silence has been seen by them as the mark of what one is forbidden or too afraid to name. A form of identity-denial, silence has been equated with death itself, as in the iconic Silence = Death poster from the AIDS crisis. However, what happens when "breaking silence" and "coming out" turn into injunctions to speak and "techniques of subjugation" (W. Brown 1996, 186)? What if the unsaid were neither necessarily silenced nor secret? What if, rather than denying identity, it were the condition upon which alternative identities would emerge? If, for instance, queerness is fluidity, unforeseen and "unforeseeable change" (McCallum and Tuhkanen 2011, 8), isn't it always yet to be known, and isn't "coming out" necessarily incomplete? Must not queerness therefore unsay itself as it names itself? These are the questions I pursue in my first chapter, which explores silencing as the site of identity negation and identity creation and as an enactment of a freedom that is not simply from but to.

Chapter 2 argues for the importance of the right to silence as a protection and empowerment against domination as well as something essential to expressive freedom. I support this claim by examining the ways in which the right to silence underpins other fundamental rights and associated freedoms, chief among which is the right to free speech and expression. The necessity, but also the limitations, of the right to silence in securing freedom of speech and expression is assessed through an extended discussion of several US Supreme Court decisions and opinions, starting with what is, perhaps, the most famous among them: the *Miranda* opinion.

In chapter 3, I turn to the social life of silence. I discuss both democratically desirable forms of self-imposed silence or verbal restraint that enact democratic equality and mutual recognition as well as democratically undesirable forms of self-silencing, which distort the perception and formation of public opinion. Political debate is hindered where the conditions are not met for citizens to be prepared to talk openly about matters of public concern or where systemic, structural silencing prevails. I examine when and how silence can express a form of empowered refusal of such conditions; how active, listening silences that offer uptake can enable us to be with others across difference while "actually hearing our distance from one another" (Bickford 1996, 154) and dogged, unresponsive silences do the opposite; and how silence and silencing may be tactically used to obstruct attempts at silencing.

Chapter 4 follows Adrienne Rich's prompt that silence is a socio-political phenomenon endowed with a history and a form. I devote the chapter to the exploration of one of these historical forms: namely, the feminist protest tradition and its role in pushing for democratic inclusion. In examining the multiple and at times conflicted unfolding of this tradition of protest *in* and *through* embodied silence, the chapter shows the ways in which these protests have reclaimed and deconstructed silence as a gendered trait to protest power, trouble received notions of political subjectivity, and enact new possibilities for being and acting politically.

While chapter 4 focuses on moments of transformative political action that have the staying power typical of "constituent moments" (Frank 2010), chapter 5 takes up constituent power as the power to enact a constitution or give rise to a new legal order. We tend to think of constitutions as things made up of words. They attest to the performative power of speech acts in helping create reality. As the rule book for a state, a constitution may seem to achieve its most perfect form when it codifies everything and eliminates any silences. But if we acknowledge that we do not have unlimited foresight and that it is of the nature of democracies to leave room for others to continue to rework the constitution, then we may see how leaving or including silences in constitutions may be justified, even required, on democratic grounds. This chapter looks into the variety of silences that may be enlisted by constitutions to ensure that they remain open to learning, adaptation, and politics itself.

I devote chapter 6 to the problem of representing silence in politics. Hanna Pitkin famously defined representation as *re*-presenting, that is, of making present what is absent (1967, 144). Following this definition, the task of representation is that of conferring presence, and in democratic theory and practice, political presence typically means voice. Accordingly, democratic representation focuses on *voice*: it conceives voice as that which is represented and as the prime mode of representing. Chapter 6 argues that this focus is problematic and turns instead to *silence* to ask two fundamental questions: Can representation empower citizens from their silent positions? And can representatives make the represented present by choosing silence? In addressing these questions, I critically engage and strengthen constructivist views of representation by developing criteria to assess the legitimacy of claims to represent—speak *about* and *for*—silent constituencies, namely, the claim to represent an (alleged) silent majority.

Chapter 7 closes the book with a discussion of environmental silence. The figuration of "nature" as inert, law-bound, agency-less, and voiceless is one of the foils against which the political domain defined itself as the domain of action, freedom, agency, and speech, expelling "nature" and "naturalized subjects" from its ranks in the process. How might "nature" be brought back in? How must democratic politics and its institutional mechanisms change for this to be possible? In this last chapter, I discuss the complexities that surround constituting an ecological politics that gives "nature"—a purportedly "silent" entity—political status and clout.

In this way, the book presents a bold argument for the democratic value of silence, showing when and how it may advance democratic values and practices and when and how it may undercut them. To make my case, in the first chapter, I begin by interrogating the entwinement of identity formation and practices of silence.

# I

# UNSAYING

Silence is my sword; it cuts both ways.
—Marlon Riggs, *Tongues Untied*

In her essay "In the 'Folds of Our Own Discourse': The Pleasures and Freedoms of Silence" (1996), Wendy Brown offers a reappreciation of the political value of silence. This is set against what she calls the "fetishizing" of "breaking silence" within progressive movements. Brown's intention is not to downplay the importance of breaking oppressive silences but rather to problematize the belief that "speaking out" is always necessarily, or unproblematically, emancipatory. As such, while she acknowledges that it is vital for marginalized groups to take up the speaking position to fill the silences of dominant discourses with their "explosive counter-tales," she enjoins that "this ostensive tool of emancipation carries its own techniques of subjugation"—namely, through (re)traumatization or (re)capture by regulatory discourses when "speaking ourselves" (W. Brown 1996, 186, 187).

To establish her argument, Brown mounts a critique of the common conceptualization of speech and silence as mutually exclusive. This typically sets speech as the marker of agency, truth, and emancipation against silence as the marker of passivity, lies, and oppression. However, as Brown rightly notes, the relationship between speech and silence is far more promiscuous and complex. Speech and silence are both parts of discourse, which structures and construes social reality. It is thus not only the case that speech and silence are complementary, interact with one another, and give shape to each other. More than this, speech and silence are effectively integral to one another, each other's constituent parts: all speech presupposes a silencing, and just as "speech harbors silences," so do "silences harbor meaning" (W. Brown 2005, 83). Thus, both speech and silence are places of potential freedom and/or unfreedom, deliverance and/or violence (Dhawan 2007). Rather than something outside discourse, silence is "a relation to regulatory discourses, as well as a possible niche for the practice of freedom *within* those discourses" (W. Brown 1996, 188). Even though they sometimes provide a protective alcove, silences are not necessarily freer from power than discourse is. Nor are silences necessarily freer from power when they harbor meaning and function like speech in discourse. While all these caveats should be borne in mind, it is important not to overlook the possibility that "the capacity to be silent" can be a "measure of our desire for freedom" (W. Brown 1996, 196). But, Brown forewarns, if silence gestures toward freedom, this is a negative freedom, freedom *from*.

In this opening chapter, I want to push forward some strands of Brown's argument while starting to probe her conclusion that silence is, at most, a "freedom from," which is never quite yet a "freedom to" (W. Brown 1996, 197). The structure of the chapter is twofold. First, I delve into what Brown classifies as the ambivalent freedom in silence—the double-edged sword of the unspoken—in connection with Marlon Riggs's experimental documentary film *Tongues Untied* (1989). Second, I distinguish between silence as "not-saying" and silence as "unsaying" to show how, *pace* Brown, the latter can support a freedom to become, which can also be a freedom to make oneself and the world anew.

## Silence as Oppression and Reprieve

It is as oppression, or at best resistance to it, that silence figures prominently in Marlon Riggs's pioneering 1989 essay-documentary, *Tongues Untied*. In Riggs's own words, the work is meant to "shatter the nation's brutalizing silence on matters of sexual and racial difference" (Riggs 1996, 185). A blend of first-person testimony, performance, rap, and poetry, *Tongues Untied* epitomizes the very liberation of expression it seeks to bring about. Its multiple forms of expression converge in breaking through the silence surrounding the Black gay community—its existence, its activity, its injury—to upend misconceptions that continue to exclude Black gay men from being included in the very communities to which they belong. To this effect, *Tongues Untied* shows and voices the experience of Black gay men living a threefold excommunication: from the dominantly white, heteronormative, and patriarchal

American society; from a Black community rife with homophobia; and from a predominantly white gay and lesbian subculture, itself tainted with racism. Against the background of these intersecting excommunications, effected by hegemonic discourses and their norms, *Tongues Untied* offers an alternative: a transgressive performance of what it means to be gay, of what it means to be Black, of what it means to be American, all in the hope of opening an opportunity for the three communities (and individuals within them) to reimagine themselves and their mutual relationship.

Given this, it ought not be surprising that such an iconoclastic work was subject to an attempted external silencing. Blocking access, questioning the filmmaker's authority, and cutting off funding were all instances of this effort. Some television stations refused to air *Tongues Untied*, and those that did agree to broadcast the documentary scheduled it for very-late-night slots to make sure that "no one ran across [it] by accident."[1] Dominant definitions of cinema, including definitions of gay and lesbian cinema, worked to de-authorize experimental artworks like *Tongues Untied* as not quite cinema (and cinemamakers like Riggs as not quite professional). Lastly, the film was identified as "pornographic"—that is, as abject. This identification was part of a censorship campaign and part of a call for restrictions on public funding. Acting on the material conditions of cultural production so that similar work would be cut off from its life support was perhaps the most effective way of preventing more tongues from being set loose and other marginalized communities from exercising their right to speak and be heard in public discourse.[2]

*Tongues Untied.* The title of the documentary is explicit about its intent. Untying is the loosening of the ties that fasten something, that restrict its movement. This something is the tongue, the muscular organ on which the formation of certain sounds and phonemes in speech depends. But here the tongue stands for repressed speech. The quasi-physical experience of having one's tongue tied is integral to the phenomenology of being silenced. This is the reason why the synecdoche is so powerful, with the tie marking silencing as an enforced, then internalized, inability to speak, to speak up, to tell one's stories, with the contents and in the formats that one chooses—and to be listened to.

· I've been referring to the "tongue" in the singular. But in the title, it is plural—not just one "tongue," but "tongues." The plural is important here, because in *Tongues Untied* it is a community that is meant to come to voice. The plural formulation suggests at least two things. First is the community's internal diversity, the many voices out of which the Black gay community is made. The documentary film relays the experiences of numerous Black gay men so that Riggs's personal testimony does not silence them by offering "a regulatory truth about the identity of the group" (W. Brown 1996, 192) or a limitation of the open-endedness of Black sexuality. There is a second meaning expressed in the use of the plural, too. The untying of tongues requires the work of democratic association. "Untied" and "united" are words made from the same letters. The plural is a potent reminder that untying requires "connecting with specific others, working something through, or transforming understanding or experience" in ways that create the political space where speech can "be claimed to break a political silence" (W. Brown 1996, 196).

The opening montage of *Tongues Untied* shows scenes of police violence over Black men. This is accompanied by the rhythmic poetic refrain, "Brother to Brother, Brother to Brother, Brother to Brother." The refrain builds up, as voices join in, into a movement that invokes the unsuspected power that may emerge if the refrain's longing for recognition is answered. Recognizing one another as members of an oppressed community, a community in search of redress, just may generate the kind of mutual support necessary to sustain political action, possibly even revolutionary action, opening the horizon of a new political subjectivation. This desire is expressed by the film's concluding statement: "Black men loving Black men is *the* revolutionary act."

For the Black gay community, speaking is restricted to specific others, brother-to-brother, as this is a community of people keeping one another's secrets and using silence to shelter themselves from power. But "Brother-to-Brother" also has a wider appeal. It is about the relationships between Black men, gay and not, with their histories of oppression and disenfranchisement inescapably interwoven. To mark this, *Tongues Untied* reinscribes Black queer history within African American history. It relates current gay rights activism back to civil rights activism in a reminder that the arc of history is long and that joining forces is necessary to bend it toward justice. Voice empowerment depends on the historical widening of self-knowledge and on the wider circles of solidarity this knowledge might engender. The "Brother to Brother" chant has an expansive, repetitious, polyphonic quality, gesturing toward the possibility of ever wider circles of brotherhood. This potential for expansion is underpinned by Riggs's displacement of the idea of the self as unified or perfectly identical with itself. A greater recognition that the self, every self, is an inner plurality would enable members of different groups to acknowledge that, though their fights for justice and emancipation may not be the same, they cannot be alien to one another.

*Tongues Untied*, we have seen, features the tongue-tie as the image of silencing as oppression—silence externally imposed and assimilated through habituation. "To be marginalized is to have no place from which to speak," writes Kobena Mercer, "since the subject positioned in the margins is silenced and invisible" (1994, 194; see also H. Young 2000). And thus, in the film, moments of image and word, of visibility and speakability, are repeatedly interrupted by the insertion of a black screen, conveying the erasing power of enforced/internalized silence. While *Tongues Untied* represents this power, it also breaks away from it, exposing silencing as oppression and providing the Black gay community a place from which to speak, a place in which to come to visibility. Riggs aspired to create an artwork destined to be brought out of the art house into the school, the church, and the bar, effecting a new distribution of the sensible by changing the spectrum of sanctioned sensibilities—that is, by overcoming the unspeak/ability of the shamed and the shameless, the abject (Rancière 2004; Keller 2008, 912).

Accessing speech platforms, having one's image seen and one's speech heard, is valuable in instrumental ways: it enables us to influence courses of action, to have a say in what gets done and in who gets it done for us, and, eventually, in getting what we need. But in *Tongues Untied* the prime concern is more fundamental, with image and speech posited as constitutive and performative—as effecting and affecting subjecthood and identity. Speech can bring into existence that which it names. It can also provoke a disintegration of the self—can harm, degrade, humiliate, dehumanize, disempower, and subordinate—in one word: *silence.*

The documentary shows most clearly the silencing effects of speech. The perlocutionary force of a certain type of speech—namely, homophobic and racist slurs and prejudicial stereotyping—is capable not only of silencing but of other forms of violence as well, including induced self-hatred and even killing (West 2012). Reflecting on his experience growing up, amid multiple voices denigrating him ("Uncle Tom," "motherfuckin' coon," "punk," "faggot," "freak," "n[——], go home"), Riggs comments, "Cornered by identities I never wanted to claim, I ran fast—hard—deep—inside myself, where it was still. Silent." Where the chief perlocutionary effect caused by speech is the shaming and intimidation of its targets—who know any response will be ignored, misinterpreted, or met with (further) violence and may thus feel incapable of mustering a rejoinder—they will self-silence to try to preserve themselves. In situations of great vulnerability, silence can offer a modicum of protection. But much of the harm will have already been done, including the inducement of a lifelong tendency to censor one's speech and expression, something fostered by feelings of fear and shame or deference to the sensibilities of others, even if not under their direct pressure. In the documentary, examples of silencing speech work alongside examples of speech not spoken, speech held back, repressed speech metastasized as anger, as internal combustion: "I listen for my own quiet implosion," the voice-over reveals.

A case in point is the silencing effect of prejudicial stereotyping. In a seemingly benign scene, we observe Black men walking, playing, and talking. But the voice-over provides a deeper, darker insight:

> Silence is what I hear after the handshake and slap of five, after, "What's happening?" "Homeboy!" "What's up, cuz?" "How ya feel, girlfriend?" "Blood!" "Miss Thang." When talking with a girlfriend, I am more likely to muse about my latest piece or so and so's party at club Shi-Shi, than about the anger and hurt I felt that morning when a jeweler refused me entrance to his store, because I am black and male and we are all perceived as thieves. I will swallow that hurt and should I speak of it will vocalize only the anger by saying, "I should've busted out his fuckin' windows."

Silencing occurs when one is prevented from carrying out a communicative action. This can happen when one is prevented from attempting the action itself (for example, through intimidation) or because of one's internalized incapacity. In this scene, the obstacle to communicative action is internal: the shame, the anger, the hurt provoked by the young Black man's social stereotyping as a "thief" (and the subsequent misconstrual of his intentions). The result is a tied tongue, but, in this case, tying is more adequately characterized as a "speaking away" than as a not-speaking. The young Black man is not simply not-speaking but rather not-speaking *by speaking*; he is not-speaking about something painful by speaking about something trivial. The denial of racialized shame is implicit in the very act of not naming and not speaking of it, as "it is after all the very nature of shame to stifle its own discourse" (Wicomb 1998, 92). Stifled discourse is one of the ways in which the everyday micro-aggressions of systemic racism manifest themselves and are swallowed. At certain junctures, however, unexpressed anger will inevitably translate into violence, against self or others. After images of riots and police violence, the voice-over comes back: "Some of the anger will be exercised but the hurt, which has not been given voice, prevails and accumulates." As the hurt lives on, silence continues to be a mode of survival, a way of putting the hurt on the back burner and coexisting with it: "Silence is a way to grin and bear it." This is a silence that enables living, but the living it enables discounts much life. In Wendy Brown's apt summary, this silence is "a defense in the context of domination, a strategy for negotiating domination" rather than an overcoming (1996, 197).

From this the conclusion could easily be reached that in *Tongues Untied* silence is something one suffers, a site where not much else happens. But Riggs shows otherwise. This silence that provides shelter from power is not just omissive. Rather, within this silence, a rich, distinctive Black culture evolves, with its fashion, dance, music, scholarship, cinema, politics—and its silent language.

In one memorable scene, Black gay men introduce the audience to the art of "snap-ology," or the variety of ways in which to snap their fingers, with "precision, pacing, placement, poise." The "Medusa snap," the "sling snap," the classic snap, the "point snap," the "diva snap": in the Black gay community, "a sophisticated snap is more than just noise." It is a whole new gestural and sound-full language developed at the click of one's fingers. Ingeniously evolved and finely textured, the snap is the means of communication among silent/silenced Black gay men. It bonds them and protects their communication from public scrutiny. It offers them a (nonverbal) voice, and a subversive one at that. This much is shown in the "Snap Rap" sequence. There, the conventions of rap as a musical genre associated with particular representations of masculinity are upended by their inscription in the discursive practice of "snapping." As Riggs himself points out, "the Snap! can be as emotionally and politically charged as a clenched fist; can punctuate debate and dialogue like an exclamation point, a comma, an ellipsis; or can altogether negate the need for words among those who are adept at decoding its nuanced meanings" (1991, 392). Snapping is undoubtedly a survival practice, a way of eluding control imposed on words by encoding meaning, and a site of resistance. But to reduce the snap to this is to overlook the creative ways in which enforced silence is not only being reworked, transformed, and given new meanings but occupied, defining new contours within which one can be, act, speak, and wage one group's internal politics. To insist on inscribing agency within a narrow domination/resistance binary, as Wendy Brown does, risks producing the very outcome she wanted to escape: to disregard the rich, active subjectivities being produced and to limit the group yet again to a single, reactive (rather than productive) account of their identity.

In his depiction of the snap, Riggs simultaneously invokes the construction of silence as passive and throws it into question (Petty 1998). The ambiguity of silence's power is foregrounded in the scene where Riggs dances naked against the background of a poem: "Silence is my shield; it crushes. Silence is my cloak; it smothers." The poem gives silence a paradoxical quality, both protective and destructive—a place of refuge and a place of annihilation, including self-annihilation. As the poem is declaimed, Riggs's movement evolves into a martial art–like dance, with the martial elements overlapping with the defensive protection of his face: "Silence is my sword; it cuts both ways. Silence is the deadliest weapon." The poem finishes with these two verses, and in them, the "who, whom" question—who does what to whom—is left deliberately unresolved: Who cuts? Who is cut? Who will ultimately succumb to silence, the deadliest weapon? Even at the height of the AIDS epidemic, the film's politics of silence offers reasons for hopefulness by demonstrating the tenacity and ingenuity of the Black gay community.

## Silence as a Site of Becoming

While cognizant of the ways in which silence can be used as a weapon of resistance, and even as a medium of self- and community formation, *Tongues Untied* takes speech as the fundamental form of empowerment. Where silence is primarily imposition and/or habituation, to come to speech, to be "heard, seen, recognized, wanted as a speaking being in the social and public realm," as Wendy Brown puts it, is critical for emancipation (1996, 197).

But it is no guarantee of it. "Cornered by identities I never wanted to claim, I ran—fast—hard—deep—inside myself," Riggs declares. Dominant gender, racial, and sexual identities corner—they force one into place, leaving little discursive scope for self-construction, for challenging racial, gender, and sexuality norms. The appropriation and reinvention of language is thus necessary for the expansion of this conscribed discursive space and for the coming into being of a subject who is not just claimed—but claims. Still, the fact remains that the affirmation of identities, the affirmation of identity difference itself, comes always with the danger of their fixation into new regulatory discourses and norms.

Take, for instance, "coming out," the speech act meant to articulate and affirm one's sexual identity, not simply in the constative mode of reporting that one is out but in the performative mode of coming out in the first place. Subjects are effects of speech, and this makes it easy to see why one may find empowerment in naming oneself as lesbian or gay. As eloquently printed out in the famous ACT UP T-shirt from the 1990s: "I am out, therefore I am." To come out means here to own up to one's sexuality, to give it a name, to give it an existence before oneself and before others and thus a sign of personal growth and political maturity. If "coming out" is deemed politically responsible, to stay closeted is taken for its opposite: "an act of silence indicative of shame and self-hatred" (Adams 2010, 238). The paradigm of coming out assumes therefore a progressive course: from the closet (shame, fear, secrecy, political immaturity) to outness (pride, courage, openness, political maturity) (238).

While "coming out" may be empowering to many, when turned into an imperative it metamorphoses into a new normativity, a homonormativity, establishing the terms of authentic LGBTQ living and realization. Unwittingly, this new normativity may disavow other forms of gay existence, especially, but not exclusively, among minoritized gay people who see themselves condemned to a perpetual "gay minority" or "closetedness."

Declaring in speech one's sexual identity is an important way of gay subject formation, but it is not the only way, nor should it be the telos of gay actualization. To not verbally articulate one's sexual identity need not imply its denial. It is not equal to "not-not coming out," hiding or lying (Guzmán 2015, 145). In his study of Dominican immigrant gay men in the United States, Carlos Decena contrasts the proud and out posture of dominant same-sex white personhood with the tacit homosexuality of Dominican gay men, whom he conceptualizes as "tacit subjects," "assumed and understood, but not spoken" (Decena 2011, 31). Their tacit homosexuality is sustained through "overlapping layers of collaboration and complicity" from the social circles within which these men exist (31). That they do not speak (out) their sexual identity does not mean that they repress it or hide it away. Tacit homosexuality constitutes instead a different way of being out by keeping one's sexual identity "unaddressed yet understood" (21). As Decena puts it, "what is tacit is neither secret nor silent": by "secret," he means concealed, and by "not silent," something that is enacted, communicated in bodily deeds bereft of words, sometimes even given off by them (19). As such, these men carry out their interactions, especially their interactions in family, under the assumption that their sexuality is "knowable in a tacit way," that their audiences have the requisite competency to interpret and decode their behavior, that they are able to "get" their "code swishing" gestures (20, 15). The speech act of "coming out" can have little to "nothing to do with the acquisition of new information," of course, and all to do with self-naming (Sedgwick 1990, 3). But because their sexual identity is tacitly out, to articulate it in speech can feel redundant or can even be actively resisted as a form of re-marking and re-closeting. As one of Decena's interviewees puts it, when you feel compelled to clarify your sexual life, you are going along with the social stigma that "you are queer and you have to explain it" (Decena 2011, 32).

Like *Tongues Untied*, Decena's study of Dominican queer men shows the unsaid to be not just a mark of unfreedom but a place of agency and outness. Cautioning against the potential of the "coming out" imperative devolving into a new regulatory discourse that hauls gay men of color into closetedness, both studies bring out their creative utilization of resources at these men's disposal to gesturally enact their sexual identity and foster community while exercising a degree of agential control over their identity's disclosure as they move through the different social circles they straddle. Their code-swishing, code-mixing, code-meshing, and code-switching are integral to their being queer. These gestures present them to the world as queer and do so differently from (and sometimes *besides*) what language could verbalize. Their performance does not warrant the slippage between silence and invisibility typical of the "coming out" rhetoric: theirs is a visible, dissenting performance of gender, "blending and bending" (hooks 1992, 147) accepted scripts of normative masculinity, normative femininity, and normative gayness.[3]

The formulaic "coming out" narrative privileges queer visibility as verbalization over nonverbal ways of expressing identity. As a result, it squeezes out a wide range of other possible ways of living a gay life and reinforces fixed binaries of unknown/known, secrecy/disclosure, private/public, in-ness/outness, negation/affirmation, disavowal/avowal, shame/pride, silence and speech. But while it is important to appreciate the ways "coming out" may be an "ostensible tool of emancipation carr[ying] its own techniques of subjugation," it is equally important not to romanticize tacit subjects by downplaying their disempowerments (W. Brown 1996, 186). In *Tongues Untied* as in Decena's study, silence about their sexual identity is a way for men of color to outplay the dangers of speaking, to negotiate race, sexuality, and power in their daily lives. The explicit naming, acknowledgment, or discussion of their homosexuality is not an option open to them, as it would likely expose them to violence or bring about the rupture of the crucial social and familial bonds that sustain them. Their tactics for living their sexuality "are not quite affirmations or quite completely negations," explained and traversed by multiple oppressions, including the gay "coming out" politics that sees them lying by omission (Villiers 2012, 6).

What their example shows is not that expression without words or speech is freedom but that a gay politics of "coming out" can itself be oppressive, expose one to a different set of unfreedoms, risks, and constraints, and occlude more than it illuminates with its neat speech/liberation/empowerment and silence/oppression/disempowerment opposition. Even queer men and women facing a real choice between speaking or not speaking out their sexuality and gender identity may wish to explore it outside the opposites of "outing speech" and "closeted silence," within a more "neutral space" that "absorbs the division between speech and silence" (Villiers 2012, 22–23; Barthes 2005). Rather than a form of identity negation, disavowal or disowning, the cultivation of non-disclosure, non-transparency, imperfect legibility, or even deliberate opacity need not betray a reactive desire for "privacy" or a repressive silence that is "fully complicit with homophobia and the closet" but constitute instead a form of identity that positively engages silences in identity production while resisting the imposition of regimes of truth imbued with power (Villiers 2012, 64; see also Asenbaum 2018).[4]

Notwithstanding their productivity, the ambiguities of silence continue to be tied singularly with the notion of freedom *from* (detection or interference), which explains silence's regular pairing with rights such as the rights to privacy and anonymity, as we will see in the next chapter. What is missing from this account is that self-identities can also be constructed upon "not-doing or not-being certain things" (S. Scott 2018, 7) and that silence can therefore constitute a positive, commissive form of identity performance, entailing freedoms *to do* and *to be* a more nuanced queer self, cultivating ambiguity, expressing oneself through dis-identification and/or self-expression in nonverbal signs. A critical engagement with language's impulse toward determination may even be necessary to free queerness from the straitjacket of identity and to embrace "the open mesh of possibilities, gaps, overlaps, dissonances and resonances, lapses and excesses of meaning" that opens itself up "when the constituent elements of anyone's gender, or anyone's sexuality aren't made (or can't be made) to signify monolithically" (Sedgwick 1993, 8).

In her essay "Not You/Like You," Trinh T. Minh-ha discusses the pathologies of identity that Wendy Brown places behind the notion of an authentic self, waiting to be released by breaking silence. "Identity as understood in the context of a certain ideology of dominance," Trinh writes, "relies on the concept of an essential, authentic core that remains hidden to one's consciousness and that requires the elimination of all that is considered foreign or not true to the self, that is to say, non-I, other." For Trinh, where silence is deliberately unresponsive to calls to identify, it provides a way of undercutting such negative identities while enabling forms of self-othering that evade and confound fixation, including fixation *in* and *through* speech. In other words, conceived as not simply "a will not to say" but as a positive "will to unsay," silence presents a form of articulating difference, which "undermines the very idea of identity" as a fixed category (Trinh 1988).

Identity tells us what we are but also what we must be, that we must be one thing or another, and that whatever we are must be nameable. Silence, with its "ever-changing meanings" and "its resonances of possibility," has a mongrel quality (Duncan 2004, 30). Its in-betweenness means that it has an ability to hold more than one thing at once. As a praxis of "unsaying," upholding processes of multiple becoming, silence represents a rejection of identity as something requiring verbal and nonverbal "conformity to oneself," as something imposing a choice between "living a lie or being authentic" (Jungkunz 2012, 143). Silence as a will to unsay thus pertains to transformation, fluidity, and becoming rather than to stable, established forms of being. And here as elsewhere we see that the dichotomy between "freedom from" and "freedom to" is a false dichotomy. Freedom, properly understood, is always about "*what* is free or unfree, *from* what is it free or unfree, and what is it free or unfree *to do or become*" (Hamilton 2014, 28; emphasis in the original). Rather than simply a form of not-saying, silence can affirm one's freedom to become in "unsaying" the compulsions of self-defining speech.

## Apophasis as a Way of Unsaying

"Unsaying" can be an effect of speech and not of its absence—or, indeed, both. Take, for instance, the increasing use of gender-inclusive pronouns, such as the singular "they/them/their" instead of the gendered pronouns "he/him/his" or "she/her/hers." To use the singular "they/them/their" is not simply not-to-say a specific gender, "he/him" or "she/her," so as to keep gender neutrality. It is also to unsay the gender binary (for those whose gender identity is nonbinary) and/or to unsay traditional gender categories and their hierarchies (when referring to a person of unspecified gender). The universalization of the use of the singular "they," which is taking hold in the English language, completes this process of unsaying as a "levelling-up progress of equal dignity" across gender divides (Bejan 2019).

Both saying and unsaying, affirming and denying, may be required in dealing with identities, their constitutive and smothering powers. The concept of *apophasia* or *apophatic* speech, which is itself a form of "saying away" or "unsaying," is of help here. Apophasis is derived from the Greek *apophanai*, meaning "to deny." *Apophanai*, in turn, derives from *apo*, meaning "way from" or "off," and *phanai*, meaning "to say." Hence, apophasis can be rendered as "speaking-way," or, to be more precise, as a form of "not-speaking by speaking rather than speaking by not-speaking" (Wolfson 2005, 220). As a rhetorical device, apophasis brings up a subject by either denying it or denying that it should be brought up. Apophasis therefore entails a certain form of denial or negation of the content of specific propositions that are said. But apophasis is also a theological term for the attempt to speak of and approach God by way of negation, unsaying, un-naming, or de-nomination, by saying what They are not. Motivated by an awareness of the limits of language and expression, of the incapacity and impropriety of finite, language-bound attempts to predicate anything of God, apophasis gestures toward the unsayable at the limit of language itself. However, even when it gestures toward non-speech it still expresses itself linguistically in languages of "unsaying." Within negative theology, also known as apophatic theology, divine attributes necessitate unsaying because they amount to "theological *idols*" mistaking "finite construction . . . for the infinite" (Keller 2008, 912). In other words, the turn to apophasis represents the acknowledgment that all definitions are "approximate delimitations of what is not as such any object that can be defined" (Franke 2015, 33). As such, apophaticism is, first and foremost, an engagement in "a theological critique of theological idolatry" (Keller 2008, 912).

Why bring apophasis into a discussion that is focused on questions of identity? Because taken as a self-critical principle, or a form of speech that "turns back upon itself," as I understand it here, apophasis can help liberate identity discourses from their regulatory essentialisms by allowing them to resist their own idolatry and their own silencing effects (Sells 1994, 3; Keller 2008, 906).[5] But how may this be the case if apophasis seems to sacrifice affirmation for negation and to equate silence with the unspeakable? Contrary to what may seem to be the case, apophasis effectively undercuts, rather than restates, the affirmation/negation dualism, as it springs from a paradox. As the infinite, God "can neither bear finite names nor exist *for us* without them": in effect, as infinite, God "is rightly nameless and yet has the names of everything that is" (Keller 2008, 913; Braaten 1967, 92). The ultimate expression of apophasis is silence, but the silence, the beyond language, toward which it gestures can only be discerned linguistically, and rather than representing a closed door, it constitutes a disclosure, an opening to a place where contradictions coincide, where dualisms are subverted.[6]

Turning now to our racial, gender, and sexual identities, they too only truly exist when named and affirmed (by ourselves and others), and yet there is always an excess to them that at once requires and escapes any naming or affirming. If identity affirmation is to resist fixation, if it is not to degenerate into the idolatry of the self-identical, then, as in apophatic discourse, a "self-conscious strategy of unnaming" and undoing must go along with the naming (e.g., of the subject "women") and along even with "the exuberant multiplication of names" typical of apophatic speech (as in, for instance, the evolving acronym LGBTQIA+) (Keller 2005, 113). This continuous unsaying is, then, a "saying anew": namely, of identity categories as not "unquestionable boundaries" but "porous passageways" through which "a subtler sociality, a relationality in which we at once undo and embrace each other, becomes dimly visible" (Keller 2008, 925, 916, 925). In view of this, silence emerges as no longer simply a niche for the practice of negative freedoms—protecting subjects from interference and domination by others—but as a medium facilitating the performance and expression of new forms of identity and sociality.

## From Unsaying to the Power in Not Saying

Even though the compulsory narration of the self is a demand unevenly placed on marginalized or minoritized groups, it is becoming a generalized requirement within a democratic culture ruled by ideals of transparency, openness, and candor. The flip side of this is that that which is kept private, or secret, is automatically taken for "a dissimulation and thus a lie" (Dufourmantelle 2021, 63). In similar fashion, the keeping of silence is considered as suspicious and taken for deceit, suppression, or (self-)repression—the sign of one's living in denial, inauthentically, and thus sealing off from others what ought to be owned up to, openly spoken about, and shared.

At the limit, the logic of the open, transparent, or candid self can be deemed to give others—including corporate others and states—a claim over our secrets, over our privacy, over our personal data. This much is suggested, for instance, in Mark Zuckerberg's public disparaging of privacy as anachronistic: "People have really gotten comfortable not only sharing more information and different kinds, but more openly and with more people."[7] Even as the Facebook founder declared our voluntary abandonment of privacy, default settings on the site were being changed "to compel users to share more information publicly" (Véliz 2020, 23). Yet even if the data economy works by shunning publicity, the invocation of the figure of the transparent self, with nothing to hide, gives the data economy a moral and ethical upper hand, a veneer of legitimacy.

This is an example of how the ideal of the open self can feed, to use Wendy Brown's words, "the very powers we meant to starve" and, as a result, deepen inequalities in our societies (1996, 186). I am speaking here of inequalities between those of us who have the privilege of discretion and those who do not; those who have a say in what counts as knowledge about themselves and in what others are allowed to perceive and infer about themselves, and those who do not; those who have control over their lives and choices—political choices included therein—and the choices of many others in their societies, and those who do not (W. Brown 1996, 186; see also Dufourmantelle 2021, 68). In societies where everyday activities are mediated by digital technologies, these differentials of power are now immense. Very few can escape or exercise any meaningful degree of control over their digital existence, and whoever "has the most personal data will dominate society" (Véliz 2020, 7). The question this raises is thus not merely an individual question about who controls my personal data; it is an all-encompassing model of individuation, sociality, and politics that is at stake.

Silence, privacy, and secrecy are, of course, different concepts. But, as we shall see more clearly in the next chapter, they are closely associated. All of them entail, to some extent, a voluntary limitation of communication but they also, more fundamentally, imply questions of access and control— namely, editorial control over ourselves, our choices, our expressions, and our disclosure(s).[8]

Critically, there can be neither self nor society without this control as facilitated by silence, secrecy, and privacy. Both secrecy and privacy refer etymologically to setting aside, setting apart from, separating out. They presuppose acts "of reserve, of separation, of relegation to silence" and, through them, "a power" (Dufourmantelle 2021, 25). This is the power to keep a "reserve guarded in ourselves" and protected from others, which is not only the basis of individuation but also the foundation of social relations (27). Our development of social bonds, of relationships with others, is premised on a degree of control over our self-disclosures as well as on the belief that others will not reveal or divulge everything we say. Simmel saw this most clearly, as he observed that human association is as much conditioned by the capacity to speak as by the capacity to keep silence (1906). Silence, secrecy, and privacy are therefore no mere private matters but matters of paramount social and political concern: a "culture of exposure damages society" and "endangers democracy" (Véliz 2020, 39). The latter will become more apparent in the next chapter, as we consider the relation between the right to silence and communicative freedom.

## 2

### SILENCE'S FREEDOMS

Silence, you know, is something that can't be censored. And there are circumstances in which it becomes subversive. That's why they fill it with noise all the time.
—John Berger, *Will It Be a Likeness?*

In 2020, pianist and composer Anthony Davis received the Pulitzer Prize for his opera *The Central Park Five*, the famous criminal case showing systemic racial bias in American law enforcement. In the mid-1970s, Davis himself was targeted by the police in a case of mistaken identity. As he drove with his wife to Boston for a concert, a police officer put his siren on and pulled them over. "And I was going to say," Davis recollects, "'Well, what is going on? I'm going to be late for my concert'" (cited in Kramer 2020). But Davis's wife cautioned him against this, as she looked back at the police car and saw that the officer had his gun drawn.

Almost forty years later, the Miller Theatre at Columbia University commissioned Davis to write a new composition. His earlier encounter with law enforcement impacted Davis so much that he decided to write the piece about it. *You Have the Right to Remain Silent* is the result, a piece in four movements—"Interrogation," "Loss," "Incarceration," and "Dance of the Other." As the title indicates, the piece takes its inspiration from the *Miranda* warning—that is, the warning that a police officer is required to give to those she arrests. Fragments of the warning appear throughout the piece.

## The Right to Remain Silent

*Miranda* warnings make for some of the most popular Hollywood images of the right I want to discuss in this chapter: the right to silence. Compared to the attention given to the right to speech, it is remarkable how little attention has been paid to the right to silence. My contention, in this chapter, is that the right to silence is a fundamental democratic right, one that underpins other core democratic rights—chief among which is the right to speech and expression.

It is possible to distinguish three different ways in which the relationship between the right to silence and freedom of speech can be understood. First is the position I advocate in the first two subsections of this chapter, namely, that the right to silence enfranchises speech, being a necessary condition of speech's freedom. Second is the position that I reject in the third subsection: that the presence of free speech enfranchises silence. And third is the position I advance in the last subsection, that is, that silence may warrant protection as a form of creative expression.

In making my argument for a democratic right to silence, I engage some well-known US Supreme Court decisions. But rather than interpreting the rulings, a task best left to the legal theorist, I theorize *with*, *beyond*, and *against* them. They enable me to foreground the importance of the right to silence and to advance a positive relationship between silence and fundamental democratic freedoms, such as association, speech, and expression.

Generally conceived, a right is an entitlement to act or be treated (or not to act or be treated) in a particular way. Despite its conventional nature, the right to silence has been sometimes understood as a natural or moral right not dependent for its existence on social convention. Even in the case of the right to remain silent during criminal proceedings, some have deemed it *prior to* and existing *outside* a conventional game, rather than a right bestowed *within* it (Skerker 2010, 80). This is premised on the idea that the state must be limited by a *cordon sanitaire* of reserved moral rights protected by the right to silence (self-defense, but also privacy and autonomy).

The notion of the right to silence as a protection against the arbitrary use of coercive power is central to the 1966 *Miranda* opinion, which lies at the origin of the legal phrase after which Davis named his musical piece: "You have the right to remain silent." The opinion, however, inscribes the right to silence squarely within a conventional game, among the procedural safeguards necessary to secure fair process and avoid miscarriages of justice.

The Court's chief concern is avoiding domination, in the basic sense of exposure to a dominant agent's arbitrary power. In the interrogation room, with individuals cut off from the outside, the *Miranda* opinion states that police can sometimes be found making coercive, deceptive, and manipulative uses of interrogation techniques to obtain "evidence" and fabricate the "truth" of confession or self-incrimination.[1] Hence, the Court upholds the right to silence as a necessary protection against domination through compelled speech—that is, against testimony or confession obtained in defiance of the will of the accused.

The *Miranda* opinion uses the word "choice" multiple times and refers to the right to silence as a right meant to protect the enjoyment of undominated choice. A choice right is "a right to both X and not-X, where not-X means refusing to do or accept X" (Blocher 2012, 765). Thus conceived, the right to silence is a "necessary condition for making expressive choices" (Armijo 2018, 325), or, as the Warren Court puts it in *Miranda*, for making sure that any statements uttered by a suspect are "truly . . . the product of his free choice."[2] It supports non-domination in that it expands the choices of the questioned and upholds their capacity to *refuse* the police's demand for response or even—at the limit—the police's interpellation of one as a suspect.[3]

While empowered silence and choice are inseparable, the conceptualization of the right to silence as a choice right should be handled with care. For people facing criminal allegations, the freedom to choose whether to speak or not is, arguably, very limited. Within the context of custodial interrogation, the pressure to speak is enormous, not least because suspects know that refusal to speak is likely to be perceived as an act of noncooperation by the authorities and may affect the level of the charge brought against them.

Moreover, real freedom of choice requires more than simply nonfrustration or noninterference. The right to silence would be of little import if it concerned freedom as mere opportunity to choose between speaking and not speaking rather than the quality of one's agency—that is, one's power to act and to do so in a self-directed manner. The *Miranda* warning accounts, at least partly, for this difference. First, it seeks to empower one's use of silence by determining its significance in advance by legal codification. Namely, it establishes that the choice of silence within the criminal process cannot be interpreted as evidence of anything and that no adverse inferences can be drawn from one's choice of silence.[4] The second way in which *Miranda* furthers empowerment is by securing a right to counsel, which will enable a more informed determination of whether (or when) to speak or not to speak. The right to counsel secures "the power to exert some control over the course of the interrogation," and this offers an additional safeguard against domination.[5]

Still, it is important to note the many ways in which one's choice of silence can be vacated. Here I advance two factors: belief systems and systemic vulnerabilities.

In the dominant belief system, silence equals guilt. *Miranda*'s attempt to corral the choice of silence within safe bounds may not be sufficient to resist established opinion's contrary force. In this sense, the Mirandized face a stark choice between, on the one hand, speaking and facing the risk of being interrogated to the point of (self-)incrimination and, on the other, keeping silence and facing the negative inferences drawn from the refusal to speak.

Potentially vacated by the belief that those who remain silent cannot be truth bearers, the choice for silence can also be vacated by systemic vulnerabilities. On the Warren Court's admission, the urge to confess may be motivated by the accused's "weaknesses." What Peter Brooks calls "inextricable layers of shame, guilt, self-loathing, [and] the desire to propitiate figures of authority" (2000, 18) are all known to put the vulnerable, most notably juveniles, the mentally disabled, or those suffering from mental illness, at higher risk of (often, falsely) confessing, even when given the opportunity *not* to. It takes power—and not just opportunity—to resist the compulsion to speak.

Furthermore, asymmetries of power between groups in society are radically accentuated in interrogation rooms and courtrooms. For people other than those expertly counseled or hardened criminals, interrogation presents itself as an intimidating speech situation in which their subordination—along socioeconomic, racial, gender, and disability lines—is easily reinforced by "subject[ing] the individual will to the will of his examiner," making those being interrogated give credence to what the examiner says they have done, to what the examiner says is true, and to who the examiner says they are (*Miranda v. Arizona*).

These asymmetries have been compounded by the requirement that the right to silence, to be effective, has to be explicitly and verbally claimed.[6] As a result of this requirement, any invocation of the right to end an interview must now be clear and unambiguous, but a waiver of the right to silence may be inferred from a suspect's speaking to the interviewing officer. This shifting of the burden of proof flies in the face of the known fact that suspects tend to adopt an indirect, and thus seemingly equivocal, mode of expression. Importantly, this is even more true for suspects who are women or are from an ethnic minority, as members of these groups tend to adopt less direct or assertive speech patterns. Yet while indirect or tentative assertions of the right to silence are likely to be ignored, confessions and other inculpatory statements are used to prove that the suspect waived that right. In the context of custodial interrogation, the right to remain silent is thus increasingly "the province of those fortunate enough or educated enough to say the right words" (Strauss 2009, 824).[7]

Silence is sometimes deemed "democratic" because it is equally accessible to all. But this claim is deceptive. As we have seen, our power to say and not to say comes from, and is disabled by, relationships of power, systemic vulnerabilities, and the forms of domination they foster. There is no *effective* right to silence apart from a consideration of these factors.

While the *Miranda* opinion sees the right to silence as effective if it guarantees that one's speech is "truly the product of free choice," Marianne Constable links the right to the preservation of "the trial as a space for proper speech," where "proper" means more than simply "free choice" (2005, 150). Under the extraordinary speech conditions of an in-custody interrogation or trial, she explains, the suspect or accused must be made aware that their statements and silences may take on a different import than they would in ordinary speech. This is critical for self-protection, of course. But, Constable stresses, it is also *more* critical for the possibility of justice, given that justice depends on *felicitous* or *effectual* speech rather than simply *free* speech (267).

This much, she claims, already transpires from the type of speech act at issue in *Miranda*. *Miranda* is an illocutionary act, a warning. As such, its aim is to put the addressee on notice about the risks of unguarded speech or speaking freely, given the specific and unexpected ways in which words may be heard in a legal setting. Where felicitous, the warning should make the addressee aware of "the need to proceed more carefully, or not to proceed at all" (150). If silence is adopted as a result, she claims, not much should be read from it. It might simply be the appropriate response given that one faces a special speech situation in which ordinary conventions "are not and cannot be met" (165). In Constable's reading, therefore, the right to silence is there to secure minimal conditions of felicity in interrogation and trial testimony, thus ensuring "that the statements of an accused who does speak have value as speech and thus as evidence" (173).

Constable is right to stress the importance of *felicitous* speech and of silence as a procedural right helping one navigate a heavily coded speech situation in which words can easily be misinterpreted or backfire. But she is guilty of falling under the illusion that the conditions of justice have been satisfied once silence is enfranchised. This is true even if the right to silence would make us robustly free from interference, since the right to silence may be necessary but will never be sufficient for free, let alone felicitous, speech.

There is yet another reason why Constable's expectations are unduly high. There is a paradox about *Miranda*'s silence. For its beneficiary's protection, its meaning is predetermined: that is, no meaning can be carried forward from the exercise of the right, since no adverse inferences can be legally made from it. But precisely because *Miranda*'s silence is so heavily coded, it is also barred from meaning anything else, namely, from enacting oppositional meaning by refusing to recognize "the legitimacy of the legally constituted speech situation" (Schaap 2008, 292). Hence, once silence is coded as a procedural right securing the fairness of court proceedings, it will struggle to be used by the "accused to contest the justness of the conditions of speech in the courtroom" (292) or the fairness of the legal procedure.

The relevant distinction here is one between, on the one hand, a silence that is a stipulated move within an existing language game, and is thus to be "interpreted through a pre-existing framework to which silence is a reaction," and, on the other hand, "silence as productive of specific language games," where the situation of interaction is disrupted and produced anew by the adoption of silence (Guillaume 2018, 477). Where the right to silence is taken as constitutive of the justness of the speech situation, exercising that right signals one's entry and acceptance of a preestablished language game; equally, making the alternative choice, to relinquish the right to silence, automatically authorizes the use of one's statements as evidence. This is a trade-off that Constable fails to notice.[8]

Both extremes are equally unhelpful, making too much or too little of the procedural right to silence. Despite its limitations, there are good reasons why the right to silence deserves a special place in trials and police questioning. Where buttressed by adequate legal counseling, the right to silence can militate against domination or overreliance on compelled speech in situations in which one's vulnerability is considerable—and especially so for those already structurally vulnerable. This is all the more important since both trial and interrogation are speech situations in which acting by the normal speech requirements—truthfulness, candor, free speaking, and so on—can have unexpected, negative consequences that are not easily undone. Under such circumstances, having a right to silence can empower a more "reflective non/participation" of the accused, following expert legal advice, and an internal consideration of reasons for speaking and not speaking (MacKenzie and Moore 2020, 441).

This warrants the inclusion of the right to silence among the general rights of defense (J. Jackson 2009, 863). Defense rights perform protective and participatory functions, and the right to silence can be seen to perform both (Roberts 2008, 333). As a right *against* self-incrimination or *against* enforced disclosure, the right to silence is primarily a protective right, entitling the right-holder to have the duty-bearer *refrain* from doing an act (namely, compelling their speech). But it can also be viewed "more positively as part of the framework for the exercise of effective defense rights" (J. Jackson 2009, 853). This exercise requires the weighing of the costs and benefits of participation and nonparticipation throughout the criminal process and the ability to act on the result of that deliberation, by speaking for oneself or performing silence in a commissive manner. As such, rather than simply a freedom from interference, the right to silence can promote a degree of control over one's actions—as to whether to participate (or not), to collaborate (or not)—when it is most needed.

Right to Free Speech = Right to Silence

My discussion of the right to silence as a defense right has already started to intimate that there is a tight relationship between the right to silence and the right to speech. But while few would deny that the right to speech is a cornerstone of democratic government, the right to silence is hardly ever characterized as a core democratic right. This is, however, the argument I want to advance in this section.

I take discussions of the First Amendment of the US Constitution as my point of departure. The First Amendment affirms speech as the route to citizen empowerment and improved democracy. This is primarily because speech constitutes and grounds a series of democratic freedoms: besides the freedom of speech itself, the freedoms of religion, press, assembly, and petition. Despite the lack of explicit mention of the right to silence, I want to argue that it is necessarily implicit in any constitutional provision of freedom of speech and expression.

I follow two famous landmark rulings of the US Supreme Court, *West Virginia State Board of Education v. Barnette* and *Wooley v. Maynard*, in affirming the right to silence as the necessary correlative of the right to (free) speech.[9] Both rulings concern religious freedom and address the legitimacy of state-imposed discursivity: namely, in *Barnette*, saluting the American flag and reciting the Pledge of Allegiance in school, and in *Maynard*, displaying a state's motto upon license plates. In both cases, appellees were religious citizens objecting to discursive impositions they believed to be offensive to their beliefs. The rulings concurred, taking the impositions to infringe on core freedoms protected by the First Amendment—of thought, religion, and speech. Equally, if not more, important to us, the Court stated these freedoms to entail *both* the right to speak freely *and* its reverse: the right to refrain from speaking at all.[10] One cannot be without the other.

The Court condemned state-imposed discursivity on account of the injury individuals suffer when forced to speak or act in a manner contrary to their personal views. In the words of *Barnette*, "compulsion . . . to declare a belief," compelled "affirmation of a belief and an attitude of mind" that are contrary to one's mind, unconstitutionally violates the "individual freedom of mind."[11]

Elaborating on the Court's ruling, I submit that what is at stake is not just the right to mental privacy, protecting individuals from unconsented intrusion into their beliefs, but a conscience- and autonomy-related right to speak (or not speak) one's *own* mind. In other words, compulsory discursivity is wrong because it compromises the reflexive integrity of speech—that is, the reflexive integrity between one's mind and its outward expression. When we say that a speaker speaks *as herself*, we mean that reflexive integrity is being observed, that "the content of expression, what is expressed" constitutes "a freely chosen intention of the speaker" (Hall 1985, 161). Integrity of expression and meaning is premised on sufficient agency, so that the speaker may be considered the author of her expressions, which will then be rightly considered her *own*. Protecting the speaker's agency entails securing them sufficient control over their expressive choices. However, where a person is deprived of the freedom "to be vocal or silent according to his conscience or personal inclination," as described in *Barnette*, this control is absent or, at least, greatly impaired.[12]

To put it loosely, free speech is speech originating inwardly in a freely formed intention of the speaker. Compelled speech mandates external conformity regardless of the speaker's intentions or what the speaker might believe or think. For this reason, instead of allowing expression, compulsory discursivity risks producing its opposite: a *silencing*. While speakers are required to literally utter words (or produce gestures, since the Court likens gesture to speech), their words may be speaking against their minds, and, when this happens, speech is silent. It leaves speakers saying nothing—or muted—*as themselves*.

This is where the right to silence enters. Silence protects one from being forced to speak as another. But the relationship between silence and speech goes deeper: silence is a *necessary* condition of a free relationship with one's words and thus a *necessary* condition of speech's reflexive integrity (Hall 1985, 162). Reflexive integrity "presupposes that one's expressions are one's own," and that presupposes, in turn, that one is "free in relation to one's words" (162). To be free in relation to one's words, one must be free *not* to speak them at all. Freedom of speech depends, therefore, on one's freedom to choose silence.

Rather than conceiving speech and silence as two separate rights, then, one may want to look at them as two aspects or descriptions of the same right, for without the right to silence the right to speech would be vacated. If this is not to happen, the right to silence must include not just withdrawal from speech but also "editorial decisions about what to include or exclude" in and from it, respectively (Horwitz 2010, 181). In other words, freedom of speech and expression requires a robust right to silence, including the right to decide whether one will or will not speak as well as what to say and not to say, where and when to do it, and before whom.

The co-constitutedness of the rights to silence and speech is apparent from the cases brought before the Supreme Court. Both are cases where words are imposed externally against the speaker's will and where not speaking has clear, attached penalties. But—and this but is important—even if the words one is made to speak are spoken willingly, the very fact that there is no penalty-free option for leaving them unsaid detracts from one's free relationship to them. As Philip Pettit explains, it would "make it too easy to be free in a given choice" if one were not made unfree "by having an option removed or replaced, if you happen not to want to enact it" (2011, 696). A related and significant conclusion follows. The right to silence is more than something one must resort to when other options are unavailable. It is more than simply a freedom *from* or a form of resistance *to* the terms of power. At its most fundamental, the right to silence is *constitutive* of the very possibility of practicing freedom *with/through/in* speech.

The right to silence can be seen as protecting speakers' proper authorial relation to their speech acts, but it can also be seen as something protecting audiences from misleading communication. In *Barnette*, the focus is the former. There are two main reasons for this. First, individuals compelled to salute the flag or recite a pledge would have been free to subsequently disavow those acts and clarify their stance publicly without incurring penalties.[13] Second, observers aware of the context in which speech acts were performed (namely, compulsion) would have good reasons to (1) believe that the requirements for sincere, intentional communication were absent; (2) not take communication to be going on, or see it as emanating from the state rather than those compelled; and (3) refrain from associating external signals (of patriotism) with the performers' beliefs or viewpoints (Blasi and Shiffrin 2004, 456).

But if *Barnette* is justified in not putting the stress on the risks of misleading communication, those risks should not be dismissed. Enforced communication will sometimes be taken at face value. What is more, it bears societal risks even where it does not necessarily mislead. As Václav Havel rightly noted, an empty ritual ("words without belief" or gestures "barren of meaning," as *Barnette* puts it[14]), even if known to be such, can create its own reality. By performing the officially mandated culture—even if there is no intention to communicate, even if attention is no longer paid to its substantive content—"individuals confirm the system, fulfil the system, make the system, are the system" (Havel 1985, 44–45). Performative citizenship, however empty, can create its own frightening reality.

If citizens are harmed when conditions of reflexive speech are eliminated, the elimination itself speaks of an improper relation between a state and its citizens. Where a state compels its citizens to enact state-sponsored views in their own voices, citizens are taken as mere instruments in state communication, or, to put it in Kantian terms, as mere means to the state's ends. Even if the state's ends and/or messages are worthy ones, citizen adherence to them should be gained through persuasion, not compulsion, as only the former shows respect for citizens as moral agents, capable of self-determination and independent judgment about what to believe, why to believe it, and about whether, when, and where to make their beliefs public. Persuasion acknowledges the separation between state and citizen selves. Recitation eradicates it, eliminating the possibility of a relation that is not a relation of domination. In a democratic community of inquiry, the integrity of speech production—as well as the integrity of thought production—depends, as the *Maynard* case puts it, on the recognition of "the right to refrain from speaking at all."

Among the core freedoms that the right to silence sustains, the Court lists the freedoms of thought, conscience, religion, opinion, and expression. Given its centrality to the rulings, it is worth unpacking the relationship between religious freedom and the right to silence a bit more. Silence can be constitutive of one's faith and worship; it can also be a way of protecting both. The right to silence can offer religious protection both as an entitlement to *not* reveal or disclose one's beliefs and as an entitlement to *refuse* to profess another's beliefs. The right to silence thus bears a relation to privacy, anonymity, and, more specifically, the protection of (religious) dissenters, in that it allows one to control whether, how, and when to express or reveal oneself and one's beliefs to others. However, to offer protection, silence must be handled with care: a noticeable withdrawal or refusal to speak, especially where speech is commanded, may betray a dissenter's views. This much was well understood by early modern proponents of the doctrine of mental reservation, who "expressly claimed an entitlement to secret identity protected by ambiguous or even silent speech" (that is, speech combining an audible statement, meant to mislead the hearer, with a silent modification that rendered the whole sentence true) (Halley 1991, 36). This is also the reason why privacy, anonymity, and dissenter-protection arguments take a back seat in *Barnette*: they face limitations when applied to compulsory public rituals involving speech acts such as reciting or pledging. In those cases, it is "abstention or exemption from the practice, not participation," that "causes self-exposure" (Blasi and Shiffrin 2004, 456).

Still, the right to silence remains essential to the protection of rights of nonparticipation or ideological non-association (Kalin 1978). Let me explain. The right to silence can be seen as a protection against being forced to speak in a manner contrary to one's personal views. But it can also be taken as a right to resist coerced participation in, or ideological association with, a specific ideological activity. Take, for instance, a country with two main political forces: an incumbent party, which supports military intervention abroad, and the opposition, which campaigns against it. The incumbent party enforces the salute of the flag and the reciting of a pledge of allegiance in schools, and the opposition affirms the right to silence on the grounds that both activities have a strong militaristic connotation and are designed to create the artificial appearance of widespread support for militarism. The primary concern here is not with how enforced speech harms individual integrity of thought or belief but with how assimilation into an ideological lexicon may skew political competition by promoting certain values and political viewpoints at the expense of others and distorting public perceptions of their level of endorsement. As a "right to resist coerced participation in or support of political or ideological activity," the right to silence can support key democratic freedoms of participation and association (Kalin 1978, 769).

Broadly speaking, the relationship between the right to silence and the right of (free) association can be cast in indirect or direct terms. I start with the former: the meaningful protection of free speech depends on group activity insofar as people are empowered to form and present their views more effectively when they come together, and freedom of speech, as I have argued, depends on the freedom to withdraw from it, totally or in part. Hence, right of association and right to silence hold an indirect relation *via* freedom of speech. But their relationship can also be established more directly. In his study of secret societies, Georg Simmel shows how keeping silent about certain things forms community by drawing boundaries between those who know the secret and outsiders (1906, 462). Besides forging oppositional solidarity, silence generates a specific type of trust between members, formed around the ability to preserve silence about membership in the group and the secrets they share. While communities structured around silence often pursue nefarious purposes (crime, conspiracy, unaccountable influence), silence can also be used for legitimate protection, socialization, and community building. A couple of illustrations are in order. In 1947, the legal team of the Hollywood Ten, a group of producers, directors, and screenwriters called before the House Un-American Activities Committee (HUAC) for their alleged Communist ties, argued that their clients had the right to refuse to answer questions about their and others' possible Communist political affiliations. The right to silence, they maintained, constituted not only a protection against self-incrimination, as recognized in the Fifth Amendment of the US Constitution, but also an essential part of the right to free association, protected under the First (see Anderson 2009). Partisans of an opinion or political belief would be unlikely to associate with one another if under the obligation of membership disclosure, knowing that sharing this information could subject them and their associates to reprisals, even if they and their activities were not responsible for wrongdoing or deserving of censure. Key in protecting political association in the face of ideological persecution, the right to silence is also integral to the reproduction and protection of certain communities and their ways of living. A case in point is the silence kept by some Indigenous communities about culturally sensitive knowledge. The 2007 *Chicot* case in Canada is a well-known example of this (Rollo 2017, 598). Asked to engage in a process of consultation, the Ka'a'gee Tu First Nation refused to disclose traditional knowledge concerning the location of traplines and burial sites on the grounds that publicity would place the sites at risk and threaten the community.[15] Their refusal produced and reproduced community. The protected knowledge was not just something of instrumental value. Its secret and sacred nature played a vital role in organizing, hierarchically ordering, and giving shared meaning to the community. To disclose it was to put the community at risk.

No Meaningful Silence Without Free Speech

In the previous section I have established that the right to silence is necessary to enfranchise speech. But what if it also worked the other way around? What if the value of free speech consisted, at least in part, in enfranchising silence? The argument has been advanced by Philip Pettit (1994), and a quick reconstruction is in order before I examine it.

Where speech is not free, many are compelled to say nothing. As important as what happens to speech under conditions of unfreedom is what happens to silence: Pettit claims that it becomes a blank, a cipher, meaningless (1994, 51). Because people cannot freely object, we cannot know whether their silence means assent or dissent. And this unreadability makes silence ripe for appropriation, for it to be "interpreted in whatever fashion the powerful wish to construe it" (Pettit 2018, 75). Where speech is unfree, therefore, silence is *silenced*. By contrast, Pettit submits, where conditions of free speech obtain, silence can speak clearly, communicating a determinate message—namely, it is an illocution of consent, telling the other "you are happy with the way things are" (75).

In Pettit's argument, free speech is primarily understood as a negative freedom, a freedom from others' interference. But, true to his commitment to the notion of freedom as non-domination, Pettit stresses that protection of speech must go deeper than the bare fact of noninterference. It must extend to possible arbitrary interference, or what Pettit calls "robust" or "resilient" noninterference. However, should conditions be in place that secure one against possible arbitrary interference by others on whether we speak and what we say, and should no independent reason suggest why one should remain silent in the face of a public stimulus, then, Pettit argues, it is reasonable to assume that the silence we hear means consent or approval.

In an interesting twist, what is argued here is that in the presence of free speech, silence is empowered. That is, silence—whose communicative power is often said to be undercut by its ambiguity—becomes a form of transparent communication. In free speech therefore lies the promise that, even if we lapse into silence, "we are not deprived of our voices" (Pettit 1994, 54). The resulting political community, as depicted by Pettit, is one where everyone, even the silent ones, will "remain active presences in conversation, active parties to potential consensus and active controllers of the things others say and do" (54). Where it is made perfectly legible by the presence of free speech, silence becomes the perfect medium for the exercise of positive freedom: namely, the freedom to participate *in*, and influence the shaping *of*, one's political community.

The reverse of this dream of an actively present community is the nightmare of its perfect transparency. There are several problems with Pettit's argument, but here I focus on just two of them: its elimination of the right to silence and the implied conception of power.

I have argued in this chapter that an effective right to silence is a necessary condition of free speech. Pettit's suggestion that free speech fully disambiguates silence effectively removes this right by fixing silence's meaning or making it necessarily speak approval. Where fixed to one meaning, silence is no longer protected as a choice.

My second objection relates to the implied conception of power. Freedom as non-domination is freedom to enjoy not merely the absence of interference but also the absence of domination. Domination is defined by Pettit as the condition of living under the thumb or arbitrary will of another—a person or a state. Thus conceived, domination entails an important, but narrow, conception of power as something a particular person or group may have over another. This conception of power is narrow because in envisioning domination in terms of imposition of will, it overlooks social-structural forms of domination, which are unassignable to anyone's will.

Where conceived structurally, domination emerges as the result of skewed power relations, preventing the self-determination of individuals or groups by affecting their preference and attitude formation and by preventing the identification, expression, and satisfaction of their interests and needs. Overlooking the workings of structural domination can easily lead to silences being misread. That is, one can miss the possibility that, even under conditions of robust free speech, a silence looking just like acquiescence may in effect be the expression of economic, social, and political defeat, making people too hopeless to voice outrage, express dissatisfaction, or articulate a challenge (Langton 1993). This type of silence reflects the absence of opportunities to exit one's current situation and can also reflect the absence of voice controls. By this, I refer to the lack of a political vocabulary to voice concerns that cannot be expressed by/in dominant political talk. No right of citizens to participate in public debate, however robust, can sufficiently engage these problems.

Pettit's concern with the silencing of silence is one that I and democratic theorists in general share. But there is something troubling about presuming, as Pettit does, that any *one* condition could ever make silence mean—and give—blanket approval. First, it risks doing exactly what Pettit sets himself to avert: co-opting silence in the reproduction of an unjust or undesirable status quo. Second, it is driven by a sovereign fantasy of perfect legibility and mutual control, which epitomizes domination.[16] Third, it is self-defeating in that the single precisification of silence as approval puts an end to what Pettit believes silence is supposed to promote: communication.

## The Right of Silence as Expressive Freedom

In the previous sections I have established that the protections of free speech must extend to silence insofar as there can be no free speech without it. In this section, I want to engage a different question, namely, whether silence could be entitled to free speech protections not just as a form of exit *from* or suspension *of* speech but as itself an expressive form.

Three theoretical justifications are commonly given for the constitutional protection of free speech under the First Amendment. These are the promotion of democratic self-governance; the promotion of the search for truth by ensuring a free marketplace of ideas; and the promotion of dignitary interests, such as individual self-realization and autonomy.[17] Free speech is deemed to be of instrumental value to the pursuit of each and all of these.[18]

The focus of the First Amendment is on the production and distribution of words—so on what grounds could the First protect silence other than as a *necessary* condition of free speech production? The question is pertinent, but two preliminary answers suggest themselves readily: first, silence can be used alongside a speech message whose communicative value it enhances, and second, silence can sometimes function *like* speech and convey quasi-linguistic meaning. Silence, where functioning in this way, thus becomes a plausible candidate for speech's protections.

But then a second question arises: is communicative silence sufficiently imbued with those elements of communication that the protections of speech seek to guard? The answer to this question can seem a bit trickier. The First Amendment focuses on speech that "communicates *something*" (Tushnet, Chen, and Blocher 2017, 99). Its prime target is thus any speech act with propositional or message-bearing content, or even speech communicating political ideas. Democracy- and truth-promoting justifications for the protection of free speech sustain this view. In them, free speech is for the sake of constituting a reasoning public through debate, discussion, argument, and so on, all of which are activities presupposing locutionary speech acts. Yet silent modes of communication are non-locutionary (cf. Acheson 2008) and do not take the form of reason-giving (Gray 2023, 824). This may seem to make them of little value in sustaining the democratic ideal of public inquiry.

Yet this is too quick a conclusion. For one, it assumes the "give-and-take" of arguments to be the sole form of political engagement. Second, it elides the fact that the value of silence can lie in its capacity to interrupt or suspend hegemonic meanings sometimes concealed under the legitimized appearance of "reason-giving" and point toward the inconsistencies of dominant discourses (something I will explore in chapters 3 and 4). Third, communicative silences are often felicitous in engaging their audiences emotionally, cognitively, socially, and politically precisely because they mean something that cannot be put into words or that dominant forms of speech fail to address or even recognize. Consider, for instance, disruptive silent practices of protest such as the refusal of Indigenous athletes to sing anthems glorifying the settler state's colonial past. Their keeping of silence constitutes the kind of "engaged and responsible democratic communication" that seeks to reinvigorate the public realm by commanding the public's attention to speech closures, the wrongs they legitimize and inflict, and the need to redress them (I. Young 2001, 688).

But if a democracy-promoting justification for the protection of some communicative silences is available in principle, silence's ambiguity as signal and its strong reliance on audience members as meaning-makers may still seem to disqualify it from speech protections.

The Supreme Court has sometimes drawn on *Spence v. Washington*, a case dealing with nonverbal free "speech" (namely, the burning of the American flag as a form of symbolic protest), to establish when an action counts as a communicative act. *Spence* separates out communicative acts by applying a double test of *intent* and *understanding*: nonverbal conduct is speech when the speaker has "an *intent* to convey a *particularized* message . . . and in the surrounding circumstances the likelihood was great that the message would be *understood* by those who viewed it."[19] In the terms of *Spence*, for silence to count as a communicative act it must pass an onerous test. First, it must constitute an active, intentional withholding of speech for the purpose of communicating a particularized message. Second, it must be recognized by the audience as such a communicative act. Third, the audience must converge on a *shared* understanding of what the silence means.

It is sometimes possible for silence to satisfy the three conditions. Structured or highly defined contexts help establish the connection between one's choice of silence and the listeners' ability to converge on one and the same understanding of it. But this is relatively exceptional: silence is normally open to multiple interpretations. Also, any attempt to distinguish between valid and invalid interpretations is premised on the assumption that the choice of silence was intended to have a particularized meaning. Yet this may *not* be the case. Silence is sometimes deliberately used to leave ambiguity unresolved.

Should communicative silence's ambiguity and openness to multiple interpretations exclude it from free speech's protections? The *intent* and *understanding* test delineated by *Spence* would seem to imply this. But the problem may lie with the test, more so than with silence (the test's stringency is recognized in, for example, *National Endowment for the Arts v. Finley*). A literal application of the test would exclude not just much (politically) communicative silence but also much speech (notably, ambiguous and nonsensical speech) and even more artwork (especially if nonrepresentational) from being shielded (Tushnet, Chen, and Blocher 2017, chap. 1). As such, the Court's position has been to extend coverage. But the Court has struggled to explain why. In a way, this is not surprising. Working with a linguistic ontology of the political and an associated understanding of meaning as representational meaning, the Court has tried to justify inclusion by finding "speech beyond words," and it stumbles where speech can no longer be found (Tushnet, Chen, and Blocher 2017, 176).

To make things harder, one could shift focus from silences whose (political) communicative intentions are relatively undisputed to consider silences that deliberately abstain from communicative intentions. Could they be entitled to free speech protections, and, if so, on what grounds? Consider John Cage's "silent piece," *4'33"*, a work that does not seem to mean, or even express, something but simply is.

*4'33"* is a silent piece with a score. For each of the three movements of the piece, the composer's sole instruction is "Tacet." *Tacet* is a Latin word that translates into English as "is silent." In musical terms it refers to a rest. The command to be silent is directed at the performer and calls for the action of *not* playing. Abiding by the piece's command requires *staging*, and the *staged* action must be conscious and engaged—that is, it must make the commanded silence *present* (a *present* absence).

Historically, the "tacet" mandate presupposed the silencing of one voice within an otherwise continuing musical form. The pattern repeats itself in *4'33"*. Two different "silences" make up the piece: the silence resulting from the intentional omission of compositionally determined sounds and the silence-as-ambient-sound that the audience is primed to hear. Carl Jung, a strong influence on Cage, captures the complex nature of this double silence perfectly: "One must be able to let things happen. I have learned from the East what it means by the phrase 'Wu wei': namely, not-doing, letting be, which is quite different from doing nothing" (1940, 31–32).

The audience is co-opted into the piece's doing. Following music hall conventions, the audience is expected to play a familiar role: that is, to sit quietly and listen in silence. Its exposure to the stimulus of the performed silence, however, is meant to influence its response to the stimulus of ambient silence.

Although the audience's attunement to the latter is externally driven, the audience's bodily, sensorial engagement with the environment is a necessary co-creator of the aural world that opens itself. On the one hand, silence could just happen if performer and audience did nothing. On the other hand, however, the resulting silence is the happening that they make happen (Muers 2015a, 336). This "they" is here ultimately threefold: the composer *instructing* silence; the musician *performing* silence-as-absence-of-intended-sound; and the audience *upholding* both the performed and the ambient sounds.

Using convention to emancipate the listening ear from convention, *4'33"* makes the acoustic impossibility of silence manifest. However, this is an effect only achievable by making silence heard in the concert hall. The audibility of silence is secured through a play of expectations. The expectation is created that concert music will be played. The audience sits and expects sound to start. The expectation is frustrated, progressively, through a play with the temporality of silence. The short first movement (33″) is just long enough to prompt the question, What's going on? The second (2'40″) induces endless, intensifying discomfort, unease in the presence of silence. The third movement (1'20″) is long enough to make one leave the room or settle into silence's soundful *presence*.

Framing upholds this presence. Frames are cognitive structures guiding representations and perceptions, determining what parts of reality become noticeable. In the case of *4'33"*, the three movements of the classical sonata, their different times and durations, frame and give direction to silence. This frame is responsible for the shifting of attention from the silenced stage to the ambient *silence* extraneous to the score. As the shifting occurs, it becomes apparent that "real" silence is not silent after all. Filled out with a myriad of unintentional noises, it has a presence in its own right.

Cagean silence is a particular entity. His definition of silence as all the sound we do not intend is pregnant with consequences. For just as "noise against noise could produce silence," so did "silence against silence" produce, for Cage, (unsounded) music (Kahn 1997, 577). And thus categories of music and silence, and silence and noise, are so thoroughly dissolved that no sonorous (or potentially sonorous) place is left outside music (558).

Cage is acutely aware of how silence changes within a piece intent on freeing silence from all musical intention. To appreciate the change, we need a comparison with the norm of composition.

Sounds and silences are the traditional materials of a musical composition. They are expected parts of a conventional music structure: "There can be no right making of music that does not structure itself from the very roots of sound and silence-lengths of time" (Cage 1970, 81). Because of its "confrontation with the construct of silence, its need to be other," however, "music itself refuses silence" (Toop 2011). And thus we get to sound and silence understood in binary terms: distinct from one another as, respectively, the presence or absence of a deliberately produced sound. Thus understood, musical silence amounts to what Dauenhauer classifies as an "intervening silence," "as the rests that punctuate a musical phrase," the silence that "terminates one sound phrase and, in some fashion, clears the way for the next sound" (1973, 11). But precisely because such rests are sites of expressivity and musical articulation, silence is, effectively, already probing the binary logic of opposites by dissolving one into the other—gap as expressivity, absence as presence, silence within/as music.

But what happens to silence—and to our perception of it—when this structure ceases to be part of the composition altogether, and composition becomes a purposeless process? "Formerly," Cage explains, "silence was the time lapse between sounds, useful towards a variety of ends, among them tasteful arrangement, emphasis, expressivity, pause, punctuation, or even overall architecture," predetermined or evolving (1961, 23). But where musical goals are no longer pursued, "means become meaningless, because nothing is meant to be happening, whatever happens happens" (Kahn 1997, 596n93). As a result, "silence becomes something else": no longer just an abeyance or temporary suspension of the musical listening to sound but "sounds, the ambient sounds," whose nature is "unpredictable and changing" (Cage 1961, 23).

Rather than re-creating the binary silence-sound of traditional music, 4'33" seeks to undercut it. Silence as noise is *the other* of traditional music, yet it is always in effect already *in* music. What happens in 4'33" is that it is explicitly brought *within* it (Cobussen 2003, 281).[20] In so doing, the piece shows that silence is not emptiness but a plenitude of sonorous life. Hence, if the sounds brought within the piece are called silence, it is because they "do not form part of a musical intention" (Cage 1961, 23). Rather than being part of a given structure, they represent a rupture with it.

But this is, of course, only half of the story. For in 4'33" silence is also part of the musical intention—and indeed structured by it. This may not be immediately apparent. After all, the sounds to which the audience is made to turn are beyond the control of both composer and performer and are not organized in terms of pitch, volume, harmony, and so on. However, the fact that sound is not specified does not prevent it from being intended at a nonspecific level. In effect, the act of silencing the performer to create an empty duration containing no intentional sound constitutes, in and of itself, a radical organization of musical sound, perhaps the most radical of them all. To argue otherwise "is like saying that the (legal) restriction of (personal) freedom depends on nothing more than an absence of (legal) organization" (Seymour 2013, 533).

I am now in a position to return to my original question: whether it would make sense to extend the protections of free speech to works like *4'33"*. While some artworks have distinctive communicative qualities *intended* by the artist and widely *understood* by the targeted audience, many artworks, probably the majority, struggle to meet *Spence*'s double requirement. Intent is an underinclusive criterion, as many artists produce work that is "not intended to convey a specific message," idea, or concept (Tushnet, Chen, and Blocher 2017, 25). It happens similarly with the criterion of understanding. Artistic expression typically lends itself to multiple, changeable, and even conflicting interpretations, and the reception of artworks—especially those of an experimental nature, such as *4'33"*—is often marked by incomprehension.

Engagement with *4'33"* is not about *understanding* a message *intended* by the composer. *4'33"* is a non-referential work, intent on enabling an experience of the aesthetic qualities of unintended sounds rather than on projecting meaning. Its silence has sensorial and cognitive, rather than communicative, qualities. It calls for a renewed mode of attention, a new mode of being in the world, one that sensorially reconnects the audience with the unrepresentable, incommunicable, and un-hearable aspects of everyday experience. It also thereby makes a critical intervention about, and in, the concert musical form as well as about the nature of music itself.

Cage had no qualms about his aim to displace notions of intention, expression, and meaning from art. Directly opposing the idea of organizing sounds to express oneself or to express *something*, he contended that sounds should be liberated "from abstract ideas," that one should "let them be physically uniquely themselves" (quoted in Griffiths 1981, 124).[21] In other words, sounds ought not to be treated as means to extraneous ends—thoughts, meanings, communication, or aesthetic values of taste—but as ends in themselves.

Does this imply, as some have argued, that *4'33"* limits itself to capturing a "natural phenomenon [silence] that already exists freely in nature" (Saw cited in Seymour 2013) and is thus neither communicative nor the outcome of an act of individual expression? It is important to engage this objection because it could rule out protections being extended to the piece, including copyrights.

*4'33"* does confound notions of authorship and ownership. Whose silence is it that the piece brings to awareness? Who is responsible for its keeping?

Cage stressed that his goal in the piece was authorial suppression rather than expression—that is, to remove the will, intention, and subjectivity from the process of artistic creation. Inspired by Zen Buddhism, he believed silence to negate the will: "When silence, generally speaking, is not in evidence, the will of the composer is. Inherent silence is equivalent to denial of the will" (Cage 1961, 53). Those denying 4'33" expressive qualities are thus correct in the notion that the piece constitutes "a conscious suppression of the author's personal will" and is intent on not expressing mental attitudes (Saw cited in Seymour 2013, 18). But whether this warrants their conclusion that any claims to authorship are thereby quashed is questionable (Saw cited in Seymour 2013, 18). True, Cage was equivocal about whether the authorship of the work was his or the audience's.[22] There is little doubt that 4'33" has many producers, but only one person is responsible for the conception of the artwork and can take credit (or blame) for it. By denying himself the will to write musical sound, Cage exercised control over the shape of the piece (even if not over the heard sounds of silence). After all, the suppression of the will presupposes a will to suppress, and the disavowal of "authorial voice" in 4'33" "involves not only a conscious decision of the will, but is perhaps the most extreme and continuous expenditure of the same will" (Seymour 2013, 537).

The question remains, however, whether Cage's exercise of the will was one of intentional creation of an artwork showing distinctive artistic qualities. In referring to the creation of 4'33", Cage emphasizes the meticulous thought process through which the piece emerged, suggesting it may be a conceptual artwork seeking to challenge and probe us about what we tend to take for granted in the domain of art (and outside it). But the author's account alone cannot establish its artistic distinctiveness. For that, we need to compare 4'33" with a few roughly contemporary "silent" pieces. Take, for instance, the work of Charles Ives, another experimental composer, especially his early twentieth-century pieces *A Contemplation of a Serious Matter* and *A Contemplation of Nothing Serious*. In these pieces, ambient silence is given presence not by intentionally abstaining from the production of musical sound but by playing the sounds of nature. When placed against these works and against the broader musical tradition from which it stems (that is, concert music), 4'33" stands out as an artwork giving silence a distinctive expression.[23] What is unique to the piece is not so much that it has nothing to say—for it is obviously informed by thoughts about the nature of music, the nature of silence, the aesthetic equality of sound, and so on—but that it "says" those things "by/through/in listening" (Cobussen 2003, 282). And not just through listening: Cage evokes a new mode of listening, implying conceptual suspension and careful orientation toward "worldly things" that are always plural, dynamic, and unsettled (Myers 2013, 17).

In this light, the idea that 4'33" has a claim to First Amendment coverage starts gaining traction. Is this because it is a "word-equivalent" or an artwork with a signifying intent? No; to claim this much would be to deny Cagean silence its distinctive nature. But it seems unquestionable that the piece engages silence as an expressive choice, which means that in protecting the piece one is protecting the expressive freedom of artistic creation (Armijo 2018).

A focus on the speech value of silence alone misses this point and leads to a neglect—in the sense of overlooking and that of devaluing—of the ways in which silence is *not* like speech and does *not* act like it. Delving into Cage has allowed us to see that silence, understood as the absence of intentional sound, is not just the natural medium within which music happens. It can constitute an expressive choice, as in the case of performative-conceptual works like 4'33", or a site of expressivity, as in the case of music and other art forms involving a dimension of temporal development (such as theatre or poetry). One could say about musical silence what John Dewey said about music more generally: "There are values and meanings that can only be expressed by immediately visible and audible qualities, and to ask what they mean in the sense of something that can be put into words is to deny their distinctive existence" (1934, 74). That is to say, musical silence is a medium of expression that can be experienced and not verbally expressed. As we saw with 4'33", however, silence can also be someone's expressive choice without being itself a medium of expression. In Cage's "silent piece," the silence performed on stage is the composer's choice for enacting the underpinning concept (that is, silence as accidental sound). In addition, for this reason, the composer's expressive choice is that the silence performed bears no (other) expressive function; it is just a vehicle. The musicians' performance of nonperformance is not designed to say something or even to hold the power of direct emotional expression. Its purpose is rather to structure a situated, embodied practice of listening, enabling members of the audience to perceive and respond to accidental environmental sounds in a nonpremeditated manner.

We tend to think of democratic political agency solely in terms of words and not the senses. But the ways in which 4'33" cultivates the art of listening gives us reason to think again. Cage contemplated the possibility of "the performance of a musical piece" acting "as a metaphor of society, a metaphor of the society that we dream of" (Cage and Retallack 2012). Regardless of whether *4'33"* is a musical piece, we can consider what kind of society the "silent piece" might perform. I submit that the piece nurtures a "situated sensibility" integral to the kind of "dispositional ethics of encounter" that must underpin democratic forms of sociability, marked by "deep openness, receptivity, and reciprocal responsiveness to the otherness of others" (Beausoleil 2017, 297). In particular, the piece points to the fact that to encounter difference as difference (in this case, sounds as *sounds*, each unique, yet equal to each other), one needs to embrace a level of uncertainty and risk. That is, one needs to welcome the interruption of the regimes of perception that inform common sense, questioning "what makes sense and can be sensed" (Panagia 2009, 3), and allow "for what exceeds one's frame to unsettle and possibly reconfigure such framing" (Beausoleil 2017, 295). All of these possibilities enact a mode of democratic agency grounded in receptivity and responseability, rather than mastery and assertiveness, without which it would seem impossible to carry on with—and remain open to the reconfiguration of—our associational lives.

And so this chapter comes full circle. I started with the right to silence functioning primarily as a "negative" power of citizenship (Gray 2023, 820), shielding citizens from domination or from becoming a mere instrument of others' power, and I am closing with the practice of silence as a positive power, enacting a democratic "ethics of encounter" wherein agency is performed not "as the ability to assert one's will over and against what is encountered—but rather as the ability to act in response to what one encounters" (Beausoleil 2017, 305). In the movement between the one and the other, I placed the right to silence among our most fundamental democratic rights and foregrounded it as a necessary, but often overlooked, condition for other, more celebrated rights: notably, rights of speech, association, thought, religion, due process, and reflexive (non)participation—in the criminal process, for sure, but also in social and political life more generally. In the next chapter, I turn to the challenges and harms of social silencing as well as to the ways in which the active choice of silence and the strategic use of silencing can enact and stake claims to democratic equality and robust forms of inclusion.

# 3

# SELF-SILENCING AND SOCIAL SILENCES

Words have a head, O shrewd man, and a tail.
Do not insert thy words between words of others.
The possessor of deliberation, intelligence and shrewdness
Does not say a word till he sees silence.
—Sa'di Shirazi, *The Gulistan of Sa'di*

## Self-Censorship and the Functioning of Democratic Society

In the previous chapter, I argued that there is no right to free expression where there is no robust right to silence. This includes not just the right to choose whether to speak but what to say, where and when to say it, and before whom. Thus defined, the right to silence gives us an editorial power over ourselves, which, I have maintained, is key for autonomous agency and for protection against domination.

Self-editing is a feature of the presentation of the self in everyday life. As the self "guides and controls the impression [others] form of him, and the kinds of things he may and may not do while sustaining his performance before them," one is likely to withhold information that might otherwise have been expressed (Goffman 1956, preface). However, everyday self-editing takes a different turn when it becomes self-censoring—that is, where the nonperformance is explained by a problematic relationship of power or influence (Festenstein 2018, 326; Horton 2011, 97). Unlike common forms of self-restraint, self-censoring inscribes a tension in the self-censor "as, on the one hand, the author, and on the other, the instrument, of the censorship" (Horton 2011, 91). While censorship presupposes that censor and censored are different persons or entities, in *self-*censorship the same person or entity occupies both roles. The *self-* element hints at an action of the self over itself and the possibility that agency is involved—that there is "on some level a deliberate, conscious decision on the part of the self-censor." But this does not mean that the action is positively chosen, and it may even be that in certain cases talk of choice is somewhat fictitious, since practiced often and long enough self-censorship can become perfectly omissive, "an unreflective disposition, a habit, or a kind of second nature" (Horton 2011, 97).

The political salience of self-censorship is easy enough to understand once we consider the negative impact that it can have not just on autonomy and individuality but also, more generally, on democratic life and core democratic goods, notably expressive freedom, the quality of democratic debate, popular control, and capacity for collective agency. Let me discuss each of these in turn.

The costs of self-censoring to individual autonomy and individuality come across most clearly in John Stuart Mill's "On Liberty," in which he reflects on the tyrannizing effects of "prevailing opinion and feeling" (Mill 1989, 8). Although often taken as the paragon of free speech fundamentalism, Mill does not mistake freedom of speech for equality of voice. He is painfully aware that expressive freedom can be imperiled by the power imbalance between prevailing and non-prevailing opinions. The costs Mill attaches to pressures for conformism are both individual and societal. Conformity, he argues, stalls individual creativity and self-development by restricting the individual's freedom to speak and capacity to develop their mind, be wrong, appreciate their mistakes, and change what they think and how they live. But there are also society-wide, epistemic costs to conformism. We are fallible as knowers. Being fallible, we can be wrong about what we take to be true, yet our erroneous opinions are less likely to be corrected if challengers are silenced. "If any opinion is compelled to silence," Mill submits, "that opinion may, for aught we can certainly know, be true," yet we will never know and will keep to our error. "Only through diversity of opinion," he stresses, "is there [ . . . ] a chance of fair play to all sides of the truth" (177). This is especially so in moral and political issues, as in practical matters truth is a question of "reconciling and combining opposites" (176). Even if challenges to received opinion are wrong, they are still beneficial, Mill contends, in that they prevent us from dogmatically subscribing to the truth we already hold. All truth must be believed for a reason; thus, "even if the world is in the right, it is always probable that dissentients have something worth hearing to say for themselves, and that truth would lose something by their silence" (49). Indeed,

Mill believes that no right to silencing can be inferred from the existence of a consensus over a particular issue. "If all mankind, minus one were of one opinion," he writes, "mankind would not be more justified in silencing than he, if he had the power, would be justified in silencing mankind" (109). Minorities of opinion, even a minority of one, keep disagreement alive, and disagreement, Mill insists, is beneficial—socially and epistemically—in terms of arriving at the truth and of endorsing it for the right reasons.

It was Alexis de Tocqueville, however, not Mill, who best explained the mechanisms whereby some views become entrenched and others disappear. The transformation of majoritarian opinion into dogma, Tocqueville explains, is assisted by processes of self-silencing, in which silent unbelievers play a major role. Silent unbelievers are those "who, like the dissenter, do not believe, but, like the majority, act *as though* they do" (Ikuta 2020, 44; my emphasis). As the conforming pressure of public opinion mounts, "those who initially rejected it as false end up accepting it as general, and those who continue to oppose it in the depth of their hearts do not show it" (Tocqueville 2011, 1650). Fear of social ostracism makes them abstain from performing any speech acts—or, indeed, any type of act—that could disclose their disagreement.

It is not just individual agency but collective agency, Tocqueville stresses, that suffers from unbelievers' being cowed into silence. Their withdrawal into silence makes them invisible to one another and incapable of coordinated resistance. Even where many of them might be willing to take the risk of opposing the dominant opinion, all stay quiet, because they do not believe others would follow them. If anything, this is worsened by silent unbelievers' refusal to publicly express esteem for vocal dissenters: "If you seek only their esteem, they will feign to refuse even that" (2011, 656). Fearing that social banishment will target not just vocal dissenters but non-ostracizers, silent dissenters feel compelled to behave like ostracizers, further accelerating the spiraling of dissenting views into silence (Tocqueville 2011; Elster 2009, 39).

This is a dire outcome for democracy, with its dependence on the dynamism of public opinion. Successful action by dissenters requires social uptake. With the dissenter finding himself radically isolated, even by fellow believers, the dissenter "subsides into silence, as if he felt remorse for having spoken the truth" (Tocqueville 2011, 655). At the extreme, this self-denial creates conditions under which it is possible that nobody believes public opinion and yet a sense of public unanimity flourishes, because everybody is convinced that everyone else believes it and acts accordingly. As Tocqueville dramatically puts it, where the majority "no longer believes, but still appears to believe," given the self-silencing of some and the active feigning of others, "this hollow ghost of public opinion is enough to chill the blood of would-be innovators and reduce them to respectful silence" (651). Society's power to re-create itself suffers accordingly.

The capacity to make good and correct decisions in a democracy requires the establishment of well-reasoned opinions, including the opinion of what the public truly thinks. Social (mis)conceptions about the meaning of silence and the state of public opinion propel processes of self-silencing that induce public opinion's *mis*-formation. This is especially problematic given that public opinion is a means by which people control not just one another but their political rulers as well. Unsurprisingly, Tocqueville's analysis of mechanisms of self-silencing inspired research into two phenomena associated with the challenge of comprehending the meaning of silence: the "spiral of silence" (Noelle-Neumann 1974) and "pluralistic ignorance" (Katz and Allport 1931). Both the spiral of silence and pluralistic ignorance arise from the wrong assumptions we tend to make when others' views remain unvocalized, unannounced, or uncertain. The so-called spiral of silence denotes the fact that, where one perceives one's opinion to be unpopular, one tends to hold back its expression, while the perception that one's opinion is popular tends to have the opposite effect. The self-silencing of nonbelievers who hold back their opinions strengthens the opinion perceived to be majoritarian, spiraling whatever opinions nonbelievers might have shared further into silence. By contrast, pluralistic ignorance refers to the fact that, when views go unexpressed, people tend to presume either their false uniqueness or a false consensus. In the first case, people wrongly take their opinions to be unique and not shared by others. This leads them to suppress those opinions and try to emulate others' (perceived) views. Alternatively, individuals can falsely believe that silent others agree with their own views. This reassures them in their views and forestalls reflexive engagement.

Both the spiral of silence and pluralistic ignorance are driven by cognitive errors accruing from the ambiguity of silence. Processes of self-silencing can help received views, courses of action, and power structures perpetuate themselves unchallenged, with new views being held back or finding themselves ruled out, not necessarily because they lack justification but because people think they are alone in holding them.

While liberals like Mill and Tocqueville blame public opinion for setting off self-censorship in egalitarian societies, others have blamed self-censoring on processes of ideological closure that benefit a few. This is the case with Herbert Marcuse, who in his essay "Repressive Tolerance" (1965) develops an argument for the restriction of speech in the name of the Millian goal of making speech a truth- and utility-promoting medium (Leiter 2018). Under ideal circumstances, Marcuse concedes, unimpeded speech might benefit progress, truth, well-being. But, in real-world conditions, discursive practice falls radically short of the ideal. Our societies are deeply unequal. Unilateral control over agenda-setting and the channels of communication structures a public realm plagued by indoctrination, misinformation, and widespread ignorance. A pervasive network of assumptions and biases effectively de-platforms the views of many and implicitly privileges the viewpoint of the powerful few. The situation is such that what is promoted is not debate, critique, and dissent, much less "truth," but the unthinking acceptance of entrenched attitudes and ideas, even where they are obviously false or damaging. Once a critical concept in marginalized groups' struggle for emancipation, "tolerance," Marcuse concludes, is now "an instrument for the continuation of servitude" (1965, 88). Calls for "indiscriminate toleration"—under the guise of freedom of expression—promote rather than challenge regressive and repressive ideas.

In both liberal and radical democratic critiques, self-censorship constitutes an objectionable form of power that undercuts autonomy, dissent, democratic control, and accountability. But there are important differences. The liberal account of self-censorship focuses on autonomy and individuality, intellectual stagnation, and epistemic deficits. By contrast, the radical account foregrounds the ways in which the ideology of tolerance perpetuates a status quo of inequality and discrimination—and how our agency as censors implicates us in the preservation of the status quo. The liberal focus is on the marginalization of minorities of opinion, not on generalized false consciousness, yet pressures of conformism inevitably weigh most heavily on social minorities and disadvantaged groups, which, being particularly affected by the perpetuation of unjust social arrangements and placed lower in the social hierarchy, are more dependent on the dominant group's approval or favorable opinion. This can limit editorial autonomy and drive self-censorship. Where self-censorship dispenses with external pressure and works as second nature, it is likely to translate into a communicatively structured disadvantage intersecting with other social disadvantages. This is an issue I address in the next section.

Silencing as Structural Injustice

Silencing can be an effect of speech. It is a trait of liberal views to set speech, as a civilizing force, in opposition to the violence of silence. Radical democratic views, however, are more likely to see this as an opposition stemming "from within civilized speech in order to hide its own violence" (Wagner 2021, 6; see also Bataille 1985, 134–44). To fully appreciate this violence, we need to set aside the conceptualization of speech as representation or a mere conveyor of thought and instead embrace speech as the way in which we intersubjectively construct and assign meaning to our social reality. Produced by effects of power within a given social order, speech is itself a powerful regulatory force. It constitutes, reproduces, and normalizes rules, practices, and behaviors. These prescribe roles and places in social hierarchies, assigning some the power to have a say, or to have their voices heard, and marginalizing the speech of others.

If a certain normative violence is intrinsic to every discursive order, particular harms can be inflicted by the speech acts produced within it. This is especially so with illocutionary speech acts, which are meant to *do* something rather than merely represent something. A case in point is hate speech—or any other harmful speech whereby speakers enact norms that oppress, subordinate, degrade, demean, silence, or otherwise do violence to their targets. In chapter 1 we encountered examples of racist and homophobic hate speech that demeaned Black gay men, positioning them as inferior and thus legitimizing their unequal treatment. These speech acts did not only state things about their subjects. They did something to them, namely, they sabotaged, muted, and devalued their speech. They cultivated an environment so hostile to the voices of such men that their freedom of expression was jeopardized. In one word, they left them silenced.

Silencing, as I am taking it here, constitutes a form of discursive injustice (Kukla 2014). It takes place when individuals are denied (or significantly obstructed from exercising) their ability to perform speech acts or other communicative acts that they are, in principle, capable of performing. However, talk about silencing as something we do to one another as a result of harmful or offensive speech acts can unduly seem to reduce silencing to an interpersonal moral wrong while occluding its systemic character as something that simultaneously tracks and augments social disadvantage (Kukla 2014, 455).

Iris Marion Young provides a rich account of the dynamics of silencing as structural injustice (1990). Oppression, she claims, has key communicative dimensions. It works by undermining the oppressed's ability to develop and exercise their capacities of "playing and communicating with others, and expressing [their] experience, feelings, and perspective on social life in contexts where others can listen" (37). This thwarting of communicative capacities entails domination, or the exclusion of people "from determining their actions or the conditions of their actions," leaving it to others to determine them "without reciprocation" (38). As a communicatively structured disadvantage, silencing need neither be intentionally pursued nor generally perceived. In effect, invisibility is one of the characteristics of systemic silencing. This is explained by the fact that silencing, as is often the case with things deeply rooted in and enacting long-standing patterns of social relations, is both temporally and socially extended, internalized, and widely normalized (Medina 2012, 59).

Systemic silencing need not mean literal silence or the suppression of uttered speech. There are several other ways in which members of a group can find themselves silenced. Communicative attempts may be stopped before they even happen. This can be on account of unequal access to speech platforms or because members of certain groups are never asked to participate in communicative exchanges. Since money buys voice and amplifies it through media power, silencing can also result from a few voices monopolizing discussions. For many, the political right to voice is limited to the act of voting for representatives to speak for them. But even this right is far from equally distributed. Think, for instance, of the practices of voter suppression preventing targeted groups—for example, Black people in America—from signaling their political choices. Preemptive silencing can also occur through the processes of self-censoring we have been discussing, whereby members of certain groups shy away from communicating—either altogether or selectively, especially when in public—because they anticipate their hearers' disregard, dismissal, or outright condemnation.

While much silencing works preemptively, via exclusion or self-exclusion, in some cases communication is attempted but routinely frustrated. Speech acts can be disabled by a failure of uptake or other failures of recognition, explained by widespread assumptions and beliefs rooted in oppressive norms and social structures (Hornsby and Langton 1998; McGowan 2019; Alcoff 2000). And it is not only speakers' communicative intentions or, simply, their sincerity that may go unacknowledged. Silencing can also occur when their authority to perform a given speech act is not recognized by addressees. When this happens, a kind of illocutionary flipping might occur, whereby the speaker ends up performing a speech act that not only is different from the one they intended but further disadvantages them as well (Kukla 2014, 445–48). Take, for instance, cases where the antiracist communicative force of protests, such as the 2014–15 Ferguson protests, was deflected by the reinscription of the racist stigma of criminality through their framing as instances of rioting and looting (Medina 2023, 236). This delegitimation and subsequent debilitation of protest can then be further reinforced through processes of locutionary and perlocutionary silencing. Locutionary silencing, where the protest's message is blocked and semantically distorted (as, for example, with Black Lives Matter being reinterpreted as exclusionary, as claiming that only Black lives matter, rather than inclusionary, as claiming that lives that have not mattered, and still do not matter, ought to matter equally). Perlocutionary silencing can add to this, when, for instance, a movement's demands are presented and dismissed as unrealistic or non-actionable (Medina 2023, 117).

Other forms of silencing are more closely associated with the speaker's epistemic standing. Here the focus is not on a failure of recognition but on the discrediting of the speaker's capacity as a knower (Fricker 2007, 44). This may make a hearer give little credence to a speaker's word. For instance, women's interventions in boardrooms are often passed over in silence or only gain salience when male colleagues repeat them. And even if members of a certain group are recognized as subjects of knowledge, they may still be silenced if their capacity as producers of knowledge goes unrecognized. By this I mean the recognition of a person as an inquirer in their own right, with the ability to pose questions—including questions regarding another person's claim to pose questions—rather than simply an informant at the service of someone else's inquiry (Medina 2012, 92). Consider, for instance, Frederick Douglass's 1852 speech "What to the Slave Is the Fourth of July?" and how his questioning of the constitutional meaning of "We, the People," as a former slave and now nominally free Black American, might have sounded impertinent to the ears of many. The power in posing questions, as a fellow inquirer ("Whose 4th of July is this?"), is far from negligible in a democracy. After all, those who command the question can sometimes silence their interlocutors by preemptively suppressing "any kind of understanding that goes beyond the limited amount it [[the question] prepares us to receive" (Fiumara 1990, 37).

The privation of the resources necessary to make sense of one's social experiences, to meaningfully articulate them in speech, and to make claims and press demands on their basis is another factor undermining an agent's capacity to come to voice (Fricker 2007, 155). In particular, the privation of conceptual and interpretive resources can condemn one to silence. Take, for instance, the notion of "gender violence" and how it came to support collective activity that would not have taken place if violence against women had continued to be seen as a purely interpersonal phenomenon.

Whatever forms systemic silencing may take—and many of these forms overlap in practice—that silencing constitutes a structural speech-related injustice, which tracks the repeated, pervasive, and generalized failure to recognize and support the agency of speakers to whose claims, requests, or demands we are answerable. Silencing of this kind operates intersectionally and is responsible for consolidating relational inequality. It is destructive of the silenced's sense of personhood and belief in their own value. It curtails their ability to develop and exercise a whole range of capacities essential to human and social value, from imaginative and interpretive capacities to the very capacities to reason and speak (Fricker 2007, 44). In corroding their status as discursive agents, it also sabotages them as political deliberators, leading to their partial withdrawal from many aspects of public life, including public discourse and collective decision-making. In sum, systemic silencing is incompatible with a relational form of democratic politics, grounded in the principle of equal voice, the equal right to be heard or get a fair hearing, and the opportunity to exercise, through these, at least some level of influence over the shaping of one's political community.

Leveling the Political Field

My discussion thus far has lent support to what is, for many, a foregone conclusion: that anyone placing value on our equality as speakers and democracy's political talk culture must treat silence as problematic. While we can all recognize the truth of this insight, it does not give us the whole picture. As I hope to show in what follows, silence and silencing can be practiced in ways that support the same democratic goods that they are thought to undermine: namely, egalitarian reciprocity, deliberative uptake, and influence.

Let us consider first the obligations of egalitarian reciprocity we owe one another. Democratic speech encounters must constitute mutually reciprocal relationships. Self-silencing, we have seen, can be the expression of their opposite: unequal power relations within which mutuality is not affirmed but denied. But self-silencing may also be the kind of active commission (or doing a non-something) required in and for respecting others as equals. In *Leviathan* (1651), as Thomas Hobbes discusses the causes of conflict in nature, he notes that "every man looketh that his companion should value him, at the same rate he sets upon himself," and thus something as simple "as a word, a smile, a different opinion" can trigger conflict where taken for a "signe of undervalue" (Hobbes 1996, 88). In other words, speech can do and incite violence. It can perform subordination, and intimating that someone belongs to a lower class of persons engenders resentment, angers people, triggers social unrest, and compromises peace. Self-silencing contemptuous speech is thus necessary to sustain a civil conversation in which they truly turn toward one another, a conversation within which everyone feels recognized as honorable by their peers (Bejan 2017, 98–99; Festenstein 2023).

While Hobbes is correct in deeming the unrestrained pouring out of one's thoughts socially destructive, one should not rush to condemn all seemingly uncivil conversation. Judgments about incivility must be made carefully and always in context. After all, appeals to "civility" can rely on false assumptions of commonality that "mask relations of power in a veneer of politeness" (Zerilli 2014, 116). To put it bluntly, talk of civility presupposes equality. Where equality is what is at stake, demands of civility will likely violate the requirements of reciprocity. As I will show in the next chapter, traditionally disenfranchised groups, such as women, have been historically accused of incivility just by virtue of daring to show up in public to press their rights claims. Calls to civility were designed to prevent such groups from breaching the borders of an unfair status quo. The transformative power of uncivil speech for enlarging "citizens' sense of both what counts as a common matter and who counts as a political speaker" must therefore not be underestimated (Zerilli 2014, 131). At times neutrally cast as "public reason" (Rawls 1996, 224), civility typically refers to "norms of 'good' (i.e., rational) political communication that are not neutral, but tend to reflect the communicative styles of already powerful groups" (Bickford 2011, 1025). These norms lend legitimacy to their claims while policing competing claims and claimants as uncivil.

However, Hobbes's injunction against contemptuous speech is misunderstood if it is seen as directed toward the protection of the existing state of affairs rather than the production of a working order. The contrast between Hobbes and Mill is instructive here. Mill's concern with the stifling of individuality in democratic societies made him overlook the problems of nonconformity or the unabashed celebration of the unique (and often privileged) individual who dares to speak their mind, say the unsayable, and possibly demean others in the process. Hobbes, albeit not a democrat, was very much concerned with this figure. His stress was on conformity, something especially clear from the fifth law of nature, on complaisance, with its striking metaphor of the "stone which by the asperity, and irregularity of Figure, takes more room from others, than it selfe fills" (Hobbes 1996, 106). Hobbes believed that political society requires individuals to accommodate one another, acknowledging and relating to one another as equals. We would not be able to accept peace or play by the terms of the covenant otherwise. Egalitarian reciprocity is the basis of trustworthiness, and trustworthiness the basis of covenanting and peace. It is also something that requires inscription in everyday practices, continuous enactment through words and gestures of mutual respect, in order to create its own reality (Hoekstra 2012; Bejan 2023, 1191). Its enactment presupposes an editorial control over ourselves—what we say and do not say to one another—backed up by the social pressure to conform and the internalization of the virtues of a sociable character (Bejan 2024, 259).

The democratic significance of silent, gestural modes of interaction is brought out by Iris Marion Young when she criticizes deliberative democrats for having "no place for care-taking, deferential, polite acknowledgment of the Otherness of others." As she explains, insofar as "democratic discussion will be fraught with disagreement, anger, conflict, counterargument, and criticism," it is all the more critical that "intermittent gestures of flattery, greeting, deference, and conciliatory caring" are enacted because they help "keep commitment to the discussion at times of anger and disagreement" (1996, 130).

Self-silencing of contemptuous expression and a silent language of conciliatory caring can thus affirm mutual recognition and our status as equals within civil conversation. When reciprocity between claimed equals is at stake, so can a discursive exit. Under circumstances of great imbalance, withdrawing from a discursive relation may constitute a form of "breaking a relationship of domination" and publicly protesting the unequal terms of one's inclusion (Warren 2011, 690).

Withdrawal from participation in a discursive relation is a form of exit (Hirschman 1970). Exiting can be oriented toward individual goods, such as self-care. It can also constitute a political action rejecting specific structures and systems, motivated by a desire to reconstitute the terms of one's association with others. There is a risk, however, that a silent exit is powerless if it goes unnoticed and/or imposes no cost on interlocutors. To challenge domination rather than simply offer protection against it, an exit must make itself known as a refusal to continue in the same way, as a political claim protesting the terms of one's inclusion, and as a means of forging a new political space where these terms might be recast.

Any conversation needs a subject about which one is to converse. Bringing this subject into focus and making it a matter of common concern are, of course, what collaborative inquiry is meant to achieve. But it is virtually impossible for the inquiry to take place if the very subject about which it is concerned is denied.

An example may make this clear. In February 2014, British journalist and author Reni Eddo-Lodge published what is now a famous post on her blog. It was titled "Why I'm No Longer Talking to White People About Race."

The title marks the point of a limit having been reached. It also suggests a generalized withdrawal, but what is effectively happening is a redirection of engagement from those who "refuse to accept the legitimacy of structural racism and its symptoms" to those who do not. The end of one thing may be necessary for the start of something new.[1]

"Conversation" literally means "turning together." Hence, a conversation about race with racism deniers is a difficult affair. There is no mutually acknowledged subject about which to turn nor interlocutors open to entertain racism as a serious normative claim (Scudder 2020b, 513). This is because white ignorance implies both false beliefs about systems of racist oppression and unresponsiveness to the agency and political claims of those subject to racist oppression. Of course, one could hope that denial could be overcome and racism could be construed as a subject claiming normative status within the practice of conversation itself. But even if this were a possibility, a second question arises: whether, as a racialized subject, one should be willing to put oneself in the position implied by the terms of the conversation. After all, in many, if not most, cases, the deniers' stance toward the structural inequalities responsible for their privilege is not a mere "passive obverse to knowledge" but a "militant, aggressive, not to be intimidated" position (Mills 2017, 49). Challenging their active ignorance in the midst of conversation is likely to be met with defensiveness, if not open hostility.

Given the attendant risk of injury, it is perhaps no surprise that Eddo-Lodge presented her discursive withdrawal as a question of self-preservation or self-care. Withdrawing, she claims, gave her back the power to "set boundaries," a power that it would be virtually impossible or too exacting to hold if she engaged discursively. Rather than a withdrawal from politics, however, her withdrawal was itself a political act, motivated by a desire to create "epistemic friction" and draw attention to the stalemate that active ignorance of white privilege was bringing to interracial conversations (Schaap 2020, 566). Hence the exit needed to be public, even dramatized. In Eddo-Lodge's case, this involved a *contra-diction*: using speech to announce a silent treatment. Eddo-Lodge then redirected her energies to explore the right to build, and enact change, elsewhere—namely, on a more level playing field (Honig 2021, 103). In her podcast *About Race*, the conversation could be taken one step further.

In intentionally withdrawing from a specific interaction, in refusing to engage further with racism deniers, Eddo-Lodge was also indirectly speaking to and seeking to restructure relationships with another constituency. As she submitted in her blog post, even those who entertain structural racism as a possibility, and are in principle open to a world-disclosing interracial conversation, show their active ignorance in assuming that, under current circumstances, parties to such a conversation can enter it as equals. Any interracial conversation conceived as a mere matter of exchanging arguments, she claims, is condemned to failure. The unequal discursive terms that the parties face must be recognized and addressed before the conversation can start.

If simply continuing to play along produces and reproduces inegalitarian social relations, the democratically right thing to do may well be to refuse to enter the game "until a more equal participation in hermeneutical practices is open to all—or precisely in order to make more equal participation possible for all" (Medina 2012, 117; see also Jungkunz 2011, 8). A very public silent treatment can be the kind of power play necessary to rebalance a lopsided discursive field.

While withdrawal from conversation is normally seen as uncivil, incivility may be what is needed to expose the exclusionary violence of "civilized conversation." One form of "uncivil" behavior is speech-interfering protest, seeking to impair another's capacity to speak and/or make themselves heard. It practices silencing as a way of communicating disagreement. And it, too, can be justified on democratic grounds. This is the case, for instance, when the "conversation" has been designed to structurally privilege certain views, irrespective of, or prior to, their merit having been proved.

Take, for instance, the international town meeting held at Ohio State University in Columbus in 1998. The meeting was meant to discuss plans for war with Iraq. The event was organized at the government's request and the television network, CNN, that broadcasted it was also handpicked by the government. The right to speak was given only to those chosen by the network. As the three main speakers, senior policy advisers to the US president, made their interventions, chanting and heckling from a minority of members of the public drowned out their voices. On the face of it, their silencing of the speakers was reprehensible. Effectively, however, it constituted a democratically legitimate way for the audience to protest the preclusion of their equal right to public speech and the monopoly given to government views. It was also a way for dissenting members of the audience to resist their co-optation as "silent" unbelievers. As one protester put it, "If we had just been sitting there quietly listening, people watching on television would have thought we were supporters of the war, which we certainly were not." The only way to stop a reading of their silence as acquiescent was to be vocal. Since they were denied contra-diction, the only power left to them was the power of interruption.

## Democratically Relational and Un-relational Silences

Egalitarian conversation presupposes equality among its participants. It should also give everyone the opportunity to be a speaker and a listener in turn. Attentive listening is essential for determining when to speak, when to let others speak, and when to respond. Egalitarian reciprocity may require self-silencing. One may have the right and the opportunity to speak and yet consciously decide to keep silent to support the discursive agency of others. While making room for others in conversation is always important, it is even more so in two situations that may sometimes overlap. First, where background power relations imply an uneven distribution of speaking opportunities, privileged speakers—that is, speakers whose voices are more powerful, are more likely to get uptake, and thus are more likely to exercise influence—may have good democratic reasons to undo their privilege by refraining from speaking and allowing marginalized voices to be heard. Second, when the question under discussion has very different implications for different participants in the conversation, the least affected may want to restrain their speech to allow the voices of the most affected to exercise more influence.

Lee Mun Wah's documentary *The Color of Fear* (1994) follows a conversation between two white and six non-white men (Chinese, Japanese, Latino, and Black) about race relations in America. Their interaction displays "powerful gestures of silencing," with the most vocal white participant arrogating to himself the speaking position—interrupting, speaking *over* and sometimes even speaking *for* racialized others, while actively invalidating their authority by re-explaining, clarifying, or "saying better" what they have said (I. Young 1990, 134). The last word is always his, and it is often used just to let them know where they have gone wrong. He speaks without listening and thus produces a pathological form of recognition.

This pathology becomes especially evident once we conceive of discursive agency as relational and intersubjective rather than as an inner faculty (Krause 2015, 60). The experience of being listened to and the ability to express oneself are closely entwined (Fiumara 1990, 98). Hence, even though listening is normally taken to follow speech, the relationship may well be the other way around. That is, one's ability to come to speech may be premised on one's being listened to or having a reliable expectation of one's speech receiving uptake. This expectation is removed when one's speech is repeatedly ignored, non-engaged, twisted, or received with bafflement as something "unheard-of, simply because it is unhearable: something only suitable for lapsing into madness or irrelevance" (Fiumara 1990, 55). With the death of the expectation comes the death of the associated speaking ability.

But silence can facilitate or support it. As an instrument of listening, self-silencing is the condition of possibility of any discursive relationship, upon which depends one's capacity to develop discursive agency. If this is always the case, it is even more so across difference and structural inequality. Listening for differences implies not only hearing what another person says but attending to another's evaluations of their circumstances, needs, and interests (Bickford 1996, 33). Certainly, giving one another a fair hearing does not guarantee that conflicts will be resolved or agreement reached. But the value of that fair hearing is not purely instrumental; it performs democratic mutuality and a commitment to engage another's perspective so that one may "clarify the nature of the conflict at hand" and continue to "speak, listen, and act together across it" (Bickford 1996, 2, 171).

If silence is a "condition for and correlate of democratic listening," not all silences are a way of relating (Scudder 2020a, 134). There are silences that do just the opposite. In some silences, a listener withdraws from an interaction, refuses to participate, or becomes unresponsive out of an unwillingness to "remain open within uncomfortable moments and the uncertain ground they present, invite challenge, and risk transformation, to encounter difference as difference" (Beausoleil 2017, 295). These silences—such as the silence of the "silent treatment"—place power with the silent person, who is free to decide whether and when a relationship is to exist. As such, they can be constitutive of highly unequal power relations and damaging for those subject to them. This is not to say that the "silent treatment" is always wrong. Because power is necessary to impose it, it can be a way of rebalancing a power relation through performing and thus claiming a power one is denied, as we have seen with Eddo-Lodge's example. It can also be a way of inducing "epistemic friction" by distancing oneself from the wrongness of something said and/or of its sayer. On the whole, however, the silences that break a relationship contrast with the listening silences that establish it. Listening silences are sustained for deliberative uptake, which can be defined as the "fair consideration of the arguments, stories, and perspectives that particular citizens share in deliberation" (Scudder 2020b, 504). A genuinely listening silence therefore constitutes a leaning or movement toward another, carried out with the intent of creating a coexistential space where one can relate *to* and be *with* the other (Fiumara 1990, 101).

This coexistential space is critical in a democracy. And the silent yielding of privileged speakers is a form of self-negation for the purpose of building a space for shared action in which everyone has an adequate, if not equal, opportunity to speak and to have their perspectives checked against those of others (Jungkunz 2013; I. Young 1990, 134). They choose to take on themselves the role of listeners, and, as Gemma Corradi Fiumara puts it, as a listener one can only enter that space "in a way that is both paradoxical and committing: 'by taking leave,' by standing aside and making room" (1990, 144). The relevant commitment is to communication across inequality and diversity. But it can also be more: a commitment to having one's exclusionary identity transformed (Jungkunz 2013, 18). As Eddo-Lodge observed in her blog, "It must be a strange life, always having permission to speak and feeling indignant when you're finally asked to listen." As a member of the dominant group, one's identity as a sovereign speaker—whose speaking commands listening but does not necessarily offer it in return—is often taken for granted, precisely because it is never threatened. But if one has become sufficiently reflective about the privileges and status that come to one by way of that identity, and if one willingly represses it so that others may be equally empowered, one may well be on the path of self-transformation (Jungkunz 2011, 5).

However, self-silencing, by itself, is insufficient to establish more reciprocal relations. One might decide not to speak for reasons that threaten rather than enhance reciprocity, or, indeed, for no reason at all. The reflexivity that gives self-silencing its normative quality requires continuing "attentiveness or monitoring" (MacKenzie and Moore 2020, 439). For keeping silence may not necessarily, and not always, support another's discursive agency.

Take, for instance, "white silence." "White silence" refers to a pattern of engagement where silence is adopted as the primary, or even only, mode of engagement (DiAngelo 2020, 4). Saying without listening and keeping silent at all times are alike in that they both are instances of unresponsiveness. They contrast directly with receptive silence, that is, a silence "always in a state of listening" and therefore always aware *of*, embedded *in*, and responsive *to* context. This also means that receptive silence is a silence that will need to be made or broken in response to what comes before, according to one's best judgment as to what uptake may require at each point (Sciacca 1963, 183; see also Davis and Finlayson 2022, 1564).

"White silence" is the opposite of this. It is a default silence, signaling less a listening openness than a defensiveness. Projects of mutual understanding depend on the parties sharing with one another what they think and feel, even (or, perhaps, particularly) when this is painful and may put one's beliefs and identity at risk. Default silence is a shelter hiding something. It shifts the onus of conversation and vulnerability to others. It is made to protect one from the unpredictable articulations (the unheard-of) that a listening silence may have enabled and to insulate one from the transformative experience of proper hearing (Fiumara 1990, 145).

The specificity of "white silence" as a mode of engagement becomes even more salient when it is contrasted with the strategic silence sometimes adopted by racialized others. While silence is sometimes deemed the weapon of the oppressed, the right and ability to keep silent is often a preserve of those who enjoy power, notably the power of speech. As has been noted, "the ability to create a silence, and thus determine a new perspective, belongs to those who can speak in so far as speech represents a decision or a choice" (Fiumara 1990, 99). In interracial conversations, racialized subjects sometimes adopt silence as a way of protecting themselves from, or resisting, hostility, denial, or co-optation. But many report that "silence is generally not an option" and that "[n]ot speaking up because they don't want to—without penalty—is a privilege they are not afforded" (DiAngelo 2020, 14, 7). This felt compulsion to speak has three main sources: *urgency*, the need to reveal the impact of racism in their lives and to question the norms that structure it; *solidarity*, the fact that they see themselves obliged to speak as they speak not just for themselves but for others similarly affected; and *stereotypical expectations*, or because they anticipate their withdrawal from conversation to be blamed on "Black uncooperativenesss" or counterproductive rage.

As a result of these factors, they come to see silence as a luxury they cannot afford. This stands in direct contrast with silence as a dominant pattern of white engagement. White participants keep this silence because the flip side of their speaking privilege is their ability to keep a silence that will not be broken. In other words, they keep a default silence because they can, because not much is at stake for them in the conversation. "White silence" is therefore often experienced by their racialized interlocutors as an unfair withholding of views, as a dogged silence designed to prevent one's own perspectives on race and racial relations from being opened up to discussion, expansion, and challenge. Instead of supporting dialogue, "white silence" undercuts any dialogical relationship and prevents the creation of "a time-space in which to meet, or clash, in order to share in the challenge of growth" (Sciacca 1963, 183). This is the very time-space of democratic encounter.

Responsibility for Silence and Accountable Silences

White silence is a sign and an instrument of the continuation of systemic injustice. It shuts down necessary interracial conversations and reinforces harmful bonding patterns with members of one's own group. White silence can also be understood in another way, however, as the silence of white people in the face of racist behavior, attitudes, and micro- and macro-aggressions. In both cases of "white silence," "silence" is a not-doing that does things, most notably silencing. Hence, in what follows, I want to engage the question of responsibility for silencing and examine whether silence—and even tactical silencing—may help counter injurious and socially destructive speech.

Every conversational exchange has at least two actors—speakers and listeners—and often also a third one, an audience. All action, including discursive action, is socially distributed. As we have seen, this means that the power of the speaker and the power of the speech act itself are contingent on the presence and receptiveness of listeners (Krause 2015). It also means that when considering the distribution of responsibilities for harmful speech and its effects, we need to look beyond speakers and their speech acts to the listeners, the audiences, and their responses to what they hear.

By responses, I mean both actual and anticipated responses. If it is true that speakers create their audiences, it is also the case that audiences create their speakers (Fumagalli 2021, 1033). A seasoned hate speaker will seek to "read" their audience to assess its dispositions and determine whether and how far they can go with their words—how much they can imply without explicitly saying something, because meaning is insinuated.

In a similar manner, where harmful speech is uttered, be it intentionally or unwittingly, the reaction of listeners does much to determine its fate. But while it may be easy to see how listeners and audiences implicate themselves in harmful speech that they visibly affirm, it may be harder to envisage how they may implicate themselves through their silence. This difficulty arises primarily because silence is normally seen as an omission, not an action. However, things may start to look different if we consider how discursive agency depends on uptake and how even minimal uptake can contribute to the conditions of success of speech acts.

To make this apparent, I want to look at two concrete ways in which the silence of listeners can facilitate harmful speech and authorize its speakers: namely, through accommodation (Langton 2018) and licensing (Maitra 2012). I discuss each of these in turn.

Conversations tend to abide by rules of accommodation. These are default adjustments defining certain moves in the conversational game as correct (Langton 2018, 145). Regardless of whether listeners share in the problematic beliefs or presuppositions introduced by speakers of hate speech, in letting the comments pass, they enable accommodation. Introducing a morally problematic presupposition into a conversation ("Homeless people, many of them from abroad, live on the streets as a lifestyle choice") is the kind of move that does more than simply introduce new content into a conversation (namely, a bigoted stereotype of migrants and homeless people). The speaker establishes what is permissible in the conversation moving forward and sets conditions for the success of other, similar speech acts.

Given the "accommodation pull" of conversations, problematic presuppositions are likely to be added by default to the common background assumptions on which the conversation builds, unless hearers disrupt them by openly challenging or blocking them ("What do you mean by a 'lifestyle choice'?"). To block is to stop, to obstruct. Blocking is thus an attempt to illocutionarily silence "back-door" presuppositions and, as much as possible, preempt their harms. If problematic presuppositions are not stopped, accommodation ensues. As Tocqueville saw, this will occur regardless of whether the listeners who remain silent are believers (sharing the speaker's problematic belief) or silent unbelievers. Their failure to challenge may be "read" as a sign of belief-sharing or a more passive willingness to let pass. This suffices to provide minimal uptake and contribute to the conditions necessary to make the speech act successful and capable of producing its desired effects: namely, to subordinate and blame migrants and the homeless for their living conditions, to mark them as outsiders to the political community and what it holds in common (Ayala and Vasilyeva 2016, 259).

The other, often concurrent, way in which silent listeners may facilitate harmful speech is through licensing (Maitra 2012). Licensing refers to the tacit granting of authority to speakers. By withholding oppositional speech, which may question the speaker's standing and ranking ("Who are you to say that, or to claim that you represent me in saying it?"), hearers may tacitly license the speaker to step into an unjust position of authority over the target of their speech and even over their audience. This is especially the case where the speaker insinuates that the audience comprises like-minded individuals with whom they hold a representative relationship (Fumagalli 2021, 1032). Again, the speaker's acquisition of a subordinating authority can occur regardless of whether the members of the audience agree with, have strong reservations about, or resent the speaker's verdictive ranking and their claim to voice the audience's views. In any of these cases, should the audience remain silent, their silence functions as a license or a default authorization.

Given that speakers are empowered by listeners and that speech acts require uptake to be brought to fruition, it is not a stretch to see the silence of those who should be knowledgeable about the harms produced by particular speech acts and have the capacity to speak up, but choose not to, as a doing rather than simply an omission. Understood in this way, it may implicate them in the speech act and its effects (Ayala and Vasilyeva 2016, 264). However, the degree to which listeners are implicated depends on various factors. Those who have little to fear in speaking up, those who have good reasons to fear reprisals, and those who have their capacity to speak back diminished by the fact that the hate speech targets them and precludes their own speech are not equally responsible. Put another way, the "responsibility for silence" must be "proportional to speech capacity" (Ayala and Vasilyeva 2016, 267). In addition, the level of implication is to be judged against the many barriers that prevent the identification and blocking of "back-door" speech acts and presuppositions, which are not necessarily openly spoken. While willful ignorance cannot be an excuse, those speech acts and presuppositions may be hard to identify, and it may be even harder to know how best to deal with them (Langton 2018, 145).

Silence and Silencing Against Violent Speech

Engaging in counter-speech is demanding. It faces considerable obstacles, some of which are structural. To be effective—that is, to stop, and ideally replace, harmful speech—counter-speech needs to be audible and taken up. Audibility is, however, compromised when access to channels of communication and to specific communities of listeners is limited. Think, for instance, of social media's propensity to connect us with like-minded individuals, placing us within echo chambers. This reinforces confirmation bias, and confirmation biases undermine receptivity to counter-diction. Even if audiences are exposed to "good speech," they may remain "ignorant, biased, or won't listen" because it feels better to have one's views and identities confirmed rather than challenged, in which case "the bad speech will continue its travels into the world unhindered" (Leiter 2017, 127). Differentials in social ranking and power also mean that counter-speech is not equally open to all. Since the speech that needs countering may enforce these differentials, the authority and capacity to speak back and block the harms of hate speech can be eroded at the very moment they are exercised. After all, a "visceral emotional response to personal attack precludes speech," and hate speech is designed to produce such paralysis (Lawrence 1993, 68). Additionally, to counter speech that typically portrays some groups as unwanted in a society, the counter-speaker must hold some representative authority, and this may be impossible when counter-speakers are members of the targeted community and pigeonholed to represent just that group. Even for those who are not the targets of harmful speech and do not face structural obstacles in responding to it, counter-speech can be taxing in other ways: it is not always obvious when to engage in it, how to identify what should be countered, or even whether countering may have the opposite result of the one intended.

While the costs of engaging in counter-speech can be high, the gains can be relatively slim. Counter-speech can counteract the future harms of hate speech, but not the harms it has already caused (Leiter 2017, 17–18). Moreover, once harmful norms of subjugation, silencing, and exclusion govern conversations, they are notoriously "sticky" and difficult to verbally undo (M. McGowan 2009, 403). To seek to verbally undo claims by negating them after they are articulated can backfire, instead reinforcing them or helping disseminate them. In the face of this possibility, to verbalize a counter-position may not always be the best tactic for preventing harmful speech from producing (more) harm. Discursive disengagement and/or selective silencing may be preferable tactics.

Let me start with discursive disengagement. As we have seen with Eddo-Lodge, discursive exit can be a form of exposing the injustice of the dominant power relations structuring the speech situation and of reclaiming a speaker's power. When enacted to counter harmful speech, discursive exit is meant to mark one's distance from it and from its speakers (Fumagalli 2021, 1037). For this "marking" to take effect, however, its oppositional nature must be made clear to others.

Clarification can be verbal or nonverbal. Take, for instance, the hashtag "If you don't understand my silence, then you don't deserve my words," which social media users deploy to show their disagreement with abusive speech. In refusing to reciprocate, in refusing to engage and to provide reasons for their disengagement, they transform a "refusal in language" into a "refusal of language" (Honig 2021, 19). They perform the impossibility of communicating—or making common—with those oblivious to the violent consequences of their words or, worse, those who intend their words to have these consequences. By deeming others unworthy of their words, they refuse to give harmful speech any airtime, they ostracize its speakers, and they put pressure on those speakers to conform. Demarcation from hate speech and its speakers can be verbal, but it can be also brought about through silent performances "in which the action itself delivers the message" (Kirkpatrick 2019, 152). Think, for instance, of someone not laughing or keeping a stern silence at a racist joke, or a group of people conspicuously leaving a town hall meeting after a council member invites migrants living in the community to "go home." Their overt performance of silence makes their dissent noticeable, produces distancing, and ensures that their silence is not interpreted as weakness or tacit support.

Most counter-speech implies counter-diction, however. Yet, given that harmful speech is sticky and hard to reverse, it is important to ensure that counter-speech does not end up promoting the circulation and salience of the speech it aims to confront. Indirect forms of silencing may be instrumental to this.

Changing the subject is a way to silence (Simpson 2013, 596). The problem with this tactic is that it can be easily interpreted by observers as an expression of weakness or symptomatic of a lack of counterarguments. Also, changing the subject constitutes a form of discursive disengagement that is unlikely to be conducive to conversational progress.

This places positive counter-speech as an appealing alternative (Lepoutre 2019). Positive counter-speech projects alternative visions of society and social relations that positively value those targeted by hate speech. It differs from negative counter-speech in that it does not necessitate the repetition of the problematic view it is seeking to invalidate or refute. This is critical, since, as I have been stressing, repetition confers salience on harmful representations and their presuppositions, with the pursuant risk of accommodation. Avoiding direct negation of the countered view can be important for at least three reasons. First, in deflecting tension and avoiding polarization, it might sustain the continuation of difficult conversations. Second, it does not risk reinforcing identification with speakers and views perceived as being victimized or "under attack" (Nyhan and Reifler 2010). Third, it avoids boosting—through iteration—a vocal minority against a silent majority.

Even though positive speech may sometimes counter hate speech more effectively, there is no one-size-fits-all approach to opposing speech's violence. All tactics are insufficient on their own, and real change requires a deeper restructuring of social relations. But, as we have seen, giving hate speech the silent treatment or estranging through positive speech are important tools of the "counter-speech toolkit."

While silence can be an accomplice in wrongdoing, the idea that silence is inherently complicitous is too loosely tossed around. If anything, the equation of silence with complicity has gained traction in a world marked by the rise of social media platforms offering avenues for immediate communication and making it compulsory that we speak all the time. In particular, when politically divisive issues arise, not taking a stand is seen as itself a statement—namely, of indifference, acquiescence, complicity. But while this judgment may sometimes be warranted, it is not always so. The decision not to take a stand may be moved by the same democratic values that it is taken to threaten.

A couple of examples will help us make the distinction. In August 2017, a white supremacist rally took place in Charlottesville, Virginia. The rally turned violent when protesters encountered counter-protesters. Donald Trump, then president of the United States, condemned the violence but not the white supremacists. His selective silence entailed "not just simply the *absence* of speech but also the *presence* of non-speech" (Zerubavel 2019, 60). Trump's role made this presence conspicuous. As president, Trump had a special duty to speak against white supremacists' racist acts and for the equal standing and dignity of the attacked citizens. The white supremacists' demonstration of force was designed to subordinate and intimidate Black, Muslim, and Jewish people, and the omission of a presidential condemnation constituted a form of connivance. Through his non-statement, Trump made a louder and clearer statement. He took a side in deciding *not* to, and he thereby encouraged similar action in the future.

The responsibility to be an upstander rather than a bystander distributes differently to different citizens, depending on their specific duties as well as on their relative speech power and the likelihood that they are secondary agents of the principal's action. Responsibility for condemning the rally and challenging Trump's silence distributed more heavily to white citizens who were not targeted by the violent action and were more morally exposed to Trump's failure as a formal representative. To speak out against Trump's omission was a way for them to de-authorize him and assert that the statement he made (in not making a statement) was not made in their name.

Trump's silence, I submit, was complicitous in wrongdoing. In order to ground this claim, I need to define complicity. Complicity is normally taken to involve two elements: first, "voluntarily performing an action that contributes to the wrongdoing of another," and second, "knowledge or culpable ignorance" (Lepora and Goodin 2013, 82–83). However, omissions can count as causally contributing to wrongdoing in two different circumstances: first, if one knew or should have been expected to know about a wrongdoing that, had one spoken out about it, would not have happened, and second, if in ignoring, shutting one's eyes to, or keeping silent as the wrongdoing is happening, one supports its repetition in the future (Lepora and Goodin 2013, 45). The latter is the kind of complicity produced by Trump's silent omission. This is also what activists often imply when they claim that a silent witness to a wrongdoing is a complicit one.

This being said, citizen silence is sometimes generally assumed and wrongly accused of being indifferent, self-serving, or complicitous. Silence is no different from speech in that it can be reflective or unreflective, indifferent or caring (MacKenzie and Moore 2020). Take, for instance, the pressure people face on social media to speak out, make a statement, and take a position on highly controversial questions, complex issues, or major news events. Resistance to this pressure is sometimes condemned as indifference or complicity. But the accusation can be too quick. Indifference implies lack of interest and lack of positive or negative affect. Complicity implies contribution to the wrongdoing of another. The choice of silence must be set against the complexity of the situation and constraints on what is sayable and what gets listened to. People may withhold their speech because they care deeply and need time to form their own opinion. To arrive at a critical and informed understanding of a complex situation, they may need to gather information, listen to the voices that matter most, engage arguments on both sides, and process difficult emotions. Their refusal to give in to pressures to speak may be a refusal of a shallow politics "privileg[ing] acts of speaking over the content of speech" (hooks 1989, 14) and constitute a form of "reflective nonparticipation" (MacKenzie and Moore 2020, 443) whereby one buys oneself time to get to know, think, process—to reach a considered judgment.

It may also be the case that one already has a considered opinion but the conditions for its expression are not satisfied. By conditions, I mean here trust and framing. Trust between parties, trust in the communicative process, and trust in the handling of the exchanged contents are all necessary for individuals to feel at ease to speak their minds. Second, and relatedly, the dominant frameworks of discussion may be so constraining that it becomes virtually impossible for one's opinion to be conveyed. As such, should one speak one's position, it is likely that it will be misrepresented, distorted, or misstated. This is prone to occur where polarization toward the extremes dominates debate and one is under strenuous pressure to pick a side, to condemn or approve, and to stop at that. Judith Butler hints at this predicament when she writes, "Although one wishes to go directly to the matter at hand, one bumps up against the limits of a framework that makes it nearly impossible to say what one has to say."[2] Forcing one to make a statement under these conditions is almost inevitably tantamount to forcing one to say something one does not want to say or even does not agree with. Even if one refuses the terms of the debate as set down, one's position, if expressed, is likely to be heard as contradictory or to be "resolved" by being bent toward one of the extremes, further polarizing the debate. This tendency is reinforced on social media, which primes us for binary reactions and through which the nuance of most opinion is lost. Against this scenario, the decision not to speak out may not reflect a lack of interest, opinion, or moral or political position but instead enact a refusal to have one's position captured within, distorted by, or assimilated into a frame dividing choices into binary blocs. In these situations, the equation of silence with complicity functions as a social pressure to conform to the terms of the debate, thus denying one's right to silence: to choose whether, when, and where to speak, and in what terms. To reclaim that right is a necessary condition for reclaiming editorial control and expressing opinions that are effectively one's own. The condition is necessary but not sufficient. Secret dissenters keeping silent are likely to induce an overestimation of the extent of support for the binary, polarizing framing. It is thus key that those enjoying speech power act as "norm entrepreneurs" on communication platforms. In publicly abandoning the imposed binary framework and adopting a new, more nuanced one, they lead the way for others to follow (Tanasoca 2020, 194; Sunstein 1996, 909).

Common as it is, the framing of silence as either neglectful disengagement or complicit connivance is the flip side of the idealization of speech as reflective, engaged, transparent, and accountable. In the next chapter, I turn to gendered imaginings of speech and silence and the creative, subversive resignification of silence as a site of collective agency within the feminist silent protest tradition.

# 4

## SILENT SISTERHOOD

It is a presence
it has a history    a form

Do not confuse it
with any kind of absence

—Adrienne Rich, "Cartographies of Silence"

In April 2017, the first three episodes of *The Handmaid's Tale*—the TV series based on Margaret Atwood's 1985 dystopian novel of the same name—premiered. The following year, silent women in many parts of the world wore the handmaids' uniform of red cloaks and tunnel-like white bonnets when taking to the streets to protest against restrictions on women's reproductive rights. Their arresting image and chilly silence were powerful reminders of how, as Atwood noted, "[i]n countries that prohibit birth control and reproductive health information, the state claims ownership of women's bodies through enforced childbearing."[1] The Republic of Gilead was once an evocation, but no longer.

The handmaids' uniform gave women protesters across the world a recognizable group identity, functioning in a similar way to the purple, white, and gold tricolor of the suffragists one hundred years earlier. Connected by their uniformed bodies, the two groups of women are also connected by the silence they performed.

This is a silence with a complex history. To borrow Adrienne Rich's words, it is a silence with a history and a form (Rich 2013, 17). That silence should be an object of historical understanding is, however, perhaps not entirely obvious. Like space and time, silence is not commonly taken for a historical category but for a non-object, a non-present, an ethereal container within or against which "things"—namely, speech and its doings—happen.

This chapter resists the tendency to transcendentalize and naturalize silence as an *a priori* or a given by exploring how silence has shaped a distinct form of protest in the feminist tradition. While there is a characteristically feminist form of silence, this does not mean that it is unchanging. Silence has a historical dimension and, consequently, women's use of silence for public protest has always been and remains dynamic, multilayered, and mediated by context. The history of silence, as Rich implies, is a history of a form that is constantly shaped and reshaped by circumstances and collective agency.

In her writings, Rich stresses that disciplinary regimes of gender and sexuality are marked by silence. Within these regimes, Rich suggests, making—or *poien*—has mutated into *techne* ("The technology of silence / The rituals, etiquette"; Rich 2013, 17). After all, regimes typically mobilize and exercise power through a set of technologies—words, rituals, rules of etiquette, silencing. It is through this apparatus of regulatory norms and practices, which govern subjectivation, interaction, and even attraction, that women have been given their self, role, and place.

In this assignment process, silence is an operation of power. That silence has been a tool of women's domination, however, does not exclude the possibility that silence may subvert the very power structures it has helped consolidate. After all, *techne* has no intrinsic, existential relationship to its craftsperson. So the question must continue to be asked: If silence is an operation of power, *whose* operation of power is it? This sense of indeterminacy is echoed in the subjectless rendering of silence in Rich's poem: "Silence can be a plan / rigorously executed / the blueprint to a life" (Rich 2013, 17). In these verses, silence is agentive, not patientive. A plan rigorously executed. *Whose* plan is this silence? How is its power produced and exercised? And if this is a power capable of drawing up a life, can its form be purely resistive, as silence's form is often suggested to be? These are questions I will need to take on as I examine the potentialities for the subversion, inclusion, influence, renewal, and rebirth of silence as enacted within the women's silent protest tradition.

This is, however, a tradition that can only be understood against the backdrop of patriarchy and the dichotomic categories that define patriarchy's structure and logic. Feminism has used deconstructive methods to challenge such dichotomies and the ensuing notions of oppositional difference. And yet resistance to patriarchy can draw feminism back into binary patterns of thinking. This is the case, I maintain, regarding the place of silence in feminist theory, where it is often positioned as the negative other of speech. As with any dominant construal, this positioning has been resisted from within—in this instance, from within feminism by people like Rich. But it remains dominant, and it reinforces gendering by taking speech as active where silence is passive, speech as powerful where silence is powerless. As a result, "silence or vocal articulations that do not conform to the disciplinary semantics of proper language" find themselves "expunged from the lexicon of *polis*" and "relegated to the pre-political or anti-political: either irrelevant or subversive" (Athanasiou 2017, 260). With this affirmation of the coincidence between politics and speech, *to be* a political being is *to speak*.

Like other progressive movements, feminism is invested in a *politics of voice* as the route to political existence. By voice, I primarily mean speech, both written and spoken. Since silence has historically performed the disciplinary norm of women's subordination, it is hardly surprising that the struggle to overcome silence should be integral to the feminist struggle. From Audre Lorde's "Your Silence Will Not Protect You" (1984) to Cherríe Moraga's "[s]ilence is like starvation" (1981, 29), calls to speak and demands to be heard punctuate the feminist tradition. Indeed, much depends on the issue of voice. To borrow bell hooks's words, it is *as subjects* that we "come to voice" (1989). An act of resistance, "coming to voice" is thus also an act of self-transformation: namely, from voiceless objects—"beings defined and interpreted by others"—to speaking subjects defining and interpreting themselves (hooks 1989, 12). For groups who, like women, have repressed so much of what they might have had to say, "afraid [their] words will not be heard nor welcomed" (Lorde 1995, 42), moving from enforced silence into voice—and a public voice at that—may well mark the beginning of a liberatory process for themselves and others.

This act of speaking—which simultaneously names and establishes a new (speaking) subject—is an act full of possibility. But it also carries risks. Rich captures this well. "In a world where language and naming are power," she writes, "silence is oppression, is violence." Yet "the very act of naming has been till now a male prerogative," so the question must be raised of "how we can begin to see and name—and therefore live—afresh" (1979, 204, 35). Two important implications follow from Rich's observations. First, speaking does not suffice for living afresh. One would struggle to dismantle the master's house with his tools, let alone create the architectural project for a new one (Lorde 1984). Should subordinated groups simply come to speak with the language *from which* and *by which* they were subordinated, "they will enter history subdued and alienated" (Gauthier 1981, 162–63). Genuine disruption requires a language in which it becomes possible for women to "find" a voice and through which it becomes possible for them to sustain a genuinely liberatory praxis. Only such a language can make "paradigms shift—that we [all] learn to talk—to listen—to hear in a new way" (hooks 1989, 15). But if this is the first implication, a second follows that is of equal, if not more, importance: any blueprint for a new life rests not only on remaking language but also on undoing the prerogative of language over the exercise of power.

To say this is not to deny the centrality of language to women's empowerment. This is hardly in question. What is less clear for me is whether a feminist progressive politics—aiming not only at bringing new things into the world but at bringing forth new worlds—can or ought to focus on speech exclusively. If the purpose is to produce a paradigm shift, more and different may be necessary. While feminism has been responsible for developing understandings of political agency that do not begin and end with speech, silence has been largely excluded from such efforts. Feminist theory's typical response to silence has been to seek to overcome it as the mark of oppression, not to complicate or reconceptualize it.[2] This chapter argues for the need to rethink this move.

Primarily conceived, within feminism, as "silencing"—or an enforced inactivity or a "distinctively speech-related wrong," whereby "a silenced speaker is deprived of benefits that speech, and only speech, can provide"—silence has been ignored as an elected source of power and as a site of potential collective becoming (Maitra 2009, 310). The conclusion follows inevitably from the premise: where speech is seen as a power that is worldmaking, and silence is defined by the absence of the characteristics assigned to speech, silence finds itself entrapped in the very patterns of dominance and opposition that feminism sets itself to challenge. In this chapter, I want to break this prejudging by looking into the dynamic relationality between voice and silence within the feminist silent protest tradition. I trace this tradition from the vigil of the Silent Sentinels (1917–19), through the Silent Parade of about ten thousand African Americans on July 28, 1917, to the activism of the Women in Black (1988–).

A couple of preliminary remarks need to be made on my principle of selection. First, no attempt is made at a comprehensive overview of the feminist silent protest tradition. This explains the considerable historical gaps between the moments I have chosen to examine. Second, my selection is present-oriented, in that all three moments speak to and against blind spots of current democratic theory. These refer mainly to the potentials of silence for strategic subversion—where voice is ineffective and/or its costs too high—and for rethinking power and political agency beyond their two dominant understandings as a capacity to do or accomplish this or that particular thing *or* a capacity to exercise control over the content and direction of what gets done. My purpose in selectively revisiting the silent protest tradition is correspondingly twofold: first, to examine the ways in which this tradition re-signifies silence and confounds the speech-silence oppositional binary, demonstrating how each is simultaneously both and neither, and second, to show the ways in which its use of silence reopens to question who might be considered a political actor and what might count as political agency.

The argument unfolds as follows. The first section examines silent practices of political subjectivation within the early feminist movement. The second section turns to the 1917 Silent Parade as an example of silence as power inhering in or possessed by a situation. In the third section, I turn to the Women in Black and their performance of silence as an opening to further activity, as the condition of possibility for something to happen, namely, for mourning to attend to its current disenfranchisements and their impact upon a political community's self-fashioning. These result from the choice and construction of the objects of mourning *as well as* from the practices of mourning. As such, the section includes a discussion of another form of silence as mourning to which the Women in Black are compared: the minute of silence. In the conclusion, I show how dominant understandings of power leave the powers of silence, which are essential for democratic renewal, unaccounted for.

## A Silent Army with Banners

The long arc of the women's silent protest tradition starts with the suffragist movement and the so-called Silent Sentinels. On the morning of January 10, 1917, the first of many Silent Sentinels marched in pairs from the headquarters of the National Woman's Party (NWP) to the White House. Upon arrival, they stood in silence in front of the gates. Nearly two thousand suffragists from thirty different states would take up their stations until June 1919. The Nineteenth Amendment, granting women the right to vote, was ratified in August of that year.

The Silent Sentinels offer a perfect example of the strategic use of silence to protest exclusion and to influence the dynamics of collective decision-making processes. Their turn to silence represented an attempt to extend protest options in response to the recognition that it is not necessarily a sign of power to have a voice nor a sign of influence to be included in conversations. For women fighting for the right to vote in the United States, voice and conversational engagement had become ineffective, a hindrance rather than a help to their cause. Previous vocalized strategies—including, alongside lobbying, "noisy" acts such as heckling and chanting—had led them to a standstill. As Harriot Stanton Blatch put it to the Congressional Union's executive committee: "We can't organize bigger and more influential deputations. We can't organize bigger processions. We can't, women, do anything more in that line. We have got to take a new departure" (cited in Stevens 1995, 57–58). No more speaking. No more co-optation through discussions with President Woodrow Wilson, the members of the Democratic Party, or other powerful political actors. These tactics needed to be replaced with a silence that resists the elicitation to speak, an act that signals a breakdown of communication and openly performs defiance. The time had arrived to enact on US soil the motto of their British mentors, namely, Emmeline Pankhurst's resounding "Deeds not Words." Silent picketing was just the deed—the embodied form of direct action—that might break the camel's back.

The Silent Sentinels' use of silence as a tactic of suffrage campaigning constituted a radical break with previous suffrage campaign strategies. But, as with most breaks, this one drew upon and wrestled with the past. Specifically, the Silent Sentinels made use of two preexisting suffragist silent protest repertoires: suffrage tableaux and storefront window displays. In both cases, silence had been adopted to expand options for political participation in the face of restrictions on women as public speakers, legal injunctions against "noisy" suffrage speech, and the generalized de-authorizing of suffragists' speech through their figuration as irrational, emotional, or convulsive speakers. But their silences differed in important ways from that performed by the Silent Sentinels.

Let me start with the suffragist tableaux. These drew on the popularity of *tableaux vivants*. Lying at the intersection of visual arts and theatre, *tableaux vivants*, from the French for "living pictures," typically contained one or more (normally) female actors or artist's models silently and motionlessly acting out well-known historical events, book scenes, or works of art. They threaded a fine line between women as silent and static, sculpturesque yet ethereal objects of moral contemplation and their construction as objects of erotic desire. In so doing, they reproduced scripts of femininity—the woman as a silent, submissive, motionless, passive, sexually objectified spectacle—while also staging the female body as a bearer and a potential *maker* of meaning

(Hill 2019, 32). This added a potentially subversive dimension to the form, but it was only partly explored by the suffragists.

Unlike the *tableaux vivants*, the suffragist tableaux were not mere vehicles of extraneous male meaning. They were shaped by suffragists' own message of political dissent. They astutely explored the tension between "verbal silence" and the "speaking body" to make women's bodies speak not just as "icons" but as authors and activists interrogating their own experience of stasis (Hill 2019, 35, 32). But on the whole, the suffrage tableaux continued to trade on tangled allusions to the conservative and the militant, the classical and the modern, the domestic and the public, frozen iconicity and political mobilization. For all the potential of the form, including its blurring of higher and lower forms of entertainment, the tableaux had a traditionalist, elitist bent. They were a "tasteful" alternative to more radical forms of suffragist intervention. They offered a medium for upper-class suffragists' iconic self-assertion. As allegorical compositions referencing complex ideas or narratives, they were a resource-intensive form, requiring audience literacy. Their impact was thus limited.

As with the suffrage tableaux, the storefront window displays enacted a form of compliant disruption. They consisted of a suffragist turning lettered cards with quotations from suffrage speeches. The displays were compliant because they iterated the coding of consumption as a frivolous female pursuit and the figuration of women as wasteful shoppers. But they were disruptive, because in commercializing the political and politicizing the commercial, they allowed suffragist campaigners to explore the mass political possibilities opened up by consumer culture and consumer politics (Finnegan 1999). The silence they performed created a new order of meaning, mainly thanks to its juxtaposition with the lettered cards. Tellingly, perhaps, New York City's Women's Political Union (WPU) referred to the storefront displays as "voiceless speeches." This formulation may sound like an invitation to concentrate on the "speeches" rather than their "voicelessness" (Chapman 2014). But an exclusive focus on textuality, or speech content, entirely misses a key copresence: namely, the presence of the absence of vocalization itself. Here as elsewhere, the suffragist's silence performed a denied political voice. But its acoustics were especially resonant: a "silent sound, the soundless voice" (Dolar 2006, 17). When "read" against this "soundless voice," the cards typified and questioned the erasure of women's voice in the male order of the devocalized logos, with its privileging of semantic content over vocal utterance, mind over body, the abstract "what" over the embodied "who" (Cavarero 2005, 43). While the cards certainly "spoke," they gave women little more than a vicarious, muffled voice. The sound of their voices remained unheard—even, perhaps, unhearable. To the attentive passerby, the displays showed how "perhaps the most intrusive and compelling are the unheard voices, and the most deafening thing can be silence" (Dolar 2006, 14). But most passersby could still simply not take notice and thus ignore the missing voice altogether.

Unlike the silence of the tableaux or window displays, protests that clothed their subversiveness in acceptably traditionalist or capitalist robes, the silence of the Silent Sentinels was crisp, militant, filled with tension and intention. A contemporary witness described it thus: "Mute, but resolute, stepping boldly, they are marching on. They can be seen but not heard. And yet they speak millions of tongues—theirs is the language of the storm, wind and the volcano" (Sussman 1917, 5). Set against a military imaginary (they were sentinels, after all), their silence communicated defiance and resolve in a nonverbal mode. Beneath this first level of communication, at least three different forms of silence were simultaneously produced: silence for voice, silence as protest, and silence as refusal (Jungkunz 2012). First, silence for voice: the Silent Sentinels performed silence to put audiences in mind of women's historical silencing and its reproduction in the present through the denial of the right to vote, the right to have a "say" in how the country was run. Second, silence as protest: together with their banners, many of which reproduced official speech, their silence showed how speech itself silences and the value of silence in upholding a dissenting political voice. Third, silence as refusal: theirs was a silence that refused the terms in which they were interpellated by power. Suffragist participation in table talk had legitimized the very power that they were attempting to dismantle. "The greatest weapon in the patriarchal arsenal," they now knew, "was the injunction, not to silence, but to speech" (Luckyj 1993, 52).

In giving power the silent treatment, the Silent Sentinels deliberately broke from the National American Woman Suffrage Association's (NAWSA) more consensual—or "civil"—strategies. Many of the members of the NWP, including its most famous leader, Alice Paul, and a chief organizer of the Silent Sentinels, Mabel Vernon, were Quakers. While picketing was a tactic previously deployed by the WPU, *silent* picketing was their own invention. But the tactic was not uncontested. Harriot Stanton Blatch, founder of the WPU, for one, was not convinced: "I am not a Quaker, not a non-resistant," she wrote in the WPU monthly *Women's Political World*. Blatch associated silence with Quaker pacifism and nonviolence, and she translated both as passivity or inaction in the face of injustice. But it is easy to see how, for those brought up in the stillness of Quaker worship, the valence of silence may have been perceived differently. Silence was partly valued for instrumental reasons. A silent protest action is, arguably, easier to organize. First, silence offers a protection from power. The ambivalence of silent protest makes it hard to shut down. Silence allows protesters to confront without being confrontational. This explains why the Sentinels who were detained as part of the action were arrested on technical grounds (specifically, for obstructing the walkway). Second, silence is (at least potentially) inclusive. Silence is less resource-intensive than speech, and this meant that more than two thousand suffragists, from different backgrounds, could participate in the picketing without having to learn a script and without much planning. Besides and above these and other strategic reasons for adopting silence, however, Quaker members of the NWP would have been aware of its community-making power (see K. Ferguson 2003, 61–63). Within Quakerism, silent worship is a ritualized practice used to sustain the sense of a community's power and unity. Quakers make silence together; it is their shared ownership and responsibility (Bell 1992, 216). Finally, for Quakers, silence is not just something that might produce power, much less something meant to enact a power relationship. It is rather designed to orient participants—both makers and addressees of silence—toward new possibilities of being and becoming. The Sentinels' silence engaged the public in such dynamic processes, which were pregnant with transformative possibilities for the form and meaning of democratic agency. I will return to this at the end of the chapter.

The concern that the emphasis on silence equated with passivity was assuaged by the Silent Sentinels' explicit declaration that they were a fighting organization of nonprofessional soldiers (see Southard 2007, 401). Nothing about this was left to chance. Silent Sentinels stood at the White House gates for six hours every day in uniform—the ladies' attire of the day and the sashes bearing the NWP's colors of purple, gold, and white. They exhibited the physical courage expected from military personnel in facing all weather and in remaining immovable and silent in the face of threats, taunts, insults, and even physical violence. Their naming as "sentinels" was rich with meaning and full of purpose. Their mission was to guard or keep watch. But there was a subversive irony to it. They were not there to protect the incumbent of the White House. They were there guarding and standing for the democratic values that the institution represented. Their tactics set the president against himself, as they were merely following President Wilson's injunction in his *Constitutional Government* (1908): "Agitation is certainly of the essence of a constitutional system" (Wilson 2017, 133). They were the agitators he called for: citizen-soldiers protecting the constitutive principles of their community even if denied those principles themselves.

The Silent Sentinels' weapons were their silence and their lettered banners. The latter have merited privileged attention from scholars (see, e.g., Chapman 2014). The banners' most distinctive trait is their use of ironic quotations from the president's campaign and war speeches as a rhetorical device to enhance the effectiveness of the Sentinels' political messaging. But here I want to focus instead on the banners' dynamic interplay with the Sentinels' performed silence.

The press was quick to try to take the sting out of the Silent Sentinels' quotation practice by reminding readers that "telling a man what he said is what every woman from Eve down has always done!" (quoted in Ford 1991, 137). Where the press starts with biblical Eve, to reduce women to receivers and maintainers of male speech, I want to start with Eve's mythical counterpart: Echo, the nymph cursed by Juno to repeat the words of a man. As her physical form became disfigured, Echo became not only a vanishing voice but a voice that was pure resonance: empty, secondary, derivative. This figuring of Echo—and therefore of women in general—is conventional in the Western rhetorical tradition, in which speech becomes the province of man, and hollow, fragmented, incoherent, insignificant language that of woman. As a result, in this tradition, women, like Echo, "are doomed to perform the masculine voice back to the males who originate the rhetoric, over and over again" (McDermott 2016, 46). The press overlaid this gendered script on the Silent Sentinels' performance.

As Cavarero rightly notes, however, in Echo as elsewhere, the act of repetition can foster forms of resistance (2005). It can confirm, reproduce, and stabilize meanings and the authority of meaning-makers. But it can equally subvert, disrupt, and destabilize them. For Echo does not simply duplicate male voice, giving it back whole: she just repeats the final words. Words therefore return broken up, disintegrated. This makes her repetition capable of transmuting meaning (Athanasiou 2017, 258). She detaches words from speakers and decontextualizes them; the same words thus take on different meanings that may, in extreme cases, negate their original meaning. This is the kind of performative loop that the Sentinels' silence enabled and that was responsible for unsettling the preordained genders of enunciating agent and the recipient subject, male speaker and female listener.

Both negation and redirection of meaning resulted from the Sentinels' unauthorized appropriation of Wilson's statements. "WE SHALL FIGHT FOR THE THINGS WHICH WE HAVE ALWAYS CARRIED NEAREST OUR HEARTS—FOR

DEMOCRACY, FOR THE RIGHT OF THOSE WHO SUBMIT TO AUTHORITY TO HAVE VOICE IN THEIR GOVERNMENT," one banner read. It repeated a line of Wilson's speech declaring war on Germany. Solemnity and comicality contended in the repetition, given how dipped in contradiction it was (Chapman 2014, 20). What is being contradicted is threefold. First, the expectation of coherence between words and action, foreign policy and domestic policy. Second, the expectation of what would follow from the words—namely, the right to vote for women. Third, Wilson's authority: its legitimacy is made to depend on the voice of the women standing at his door. The exposure of Wilson's self-contradictions is designed to negate the meaning of his statement, induce public shaming for the violation of democratic norms, and encourage the violator to revise his conduct and comply with these norms in the future. But the exposure was also instrumental in generating wider public accountability, strengthening the public's shared sense of commitment to the norm and fostering solidarity with those wronged by its violation. Besides negation, however, the juxtaposition of the banners with their silence effected a redirection, whereby a nonspeaking female collective subject became the rightful speaker of another's words (Chapman 2014, 40). The ownership of democratic voice was reassigned from the president to the silent women, and at the same time, the political language responsible for their silencing was laid bare for everyone to see.

"Ladies, concert public opinion on behalf of women suffrage," President Wilson had advised the disappointed delegates of the NWP in their last meeting with him before the silent vigils started. Wilson's presidency has been deemed a "rhetorical presidency" for its tendency to bypass Congress by appealing directly to the American people to generate support for public policies (Tulis 1987). The Silent Sentinels followed in his footsteps. They sought to pressure the president to take action by harnessing public opinion directly from a place—the gates of the White House—whose symbolic value increased the weight and persuasiveness of their claims.[3] In so doing, they competed with the president for the representation of the American public while radically redefining the "voice" in which a democratic representative might speak.

Let me turn to this redefinition. As has been noted, the term "rhetorical presidency" establishes "the essence of the modern presidency—rhetorical leadership" (Tulis 1987, 3–4). Wilson believed that only a new oratorical statesmanship, centered on the figure of the president and on rhetoric directed at and to the public, could claim a popular mandate. To his mind, rhetoric alone could actively shape public opinion, thereby bringing popular will "into full consciousness" of its "unity and purpose" (Wilson quoted in Tulis 1987, 125–29). The president thus had to act as a macro-interpreter, extracting one will from a cacophony of wills. Though Wilson's own rhetoric was one of listening, his actions made it clear that his was a predetermined "listening," which spoke of a desire for mastery, executed from a purportedly epistemically privileged position. His self-figuring was thus as "a man in whose ears the voices of the nation . . . [sound] concurrent and concordant like the united voices of a chorus . . . so that he can speak what no other man knows, the common meaning of the common voice" (Wilson quoted in Tulis 1987, 135). If validating what the president said was the role reserved for suffragists when they were conversing with Wilson, revealing to the people their true voice was the role Wilson reserved for himself. His self-proclaimed mission may have been that of gathering and following public opinion. But he believed that public opinion could only be "concerted," and thus come into its own, by echoing his voice. This was the trademark of the Wilsonian presidential democracy.

Given his self-portrayal as someone speaking (for) public opinion, President Wilson was guarded about his position regarding female suffrage. When asked, he hid behind the distinction between the voice one is allowed to have as a private individual and the voice one is bound to as a public official: "When I speak for myself, I am an individual; when I speak for an organic body, I am a representative. For that reason, you see, I am by my own principles shut out, in the language of the street, from 'starting anything.' . . . I am not at liberty to speak until I speak for somebody besides myself. . . . I am not at liberty to speak as an individual for I am not an individual" (Wilson quoted in Irwin 1921, 44, 59, 116). The intention to effect a permutation of roles is clear. The role of representing all carries a duty of silence that makes Wilson look more disenfranchised than any of the suffrage campaigners when it comes to speaking his mind. His legitimacy depends on his being perceived as a follower, not an initiator. Should the Silent Sentinels manage to turn public opinion, he might follow. But not before.

In their attempt to concert public opinion, the Silent Sentinels offered a powerful counterpoint to Wilson's construal of the popular voice. For Wilson, genuine popular voice was the voice of the rhetorical president, who was "the sayer, the namer" responsible for constituting the very public that might support it (Emerson 2010, 11). Wilson's emphasis lay therefore on the individual rhetor's voice as the prime vehicle of democratic agency. The Silent Sentinels' performance of "voice" came to upend this. This performance involved both the subversion and positive appropriation of Wilson's speech and the

Sentinels' silent embodied action. We have seen that the Sentinels' use of quotation achieved two fundamental severances: it severed political voice from individual authorship (his voice became theirs) and it severed authorship from authority (though authored by him, his voice could only be made authoritative through the Sentinels' action). Through these severances, the Sentinels prepared "voice" for wider circulation and collective appropriation—both by the suffragist movement itself and by the movement's supporters. The severances made the voice "mass, collective, quotational" (Chapman 2014, 72). While this much has been acknowledged, the role of silence has been overlooked. For it was silence that produced the leveling, universalizing effect driving the creation of a more impersonal and more anonymous democratic voice. Suffragists were all too aware of the silencing effects of Wilson's style of representation. Given how resource-intensive speech is, especially for a group that has been cut off from public voice and struggles to find a hearing, should the Sentinels have chosen speech as their means of protest, a few prominent figures would have emerged as their spokespeople, or the public, discursive self of the group (Alcoff 1991, 10). But in choosing silence, they made sure that no one individual spoke for them and that their collective identity hinged not around a single speaker but around their public, disruptive silence. Precisely because silence is less resource-intensive than speech, they could draw on large numbers of women, from diverse age groups and backgrounds, to rotate in their stations. That their silence was an embodied action, performed in real space and time, by multiple actual or potential female speakers was critical in steering clear from a strictly speech-centered view of political agency, effacing "the silent gesturing female body" in favor of "the silent disembodied text" (Chapman 2014, 30). Their active performance of silence was not just perfectly embodied but a practice of participatory democracy on par with discursive speech. Their performance of silence was political because it dramatized meaningful absences of speech and because it constituted a meaningful action performed and taken up by each Sentinel. A symbol of their negation as political beings, silence was also the site of their reinvention as a distinct political being, as making silence with each other developed solidarities and a common, empowered sense of self. Within it, each was not the same as but equal to the other, holding a banner and through it holding to a voice that was at once hers and not hers—a voice they authorized themselves to "voice" and re-signify collectively. This was a voice dependent not on a single speaker, or the uniqueness of that speaker's voice, but on a collectivity of unnamed and unidentified silence-keepers. Their silence amplified the protest's message by allowing its collective resounding in ways that radically detached it "from sovereign, solitary personhood" (King 2012, 239). Through its soundless vocalization, the suffragist voice turned into a kind of propertyless commons that could be shared with other marginalized groups.

## Haptic Silence and the Democratic Sublime

But potential is not necessarily actual. W. E. B. Du Bois made this clear in "Forward Backward," a piece written for *Crisis* in which he claimed that "the nemesis of every forward movement in the United States is the Negro question" (1911, 243). While potential is only realized where it produces motion—where it translates into the act of moving itself—the potential for the suffragists to produce a new democratic subject was undercut by the movement's racism, by its refusal to see what Du Bois saw best: "Every argument for Negro suffrage is an argument for woman's suffrage; every argument for woman suffrage is an argument for Negro suffrage; both are great movements in democracy" (Du Bois 1915, 285).

It is therefore not without some ironic resonance that the first civil rights march—the Silent Parade, held on Fifth Avenue on July 28, 1917—should draw its protest repertoire, at least in part, from the silent suffrage protest genre. As leaders of the Harlem branch of the National Association for the Advancement of Colored People (NAACP) met to decide on how to protest, the field secretary, James Weldon Johnson, who was married to the African American feminist and civil rights activist Grace Nail Johnson, brought a proposal to the table: a silent protest parade. This resumed a proposal made years earlier by the prominent suffrage and civil rights campaigner Oswald Garrison Villard, a founding member of the NAACP.

Both parading and silence had become trademarks of the suffrage protest genre. But only occasionally did they come together. On June 14, 1906, as the National Democratic Convention met in St. Louis, NAWSA organized a unique parade—motionless and silent—for a plank advocating votes for women. Lining the street in their white dresses with yellow sashes and parasols, they silently witnessed the delegates walk to the convention center. Black women participated in later silent parades, such as the 1917 silent parade on Fifth Avenue in support of the Red Cross. But if there is a forerunner of the Silent Parade in July of that year, it may well be the silent protest march organized in 1913 in New York by Villard's mother, Fanny Garrison Villard, for fifteen hundred black-clad suffragists and pacifists.

Parades imply marching or moving. As processions of people in the public space, they can be a vehicle for marginalized communities to transgress what Jacques Rancière calls the "partition of the sensible"—of visibility and invisibility, of what may be perceived and what may not—and to secure visibility with a public presence (2004). However, most pro-suffrage parades tended to reinforce preexisting partitions rather than inscribe new ones. Take, for instance, the massive 1913 women's suffrage parade organized by Alice Paul for the NAWSA in Washington, DC. Delegations from the southern states threatened to boycott the parade over the question of Black participation. Although Black suffragists would eventually march with state delegations, restrictions applied, with a group from Howard University, for instance, relegated to the back of the protest. The partition of the sensible reproduced racialized categories of dominance within the parade itself.

The first civil rights parade defied established social categories of visibility and invisibility. On July 28, 1917, an impressive ten thousand African Americans marched in silence along Fifth Avenue to protest against lynching and growing anti-Black violence. They claimed visibility and demonstrated political capacity. In an editorial whose title was evocative of the Silent Sentinels, James Weldon Johnson referred to the marchers as "an army with banners." This was a minutely choreographed army, signaling the beginning of a new militancy.

The scene was set meticulously. Demonstrators marched behind a row of drummers: children first, followed by women, all of them dressed in the purest of white, a background of innocence that focused attention on the national stain. Men in dark mourning suits marched at the rear, somberly. Organized by the NAACP with church and community leaders, the parade adhered to a gendered, bourgeois "politics of respectability" (Higginbotham 1993, 187). Respectability—cleanliness, dignified appearance, and behavioral decorum—was a key dimension of an "uplift politics" designed to empower the Black community to stand up and reshape interracial relations. This was meant to debunk the racist stereotype of African Americans as promiscuous and uncouth, which was often used to justify violent practices, including lynching, and to de-authorize their political voice. Respectability was also the most salient note in the press coverage of the march. On July 29, 1917, the day after the march, the *New York Times* called it "one of the most quiet and orderly demonstrations ever witnessed." The *New York Age*, one of the most influential Black newspapers of the time, reported that same day that the demonstrators "marched without uttering one word or making a simple gesticulation and protested in respectful silence." Respectful silence is here a sentinel, a control, a gatekeeping mechanism reinforcing distinctions of status. But while chastening and disciplining on the one hand, silence also showed willpower on the other. Its ambivalence protected demonstrators from police violence and allowed the parade to go on.

To call the march silent is to note at once an embodied phenomenon resulting from the absence of speeches, shouted chants, or rallying cries and a symbolic representation of the political condition of African Americans: not heard and deprived of their most fundamental rights. Yet sound was present. The repeated, muffled sound of the drums created a coordinating—grave and menacing—soundscape that enveloped the marchers. Instead of interrupting the demonstrators' silence, it amplified its effect.

From political speeches through protest slogans to the vote/voice motto, democracy is often reduced to voicing. But democratic soundscapes are equally important. The lasting impression left on those witnessing the march can only be captured if the visceral character of its aural apprehension is sufficiently appreciated. By visceral I do not mean to distinguish the emotional from the cognitive but to understand the emotional as a critical dimension of practical reason. A contrast between the aural and the visual is of help here. As David Suisman rightly observes, while through the eye one sees the world "out there," separate from oneself, through the ear one hears the world in one's head; it enters inside one and is perceived "from the inside out" (2009, 14). This partly explains the profound emotional and physical effect of sound—in the Silent Parade's case, of the drum's sound heightening the silence. We sense the presence of silence. We feel its weight and give it an emotional quality when speaking of it as dark, heavy, or grave. This "feeling" is not limited to hearing it: "we felt it in our bodies" (Acheson 2008, 547). The dress code, the commanding presence and stern posture of the marchers, and their slow, heavy, dignified steps together produced a soundscape that inspired terror, dejection, reverence. The full spectacle was the most sublime object. "And so it was," wrote James Weldon Johnson, "that these thousands and thousands moving quietly and steadily along created a feeling very close to religious awe" (1995, 66).

Words had a presence in the march too, albeit unvocalized. Multiple banners exposed and condemned the continuing violence against African Americans. There was the biblical quote "Thou shalt not kill." There was the question asked not for the answer but for the effect: "Mother, do lynchers go to heaven?" There was the shaming of contradictions in race relations: "We are maligned as lazy and murdered where we work." There was the disclosure of the vicious irony in racial reciprocity, especially trenchant in the wartime context: "We fought for the liberty of white Americans in six wars; our reward is East St. Louis." At the very rear of the parade, just before the American flag, an enormous banner stretched from one side of the street to the other that directly implicated onlookers in the continuing violence and incited them to move beyond mere spectatorship: "Your hands are full of blood," it read. The effect of all this, as Johnson recalls, was beyond words. But it could be seen on the faces and in the reactions of spectators: "There were no jeers, no jests, not even were there indulgent smiles." As "terrible truths" were paraded one after the other, their faces "betrayed emotions from sympathetic interest to absolute pain." Yet the words were not doing the real work here: "The power of the parade consisted in its being not a mere argument in words, but a demonstration to the sight" (Johnson 1995, 65)—and, as we have seen, to the ear.

The parade may not have been "a mere argument in words," and it was all the more powerful for it. But its moving, expressive speechlessness spoke louder than words. Words could have belittled the enormity of the racial crimes being committed against African Americans. The moral aptitude of their condemnation was nonnegotiable; it required no argumentation. In sealing nonnegotiability with a very public silence, the demonstrators turned the tables on white America. It was white Americans' continuing silence that was put on the spot, a silence maintained to avoid being held accountable for their in/actions. As the parade passed by, Boy Scouts handed out leaflets. They read, "We march because we deem it a crime to be silent in the face of such barbarous acts." There was a speaking silence and a deafening silence separating the parade from its audience, and the parade made it clear which silence belonged to the protesters and which silence belonged to the onlookers.

## Silent Vigils

There is a considerable time gap between the Silent Sentinels and the Silent Parade and the antinationalist, antimilitaristic, pacifist, feminist network that is the focus of the remainder of this chapter: the Women in Black. Formed in the late 1980s by a group of women in Israel who gathered to protest against the Israeli occupation of the West Bank and the Gaza Strip, the Women in Black have since become a worldwide network with a presence across continents.

Among the various groups drawing on the silent protest genre in the interim period, however, the Women in Black merit special consideration because they define themselves primarily by their mode of action: *silent* public vigils. "We are not an organization, but a means of communicating and formula for action," they claim on the network's website.[4] Silence is thus integral to who Women in Black are—since what they *do* when they protest is deemed essentially interchangeable with who they *are*.

Hence, while it is not uncommon for Women in Black to bear banners and distribute flyers at their protests, one would misunderstand these protests if these elements were made the focal point. Banners and flyers are accessories to silence rather than the other way around. As a signal, their silence is a means of communicating that doubles as the message itself. "We protest in silence," they write, "because silence is the most potent way to express views," and, "when deliberately used, it is the most powerful sound."[5] As a formula of action, their silent vigils constitute a way of "being present differently," of creating "a new awareness simply by being there," of redirecting "attention without compelling it," and of practicing "a renewed giving of attention" (Muers 2015a, 341, 333, 340). Theirs is a silence of witnessing repressed presences, and it quite literally "takes place" in the midst of the everyday to create an inclusive interactive space that—in the words of the Women in Black—"belongs to others, a space without violence."[6]

The Women in Black's characterization of their silence as a space without violence, designed to allow others in, captures the intention behind the silence. But it does not apprehend all its registers. Like speech, silence finds itself caught "between the poles of emancipation and bondage" (Haines 2017). As something within discourse, sometimes at the edge of it but never outside it, the silence of the Women in Black would be wrongly taken for a pre- or meta-discursive haven "uncontaminated" by and free of violence (Athanasiou 2017, 280). Their silence is gendered—and a performed gender. Again, in Rich's words, it has a history and a form (Rich 2013, 17). But this does not condemn it to either. For it is also an elected power, a form of calculated disruption aimed at not letting history, and the forms it has bequeathed to us, dominate the present. To fully appreciate this productive tension, let me turn to the different silences that the Women in Black make, evoke, and provoke in their demonstrations.

*Mourning Silence*

First, we should reflect on mourning as a form of political resistance.

In the 1917 Silent Parade, the mourners were men. They were last in marching sequence—NAACP, church and community leaders at the front;

children and women in white, pure, virginal, angelic, in the middle; men marching in dark dress at the rear. They represented a community's grieving of the lives lost to racial violence. The parade performed and broke the enforced silence that makes such losses unspeakable. It brought them into public and political life by resetting the frame through which lynching was seen: not a vigilant response to crime and disorder in a community but a technology of control and a ritual of white supremacy, springing from and serving wider processes of oppression and domination.

The politics of grief and grievance is also integral to the activism of the Women in Black. The black in their name refers to the black they wear for their silent vigils as a color-coded sign of mourning. Unlike the white worn by the women of the 1917 Silent Parade, the Women in Black's black sets them off as a dark, somber, possibly even threatening force. They bring injury, violence, and death—in other words, disorder—into the everyday life of the street.

The object of their threat is their community's self-understanding. Every community mobilizes the dead into the stories it tells itself about itself. These stories have great generative power; they shape communities into what and who they are. The ways in which communities respond to and engage the dead are a measure of their commitment to democracy. Mourning can be a resource for democratic politics, but it can also be the instrument for its closure (Butler 2004). The mourning of the Women in Black threatens the community's self-understandings because it does what is often forbidden. It re-politicizes mourning by showing how it has always been political (Athanasiou 2017, 13). It is critical of modes of mourning that induce depoliticization, that place the meaning and significance of traumatic events beyond contestation, revision, re-signification—beyond politics itself. It calls into question the false consensus and the false unity produced by mourning and the violent foreclosures involved in the resulting civic identities. The Women in Black thus demonstrate a dissident mourning, a mourning of dis-identification that questions how the work of mourning is conventionally done (205). Among the modes of mourning they resist are nationalistic narratives and public rituals that construe stories of death and loss in ways that bring out injuries against the nation while consigning to oblivion those committed *by* and *within* it (70). By contrast, their dissident mourning seeks to take heed of the "present as haunted by (its) absent presences" in order to instigate "reflexivity about the phantomlike remainders and reminders" (Athanasiou 2021, 169) of historical and enduring violence, including violence against women themselves.

In having women—rather than men—as mourners, the mourning of the Women in Black acquires a new significance. It both repeats an antecedent gendered form and reshapes it. Specifically, the Women in Black evoke the figure of the mourning woman, but they do it as an act of resistance to nation-state-centered forms of identification as well as to the enlistment of women in these rituals (and the gendered assumptions of the mourning genre itself). I will now turn to this relationship between gender and mourning.

From early Greek times, the responsibility for funereal laments has fallen on women. With the ensuing gendered division of the economy of grief, mourning became a "woman-specialism," with some women hiring themselves out as paid mourners or experts in grief ventriloquism. Made into vehicles of collective catharsis, women saw their mourning, especially their mourning of the fallen at war, controlled by the state and enlisted to justify military interventions abroad and to shape civic identity at home.[7]

Set against this background, the intention behind the Women in Black's performance of mourning becomes clearer: to "convert women's traditional passive mourning for the dead in war into a powerful refusal of the logic of war."[8] To take back control of mourning means, for the Women, to turn it on its head. That is, they use it as a mode of refusal of the dictates of others—namely, the state and its official interpretation of the meaning of traumatic loss—and as a mode of reopening active critical engagement and reflection on the very logic it is meant to serve.

Their mourning shapes not just the substance of the act of mourning but also its form. Sound and the dramatization of emotion have played an important part in the public enactment and commemoration of funerary rites. But the Women in Black's mourning is silent. Their silence stands in the place of the outward sounds that have been traditionally associated with women's mourning, such as crying, wailing, sobbing, and even screaming. This is therefore a silence performed in response to both gendered conventions of mourning and what Simon Stow has called mourning's "romantic" modes (2017, 60). These consist of "aestheticized, maudlin, and deeply sentimental" forms of mourning, prioritizing the expression of emotion—in some cases, extreme emotion, even a kind of "grief wrath" (Loraux 1986, 98)—to bolster the friend-enemy distinction over critical engagement with the complexity of "the enemy," an appreciation of mourning's ambivalent and complicated nature, and an understanding of "political identity as an always incomplete and ongoing process" (Stow 2017, 60, 157). Critical engagement and reflection do not necessarily exclude sentiment, as the suppression of sentiment toward those rendered un-grievable is integral to the problem. Part of the work of mourning is getting people to grieve the apparently un-grievable and thus comprehend the messy, complex reality of violence. But sentiment must be distinguished from sentimentality. The Women in Black resist not the former but the latter. Sentimentality is seen to subordinate the real importance and complexity of the object of grief to its emotive utility to the grieving agents. This, in turn, distorts judgment by idealizing the object of grief and preventing it from being understood otherwise (Jefferson 1983). A member of the Belgrade Women in Black group expressed the contrast most sharply when she referred to the collective's silent vigils as "a cruel mourning . . . a mourning without sentimentality" (Athanasiou 2017, 89).

Women's collectives creatively reshaped the received gender of mourning in different ways. Some women protest collectives—notably, the antinuclear and peace movements—have embraced female sound, including chanting, lamenting, crying, screaming, howling, wailing, and other sounds of affect writ large. They use it to question the passivity of voice (as a mere irreflexive sign of emotion) and reintroduce it as a central affective-cognitive component of democratic practice. Others, like the Women in Black, turn to silence. Physically embodied in a public space, theirs is a silence that is truly present. But it is also a silence that is present as an absence. As such, it is best placed to instantiate and draw attention to the absent presences that shape the present into its particular form but may prevent democratic work on that shape.

The silence performed by the Women in Black is both evocative and provocative. It evokes the silence imposed on women, not least through the equation of their speech with loquacious, formless, insignificant sound. It also evokes the silence of their political communities *about* intertwined geographies of violence, how the structural violence of race, class, and gender at home—the deadliest violence, with its power to normalize everyday experiences of interpersonal violence—exists on a continuum with the silencing of enemy suffering and enemy war victims. In drawing attention to these intertwined silences and to the master narratives—patriarchal, nationalist, militarist—responsible for their reproduction, the Women in Black's performed silence looks to provoke, to "engage with and account for unclaimed injuries and memories in ways that displace, again and again, the norms that authorize who/what matters as memorable and who/what is deprived of the rights and rites of memorability" (Athanasiou 2021, 186).

## A Minute of Silence

All acts of resistance are responses to given scripts. The Women in Black's dissident silent mourning responds to other ritualistic uses of silence to mourn the dead. A case in point is the minute of silence as a practice of memorialization.

Originally established to commemorate soldiers killed in the First World War, the minute of silence has become a ritual repeated everywhere death takes on a collective significance. Its acoustic staging can be more or less intricate, but it normally includes a few recognizable features: a silence of one or more minutes, which can be framed by sound marks signaling the silence's start and end.

An acoustic event that effects an interruption, the typical minute of silence is also a bodily spectacle, with people standing still and speechless in one another's presence in public spaces. Their bodies are "acoustically connected," as they are asked to engage in a movement that is both outward and inward, both public and introspective. As individuals follow the instruction "to keep silent and to keep immobile," they stage "a collective, socially shared (e-)motion." But if the publicity of the event draws them outward, fomenting solidarity in the affirmation of community, silence also invites a "strong inward orientation," as it is meant to be lived inward (Lichau 2014, 153).

The minute of silence tends to be organized or sponsored by the state. It is ritualistically scripted and meant to uphold the dominant order. In it, silence becomes an emotional site for the (re-)narration of death in ways that create or reinforce shared meanings, emotional ties, in-group solidarities. The role of the minute of silence is to co-opt the voices of the dead—the true "silent majority," in Homer's assessment—into the making or remaking of national unity.

The very production of the minute of silence requires undifferentiated unity without remainder. The asymmetry between speech and silence is instructive in this respect. While, in principle, just about anyone can appoint themselves to speak for a collective, collective silence can only be produced through universal collaboration. In other words, it takes just one person to break the silence and jeopardize a "performative commemorative" like the minute of silence (Santino 2006). This is also the reason why the minute of silence is such a fragile creation. It requires tight control, policing, and organization. Think, for instance, of the level of social control that goes into keeping a minute of silence or of the various occasions in which the minute of silence has offered an opportunity to stage a protest and destabilize, rather than affirm, community self-understandings by becoming an obstacle to the aspired closure.

Examples of this abound. Here I focus on two: the silence held by X González at the March for Our Lives on March 24, 2018, and the evolving use of silence within Black Lives Matter. Both challenge the meaning of the minute of silence by either playing with its duration, effecting its re-signification, or simply breaking it.

A minute of silence for mass victims of gun violence is all too common in the United States. It is also often used as a depoliticizing move, foreclosing the very questions democratic citizens must ask and for which they want answers. "This is not the time for politics" is often heard in the face of traumatic death and loss. For this reason, the minute of silence has begun to be treated with suspicion and boycotted as an excuse for inaction on gun control legislation.[9] In 2018, X González, a survivor-activist of the Marjory Stoneman Douglas High School massacre, gave a speech lasting six minutes and twenty seconds on the March for Our Lives stage in Washington, DC. This was exactly the amount of time, they noted, that it had taken for seventeen of their schoolmates to be killed and many others injured. González then started listing the names of their classmates and saying the little things they would not be doing anymore. "Six minutes and twenty seconds with an AR-15," González said, "and my friend Carmen would never complain to me again about piano practice." This was followed by a litany of names and no-mores. Having spoken for less than two minutes, they stopped speaking and kept silence, staring at the crowd and the cameras until six minutes and twenty seconds were up. One ought not underestimate the impact of duration on the phenomenology of silence. Their prolonged silence gave a full, saturated presence to the victims of gun violence and their never-ending silence. As a piece in the *Atlantic* put it, González gave their audiences "dead air, in every sense" (quoted in Gerber 2018). The day had been filled with speeches, many of which were poignant, but it was González's silence—their impossibly extended silence, their unbearable silence, their shaming silence, their questioning of authorities' inaction—that left the most indelible mark. Their politicized silence was the perfect antidote to the depoliticizing effects of the minute of silence.

A similar reopening of the contested nature of mourning silence occurred within the Black Lives Matter movement. First there was the traditional minute of silence, a coming together in a show of solidarity. Five days after the shooting of Michael Brown Jr. in August 2014 by a white police officer in

Ferguson, Missouri, Americans were invited to participate in a nationwide minute of silence against racism and police brutality.

Every such minute of silence comes with the promise of not forgetting, but it is also meant to heal, to bring closure and finality. Closure implies unity, the nation's fusion—and resolution—into a unique and ultimate identity. But this unity started to crack as the temporality of silence changed. Silence became instead the unvoiced sound of resistance to closure, of the impossibility—the indignity—of letting go. This happened at an event to mark the first anniversary of Brown's death, where his father asked for four and a half minutes of silence to be observed in memory of the four and a half hours his son's body was left dying in the street. This silence relived the traumatic event; it refused to consign it to memory.

The following year, American Black athletes started kneeling at the beginning of sports events and refusing to lend their voices to the singing of the national anthem. As this silent protest unfolded in stadiums, the slogan WHITE SILENCE = WHITE CONSENT started appearing on T-shirts. This was soon followed by a "WEAR OUT THE SILENCE" campaign encouraging white people to wear Black Lives Matter T-shirts as a way of signaling the need for uncomfortable, but necessary, conversations about racialized disposability. Gestures that might seek to close down or displace those conversations for the sake of perpetuating denial were met with protest. This was the case with the 2016 Democratic primary. Candidate Martin O'Malley responded to activists shouting "Black Lives Matter" with a racially tone-deaf triple assertion: "Black lives matter. White lives matter. All lives matter" (see Butler 2015c). Other Democratic candidates, too, only reluctantly embraced the "Black Lives Matter" slogan and its entailments. In her 2016 convention address, Hillary Clinton, for instance, acknowledged "systemic racism," only to follow this with a salute to police officers. "White silence" within the party—whether generated by not saying or by unsaying what had (just) been said—betrayed the party's inability to do what was expected of it: to publicly acknowledge and stand up to structural and institutional racism. Protestors' interventions, in turn, sought to make the party reckon with its role in perpetuating structural racism and to make a full-throated recognition of it a precondition for the BLM movement's and the party's joint work. The significance of the disproportionate death and incarceration of countless unnamed Black men and women at the hands of the state could no longer be left unsaid or half said or hidden within other things that were being said or done. It needed to be spelled out if it were to reshape not just the party's ongoing relationship with the dead but its ongoing relationship with BLM—and the living.

## Silence as In-Betweenness

Along this chain of events, the political valence of the silences made and performed emerges. But what becomes apparent, too, is the difference between the minute of silence and the silent vigils of the Women in Black. I am now in a position to address this issue.

Despite its vulnerability to subversion and reappropriation, the minute of silence (especially the national minute of silence) is typically a staged event, saturated with predetermined meanings, that disciplines citizens into hegemonic civic identities. By contrast, the Women in Black's silent vigils are deliberately a far more perilous affair.

Their silence, like the minute of silence, seeks to produce an interruption. But this time the interruption goes against the grain. It stands in opposition to "normal life"—busy and sonorous—of the anonymous passersby. Hence, the first risk is that passersby fail to take notice. Their silence is also in opposition to interruptions made for the sake of continuity. It is not a pause to get back on track; it does not assume the value of the track taken. It is instead a caesura—the Latin for cutting, here to be understood more like a *discidium*, separating, tearing apart, dissenting, dis-identifying—seeking to enact a disruption. So the second risk is that as the Women in Black present themselves to their communities, they are targeted with ostracism and violence—the treatment normally reserved by communities for "internal enemies" (an epithet applied to the Silent Sentinels as well as the Women in Black; see Athanasiou 2017, 54). This risk is compounded by the fact that a silent street vigil has no space that it can claim as its own. In other words, vulnerability is the prerequisite of its performance (Muers 2015a, 340). The cost of interrupting the everyday, in the way the Women in Black do, "is allowing oneself to be interrupted by it—occasionally in ways that will throw [one's] particular performance off course" (340–41). Because silence, unlike speech, does not have a "take-home message," this leaves it even more vulnerable to being set "off course" by misunderstanding or misinterpretation (341).

But there are also other risks, this time inherent in the opening that the silence of the Women in Black seeks to effect. The Women's appropriation of public space, as the space "for the performative work of reflective and agonistic mourning" (Athanasiou 2017, 71), is not for the sake of owning it and bringing about a new closure but for the sake of contesting the terms of its current closure and inviting "a new and questioning look at the taken-for-granted" (Muers 2015a, 340). Their silence seeks to hold open, to reinstate the possibility of mourning becoming a dynamic process, serving democracy's capacity for self-critique and renewal. The distinction between a "door-opening" and a "door-closing" silence is helpful here (Tribe 1982). Silence can be "door-closing": it can mean cessation of all reciprocity, finality, and foreclosure. Take, for instance, the silence of authority. One is not properly condemned before one has exhausted all appeals. The silence heard at the end of a last appeal, however, is a "door-closing" silence, a sign of final authority and irreversible determination. By contrast, silence is "door-opening" when it creates a coexistential space that others can enter. This is how the Women in Black define their silence, as a space belonging to others, as room being made for others. In engaging silence as their mode of action, the Women in Black witness *for* and practice a new paying of attention to the dead. The space their silence creates is meant to belong to the unmourned dead. But it is also a coexistential space, for the deceased and the living. In keeping silence, the Women are looking to sustain a public space for the former's appearance and the latter's attempt to make sense of death's political meaning(s). This is a space, however, otherwise unscathed by their control. They do not populate it with their own narrative, with their own attempt to invest death with meaning. Hence, there is a risk that the Women in Black's silence is deemed inconsequential.

But is it? Well, yes and no. It is not consequential if this implies identifying solutions to problems or even obtaining particular results. But it may well still be consequential in other ways: namely, in reorganizing our political attention and holding us in the presence of hitherto absent or disavowed presences in our communities.

To grasp this fully, we need to move away from understanding silence as purely derivative of speech. Silence is derivative when taken for repressed speech or for a form of speech—a "saying" something determinate by "keeping silent." Although silence can certainly function like this, it is possible to contemplate an alternative modality: notably, that of a nonderivative yet meaningful silence, performed neither for its own sake nor for a preestablished end. This second possibility has sometimes been captured by treating silence not as sign but as gesture (Acheson 2008). Gesture seems an apt figure to capture the embodied textuality of silence, as no mere sign of some signification lying behind it but the embodiment of meaning (see, e.g., Bargu 2022, 298). However, the notion of gesture can also be invoked to set silence apart from both *poiēsis* (production) and *praxis* (action) (Agamben 2000, 7). This is achieved by not allowing it to be dominated by an end, whether external to the activity (in the case of *poiēsis*) or coinciding with it (in the case of *praxis*) (57). Conceived as gesture, silence is not concerned with the transmission of a particular something, or with doing something specific, as it is with transmission, mediality, or communicability itself (59). As a mediality, silence acts as a "productive passivity," creating an intersubjective space and activating "the potential for language, without a prescribed outcome" (McKim 2008, 97–98; see also Agamben 2000).

Is the silence enacted by the Women in Black of this type? At first glance, it might seem unlikely. The Women in Black are committed to peace with justice and actively opposed to war, militarism, and other forms of violence. Their collective has, therefore, a message and a telos. This is sometimes shown in the protest banners. Their enactment of silence, when read in the light of the banners, looks like a means to a pre-identified end.

And yet the dissenting silence of the Women in Black is not easily reducible to this or any other take-home message. Rather than seizing ownership of mourning to impart meaning to it, their silence, I submit, *is* the message. But what "message" could their silence be? The Women in Black's performance of silence deliberately exerts "very limited control, on any level, over the remaking of meanings towards which it is directed" (Muers 2015a, 340). If it performs an attempt of meaning-making at all, it is one that "allows or invites interruption," one that seeks to involve passersby in an active role (341). The key function of their practice of silence is to bear the presence of the death and the loss that remains untold. This practice represents a positive commitment to upholding the spaces where it becomes possible to establish, contest, and revise the scope, meaning, and means of mourning and grievability. It provides a mediality for different parties to engage in and through *their* differences, because the Women's silence acknowledges and makes room for the complexity and multi-sidedness of mourning objects as dynamic intersubjective processes. There is therefore no promise of healing, consensus, or unity in their silence: as a mediality, with its inherent indetermination, their silence is "as much a zone of risk as a place of comfort" (McKim 2008, 98).

## Conclusion

This chapter was an inquiry into the silent protest tradition, especially as engaged by women. I want to finish it by engaging the forms of political power and the forms of political agency that run through this tradition.

Political agency tends to be understood in terms of two broad forms of power: power-over and power-to. Power-over refers to the ability of some agents to exercise control or influence over others, or, as Patchen Markell puts it, "at least over a decision or course of action in a situation of actual or potential conflict with others about what is to be done" (2014, 117). It can be formalized by saying that A has power over B to the extent that it can get B to do something B would not otherwise have done. By contrast to power-over, power-to refers to one's ability to perform some activity. It consists in the actualization of one's "power to do or accomplish this or that particular thing" (129). In formal terms, one can say that A has power to the extent that A has the capacity or ability to do something or, in the appropriate circumstances, it will do something.

Hence, silence's potential for empowerment is normally assessed against these two notions of power (Gray 2023, 821). This, I want to argue, is not wrong as such, but it is too limited. It fails to grasp the ways in which silence can broaden and transform our understanding of power and political agency.

In this chapter, we have seen how, in electing silence as their form of political intervention, our collectives exercised both power-over and power-to. Under conditions where voice was unavailable, costly, or had become ineffective, silence expanded their repertoires of protest by allowing them to evade the power others may have exercised over them and acquire power to (protest) (Gray 2023, 821). The more power agent A has, the more they can control the options of another agent (call them B). A's power over B is diminished to the extent to which B has options that fall outside of A's control. The case of the Silent Sentinels shows this most clearly. The stereotypical construction of women as irrational and hysterical is one of the technologies of power used to deny women's agency. It had been used to push suffragists toward "civilized" speech engagement with authorities, since they were made to believe that their access to public and political recognition depended on it. Authorities capitalized on this by turning their exchanges with the suffragists into inconsequential talk. The more the suffragists' options were constrained by authorities (and by the public perceptions on which their de-authorizing of suffragists fed), the more likely it became that the suffragists would choose to do something that aligned with the authorities' will, desire, or interest—that is, the type of "table talk" that legitimized authorities but did little for the suffragists' cause. Silence was then the elective power that offered the suffragists a way out and a way back into protest. Silence offered them the power to protest in public, being less likely to be punished or dispelled. Combined with speech, and as a public form of exposing injustice, silence also gave them power over the president and other political authorities, namely, by constraining their options, especially their option of continuing to pay no heed to the suffragists' demands. They did this by publicly de-authorizing the president and harnessing the recognition and support of a third agent—the public.[10] Despite the difficulties of positing a causal relationship, it is reasonable to suggest that the Sentinels' silent public protest conferred on the suffragists some control over the political agenda and influence over decision-making—by pressing for the recognition of women's right to vote. This assessment falls under the common understanding that a movement or collective is powerful to the extent to which it advances or actualizes the power to do or accomplish a particular thing or a specific set of demands.

But, as I hinted at the beginning, this is a limited way of thinking about power, agency, and influence. One of the ways in which silence can do democratic work is by troubling received notions of each of these and asking us to think differently about them (Muers 2015a, 335). We have come to think of power as either someone's possession or as something that is everywhere. But when we look to the Silent Parade or the Women in Black's vigils and ask whose silence this is, the answer that best applies is no one's and everyone's. Their power to make silence is the kind of power that is not possessed and can only emerge *among*. It belongs to no one in particular, because it can only be produced—made to happen—through joint action and uptake.

But to say that their power emerges among is not yet to answer the question of what kind of power the emerging power is. For that, we may want to turn to Rachel Muers's discussion of silent vigils. "Not doing anything particular," she explains, is different from "doing nothing" (2015a, 335). One of the main things the silent protests I examined did was perform their "conscientious objection" and draw public attention to constitutive exclusions actively shaping collective identity (Muers 2015b, 66). In so doing, they invited "a new and questioning look" at the "taken-for-granted." This is something they achieved "not mainly by saying anything, but mainly by *being present differently*" (Muers 2015a, 340, my emphasis; see also Butler 2011). Silence understood as a signal of absent speech cannot grasp this "being present differently," since the *doings* of embodied silence no longer fall under the political ontology of speech (see Rollo 2019). Instead, they transgress the boundaries of speech and body, reason and affect, doing and being.

We may need to call on the notion of "gesture" (from the Latin root *gerere*, "to bear," "to carry or carry on," "to show," "to reveal," "to assume") to grasp how embodied silence acts politically in the absence, and sometimes even in defiance, of a speakable presence (Acheson 2008). Gesture is neither the model political action, *praxis* or doing (which is an end in itself), nor the model speech action, *poiēsis* or making (which has an end other than itself)

(Agamben 2000, 79). It is rather a means in an end, "the process of making a means visible as such" (58). As such, it serves no purpose other than to reproduce itself through the medium of the human body. Thus gesture looks and is wasteful: it is the opposite of commodity, something with a value other than use or exchange value (Muers 2015a, 339). Inclined, as we are, to assess political action solely in terms of efficacy—that is, as a means to an end, as a way of voicing demands and having them answered—we question the *point* of silent protest. What the instrumental approach misses, however, is the politics of creating a situation allowing for such a "pointless" gesture, the presence in the moment, the simply being there, which coexists "with instrumentality but is also in tension with it" (Bargu 2022, 296; see also Muers 2015a).

The silent protesters I have examined in this chapter made silence palpable and visible. They strategically used speechlessness and corporeality to dramatize and challenge their (and others') relegation to speechlessness and invisibility. Their bodies acted in concert—intruded into the public space, the space of speech, and congregated there, standing still—to question the silencing effects of hegemonic speech and the principles of justice that it articulated. Their embodied performance of silence did not only signal absent or unspeakable presences, however. It placed their bodies in relation, forged alliances, and enacted a new political subject at once referencing and subverting ascribed roles and power relations. While we have been made to believe that political action means speech and that action unaccompanied by speech is action destitute of revelatory power, their embodied performance of silence constituted and revealed a form of political subjectivation, favoring a relational, anonymous, collective subject over solipsistic leadership and sovereigntist ideals of political agency (Arendt 1958, 179).

Self-mastery is commonly taken as a central aspect of agency. Making silence in public—sometimes in the face of insult or injury—is a demanding practice, involving a considerable amount of discipline and self-mastery. But it is also a particularly vulnerable one. It embraces, through the performance of silence, a level of "ambiguity, multivalence, and uncertainty" (Beausoleil 2017, 293); it invites passersby to be active partners in making sense; it exposes the performed silence to interruption, misreading, or even simple neglect. Silent vigils enact political self-formation as a "constant practice of openness and presence" (303). Rather than being about repossessing the word, they perform the experience of "language being at a loss" (Athanasiou 2005, 47). By suspending language, they push back on current habits of thought and speech, expose their limitations and contradictions, and create an opening for their reconstitution. Importantly, they also refrain from foreclosing that opening by populating it with their own counter-diction. Instead, they hold open a "space of appearance" within which competing conceptions of political community can emerge and become the subject of public questioning, without participants knowing or—indeed—controlling in advance what the outcome will be (Arendt 1958, 198–99).

This foregrounds the ways in which the performance of silence can both assert agency and refrain from agency in ways that are powerfully affirmative of community. The purpose and direction of a political community is not something preset but construed. It needs to be figured out within practices of world-building that, in a democracy, must be shared if they are to shape shared conditions. These practices imply a particular quality of attention—borne by careful, engaged, listening silences—that brings into focus currently unspeakable or unspoken subjects and worldly objects worthy of attention and concern (Myers 2013, 96). Rather than popular sovereignty or a set of procedures for arriving at collective decisions, democracy is best understood as a common quest, and those practices that sustain it, in the face of uncertainty and disagreement. The practices sustaining this quest, making it common, give democracy the capacity to begin anew.

This understanding underpins the feminist silent protest tradition. Its beginnings can be traced to an element of Quakerism; Quakers themselves grew out of groups known as Seekers. The latter can be used as a window onto a fundamentally democratic use of silence. Seekers found in silence a way of sustaining their search for truth in the face of breakdown and great uncertainty regarding how to start again and where the search might take them (Muers 2015a). As Rachel Muers explains, in keeping silence with/for one another, early Quakers "were not 'doing nothing'—but they were not quite (yet) doing anything in particular" (335). Their quest, like ours as democrats, was not for something preexisting toward which they might work. Instead, what was to be "found" was (also) to be constituted within a new form of relationality, within a new form "to encounter one another" borne by their practice of silence (335).[11] As Muers rightly points out, their "time-wasting in the mode of paying attention" defied instrumentality and, as a result, was a "subversive act" (339). It prioritized listening over voice and understood listening as the active practice of listening for, reflecting on, and working through the vocalizations of others, even if—or especially if—they were unsettling. This kind of silence performs a receptiveness that is neither passivity (as this would preclude relation) nor limited by what falls under preexisting categories (which would preclude receptiveness). There is undoubted democratic power in this practice, but neither a power-over nor a power-to. It is rather "something like the bond that holds people in a relation of presence and attention to each other and to some aspects of their world" (Markell 2014, 127–28). In democracy, our sights must not turn to external sources of truth but, like the Seekers, to issues, goals, or things in the world we must care about in caring for one another (Myers 2013).

It is not fortuitous that this type of power should have been likened to the power we sometimes assign to a picture, a musical piece, or a scene capable of holding us in its presence even if it is no longer being seen, heard, or otherwise directly experienced (Markell 2014, 128). Instead of being possessed by an agent, this holding power belongs to the thing, situation, or political scene itself. We saw instances of this in the newspapers' description of the Silent Parade as a sublime "object," causing fear, admiration, respect, even reverence. It was something that clearly lingered in witnesses' minds and echoed in their ears well after the event. The Parade's "staying power" traveled and continues to be realized every time the political failure to put an end to racist violence is "felt and mourned and remembered in common" (Markell 2014, 134), as was the case in July 2017, when activists marked the hundredth anniversary of the Silent Parade in Bryant Park, New York, holding portraits of well-known victims of police violence. Or indeed with the Black Lives Matter silent protests that spread across the United States from 2013 onward, with a peak in 2020, following George Floyd's murder.

If failure to effect radical change might seem reason enough to elide the foundational significance of the silent protests, their staying power and their reiteration in response to the reproduction of history tells us something different: it foregrounds their importance and that of countless other partially successful, partially frustrated efforts for democratic founding understood as "an ongoing, dynamic, and contestatory aspect of political life," which "exposes and exploits the [political] system's own underauthorized nature" (Bernal 2017, 15, 101). How might founding, understood in this fashion, be reconciled with the traditional notion of founding as referring to the drafting of a constitution that authoritatively fixes—sets up or puts in place, very often through the written word—fundamental political commitments, principles, rights, and values? The next chapter addresses this question through an exploration of how silence might be integral to the making of constitutions and their democratic political remaking over time.

# 5

# THE SILENCES OF CONSTITUTIONS

In short, silence can be a constructive force. Incompletely theorized agreements are an important source of successful constitutionalism and social stability; they also provide a way for people to demonstrate mutual respect.
—Cass Sunstein

This chapter is about the silences of constitutions. It submits that constitutional silences are integral to a constitution's makeup—and, in particular, to its *democratic* makeup.

On the face of it, the claim may sound implausible. After all, constitutions seem to be all about words, especially written words. Written constitutions are now nearly universal. Although they are irreducible to their written text, in speaking of constitutions, one's mind is immediately directed to their textuality. Constitutions thus remind us of the power of the word—the demotic power of the printed word, to be exact—in enacting, organizing, and constraining power (W. Mitchell 1986, 54). As things that are made up of words and that make the world in their words' image, constitutions speak to the power of language for both rule and transformation (Colley 2014, 259).

What may be less apparent is that constitutions are as much works of silence as they are works of words. Some constitutional silences are simply inevitable. Constitutional texts are never fully comprehensive, self-determinative, or self-executing. Some of their silences are omissive, just silences of missing out or unwittingly leaving something unaddressed. Other silences are tacit, the silences of assuming something to be true or taking it for granted. To this we can add a third main source of silence in constitutions:

everything that a constitution says is at least partly silent on how it should be interpreted. Every clause in a constitution is somewhat silent about "how narrowly or literally it is to be taken; what significance is to be attributed to what it excludes along with what it includes; how its context, both elsewhere in the same text and in preceding and comparable texts, ought to figure in what it conveys" (Tribe 2018, 27). Thanks to this, if constitutions are to speak at all, they are in need of interpretation. Yet not all constitutional silences are like the ones mentioned hitherto, that is, either necessary or neglectful. There are also constitutional silences that are commissive: deliberately done and purposely chosen. All constitution-making involves fundamental decisions regarding what to say and what not to say. Some of the silences left in constitutions are therefore intentional. They result from deliberate decisions not to say, not to regulate, and not to determine.

And yet the idea that constitutional silences may be essential to constitutions' democratic makeup has been largely overlooked.[1] Not all the silences intentionally left in constitutions will, of course, be justifiable on democratic grounds. Some will be purely self-serving; others will have nefarious systemic effects. But I submit here that there is a *prima facie* democratic reason for stopping constitutions from saying it all.

In a democracy, the authority of the constitutional text as a foundation cannot be separated from the possibility of the political action it may generate. This is normally understood in terms of the possibility of revising the constitutional text, reworking its clauses, (re)interpreting their meaning, and articulating their policy implications. As Hannah Arendt most famously put it, "[A]mendments to the Constitution augment and increase the original foundations," and "the very authority" of a constitution "resides in its inherent capacity to be amended and augmented" (2006, 194). In only associating political action with the remaking of a constitution's words, however, we forget constitutional silences. Both are essential for reconciling the initial act of foundation with freedom of political action—our own and that of future generations. Ultimately, constitutional silences hold off a constitution's closure and give citizens a stake in its remaking over time.

There is some irony in citing Arendt to make my claim that constitutional silences allow for amendment and augmentation, the kind of political action that Arendt saw as conferring retrospective authority upon a foundation by allowing it to be not just a command but our own construction. The irony consists in the fact that there is little room for silence in Arendt's theory. She defined action as speech-action, and speech-action as the political itself. This left silence as either a dangerous outside, as seen from her association of silence with violence (which she deemed "mute"; Arendt 1958, 26), or as insignificant, as seen from her association of silence with withdrawal from the political and/or absence of a political existence (176).[2]

In light of this, Arendt's inattention to the democratic potential of constitutional silences is hardly surprising. This potential is the subject of this chapter. The chapter has two main parts. The second part focuses on silences that are deliberately kept in constitutions and discusses how they may help support and enhance democratic processes or, conversely, threaten to undermine them. These include "gag rules," complete silences about certain matters of constitutional relevance, the use of constitutional ambiguity to avoid saying something specific, and matters that are mentioned in the constitution only to signal their absence and make a deferral. Before I turn to these intentional silences, however, I want to engage three other silences: the silences that enable constitutions to continue speaking and generating speech-action; the silence of tradition used to fill out perceived constitutional silences; and finally, constitutions' silence about their own subject, the people, and its meaning. These silences, while not intentionally embedded in constitutions, frame and sustain our relationship to them. I start with what I have called the "silence of mediality" and the "silence of the taken for granted." Each of these is now discussed in turn.

## The Silences of Mediality, Democratic Necessity, and the Taken for Granted

First is the silence of mediality. Silence can be seen as playing a critical role in mediating the relation between the constitution and the speech-action that follows. Political discourse always refers back to a foundation, an origin, a beginning, which (being foundational) enjoys a privileged position and sets "a standard of legitimacy" (Dauenhauer 1979, 443). It is, however, of the very nature of political discourse that it has no "final terminus" in which it may find its completion. Hence, even though the foundation will always be present in subsequent political discourse, it is never fully so, as it is always unfinished (Honig 1991). It will always be present, because, as Bernard Dauenhauer explains, "What is uttered in the present, if it is political utterance, is meant to prolong, preserve, and develop what was initiated in the beginning" (1979, 444). But—and much weighs on this *but*—as much as present speech-action looks to the beginning, it never simply repeats it. In other words, and as Arendt saw most clearly, neither present nor past political discourses are fully autonomous, and neither should have strict priority over the other. Present utterances have their roots in some founding discourse, but equally the founding discourse has current efficacy, current life, only by virtue of present utterances. This mutual dependence secures a genuinely *relational* connection between present and past political utterances. Critically, this is also a relation that is supported and mediated by a twofold silence. "There is the silence which lets the founding discourse be heard anew," Dauenhauer writes. "And there is the silence which opens the way for that which, however founded it is in the origin, is new, never uttered before, and yet destined to yield to a subsequent, dependent, but new political utterance" (445). Dauenhauer points here toward two distinct forms of silence that structure the political realm and enable a coequal relationship between past and present political utterances, foundation, and subsequent speech-action. First, a listening silence, allowing the founding discourse to speak and to be used by others. Second, a silence opening the way for new communications, for further mediating activity, and for further interpretations of the original speech-action—interpretations that can conflict with one another or even, on occasion, contradict the foundation itself (444–45).

While the silence of mediality is what I have called before an "opening silence," enabling further speech activity, the silence of the taken for granted seems to do just the opposite: to close it off. The very language of the taken for granted evokes a givenness over which we have no control, one that simply compels or commands acquiescence, which we must accept without question or objection—in one word, that silences. By the silence of the taken for granted, I mean here something specific, namely, the traditions, conventions, and cultural assumptions against which constitutions are understood and against which meaning is made from their silences, gaps, and abeyances. A tradition can provide a collective framework for remembrance of the founding and a collective set of interpretive guidelines for comprehending its meaning in the present. It can therefore operate as a kind of bridge between present political actors, "what is sanctioned today," and constitutional actors, "what was initiated at the foundation" (Loughlin 2018, 929).

There is always the danger, however, that freedom and political action are dominated by tradition, if tradition—including a constitutional tradition—is taken to be fully set or predetermined. The danger is there because the binding power of a tradition depends, to a significant degree, on its becoming tacit knowledge or common sense, something assumed rather than rewoven through use. And yet the prerequisite for the survival of tradition, according to Dauenhauer, is that it "conserves and saves, but also forgets and sloughs off" what has lost its value (1979, 450). In other words, for traditions to be preserved, they must not be treated as something absolute that stands beyond the freedom of political action but as something to be transformed, revised, and augmented through it: "If the future utterances for which tradition prepares the way do not go beyond this point of departure but rather merely repeat what tradition retains, then tradition ossifies" (450). Tradition and new political utterances are thus radically codependent: tradition is necessary to secure the efficacy and bring about the effects of the new utterances, just as the new utterances are necessary for the "maintenance and vitality of tradition" (450). And this is ultimately because tradition, while not being the same as silence, is partly constituted by it and "must be [partly] silenced if it is to remain fertile" (451). In other words, the "tacit" element of our constitutional traditions is wrongly taken for that which is understood without question. Constitutional authority depends on the construction of a constitutional tradition as well as—and critically—on the latter's being an active site of knowledge generation.

The language of a constitution is often used purposively to express certain "self-evident ideas," chiefly that of the sovereignty of a people. This "people" is typically presented as something already in existence, so that the constitution may be fashioned as the vehicle of its sovereign, general will. Most constitutions do not seek, however, to define, in any specificity, the people they assume to have authority over them.[3] They do refer to "the people" or even "the sovereign people," and they may even bind this people to a particular nationality, as evinced, for example, in the 1958 French Constitution: "The French people solemnly proclaim." But constitutions will usually stop short of further articulating "the people." It is, of course, tempting to read this omission as no silence at all on the basis that the constitution need not specify "the people" because it refers to an already known entity. By remaining silent about the people, the constitutional text would, in this reading, simply defer to silent presuppositions, thus letting the latter speak for it, filling its silence.

This is, of course, part of what constitutions are doing in invoking an authorizing "we, the people." They remain undecided between the *constative* and the *performative*; a *referent*, which is positioned as something taken for granted and already in existence, is effectively called *into being* through the act of writing a constitution (Derrida 1986). One cannot be without the other. But I want to suggest that it is not *just* the case that textual delineations of "the people" are constitutionally unnecessary, because the taken for granted fills them up. The absence of such delineations is also, I submit, constitutionally *necessary* in a different sense, as part of a normatively constituent intention. In a democratic constitution, the inarticulation of the "we, the people" is normatively forceful because it leaves in the constitutional text a silence that functions as the trace or mark of the people as something that could never be "wholly subsumed in the text that represents it" (Frank 2010, 31). And insofar as the people is never wholly representable, let alone realizable, in any constitution, this generates what Jason Frank has rightly named as an "internal surplus" that feeds further speech-action (2010, 31). In other words, given its standing as an "internal surplus," the question of who "the people" are remains a legitimate subject of political contestation, that is, the subject of the kind of speech-action that is the most robust component of democratic politics.

Silence as Deferral and as Gagging

Not all constitutional silences are silences resulting from the impossibility of articulating what ultimately lies beyond definition, however. Constitutional silences may simply result from a decision not to determine what was, in principle, fixable or determinable. Constitution-making, I have argued earlier, involves fundamental decisions as to what to say and not to say; what to regulate and not to regulate; what to determine and not to determine. This means that some silences that are left in constitutions result from more or less deliberate decisions not to say, not to regulate, and not to determine.

The empirical literature identifies two main drivers of such decisions. First, there are concerns about the up-front decision costs of trying to reach a constitutional settlement, and second, there are concerns about the longer-term error costs of making a constitutional decision that proves to be, and is *shown* to be, wrong (Posner 1973; Dixon and Ginsburg 2011). As Rosalind Dixon and Tom Ginsburg rightly emphasize, up-front decision costs are especially pertinent when the issue at stake is perceived as highly divisive, because the parties involved see themselves as likely to gain or lose a great deal (2011, 639). When the stakes are perceived as being high, the parties may be reluctant to make a decision, as they understand the constitutive power of constitutional law. In addition, when the stakes are low but the probability of error is high—because information is unavailable about the likely empirical effects of different choices and there is considerable uncertainty about how things might evolve—not deciding might be an attractive strategy (638). Error costs gain saliency since constitutions lock people who lack certain knowledge about the future into long-term contracts. This brings out a question that is vital for both the longevity *and* the democraticity of any constitution: how to make sure that a constitution remains responsive to ever-changing circumstances, accumulated experience, and the freedom of political action of those beyond its makers (Loughlin 2018; Freeden 2022, 223–28). Choosing not to constitutionally determine some issues in order to make room for all of these may be part of the answer. As Benjamin Constant noted, in being selective about what they say and how they say it, constitutions might carve out much-needed "room for time and experience" (Constant 1988, 172). To this one could add room for the freedom of political action.

Constant's advice is a warning against the attempt to preempt or fill in every possible constitutional silence in order to settle or control the future. But though this warning is warranted, one should avoid falling into the opposite trap of thinking that constitutional silence necessarily adds to the endurance and democraticity of constitutions. One claim is as overstated as the other. If constitutions are to support openness and freedom of political action, certain things need to be decided and settled such that they are no longer debated, resisted, or questioned (however debatable they might become again in the future), thus producing a stable set of rules to support the conduct of politics in the presence of ongoing disagreement (Holmes 1995; Sunstein 2001). Leaving significant gaps in constitutional coverage can compromise the viability of a constitution and the workings of the institutions it sets up. Take, for instance, basic procedural questions that allow democratic institutions to function effectively. Or take instead the architecture of the most fundamental political institutions, without which it is impossible for these institutions to perform as they should: cooperate, control one another, or formulate and implement policy (Eisgruber 2001, 13). Simply leaving these questions to be decided through "normal politics" not only risks overburdening legislatures and compromising their "ability to perform other key functions" but may also effectively jeopardize "the whole enterprise of constitution-making" (Dixon and Ginsburg 2011, 649, 664). Constitutions present unique opportunities for collective reinvention and renewal, and this requires both determination and silences that can be used to engage these processes and leverage space for growth.

This takes me to a related question, which has been implicit in the discussion so far but not yet explicitly stated: the question of power. It is easy to see how there is power in decision-making but perhaps not as easy to see how there is power in non-decision-making (Lukes 1974). Constitutions define the rules of the political game, and those sitting at the constitutional decision-making table seek to shape these rules in ways that enhance their future political action just as they seek to shape overall constitutional meaning in ways consistent with their own politico-ideological projects. To decide not to decide on certain matters falling within a constitution's scope may seem like a way of renouncing this power. But this is not necessarily the case.

To see this more clearly, we may want to distinguish between not deciding for the sake of deferral and not deciding as a form of silencing. Let me take deferral first. In deciding not to decide on certain constitutional matters and to leave them instead to future decision-makers, constitution-makers risk losing control over some of the rules of the game and the future direction of constitutional meaning (Dixon and Ginsburg 2011, 638). As hinted earlier, however, this danger may be outweighed by the decision or error risks associated with filling the silence. Risk can be offset, for instance, by the benefits accruing from deferring decisions, as in highly divisive controversies, on which one may lose now but be able to reach a compromise later, and issues where important information is absent and decision-makers might be blamed for making the "wrong" choice. Constitution-makers may also prioritize the short-term gain of a seemingly successful constitutional agreement, even if this is only achieved by leaving contentious matters unattended (Dixon and Ginsburg 2011, 638–39). But if power can accrue from deferral, it can also accrue from silencing, that is, from keeping "issues from arising, grievances from being voiced, and interests from being recognized" (Gaventa 1980, vii). As Peter Bachrach and Morton Baratz have put it most poignantly, such silencing is a form of power: through it, certain "demands for change in the existing allocation of benefits and privileges in the community can be suffocated before they are even voiced; or kept covert; or killed before they gain access to the relevant decision-making arena" (1970, 44).

A prime example of the latter form of power is the "gag rule." To "gag" someone is to put a piece of cloth over the person's mouth to prevent them from speaking—that is, to silence them. Accordingly, "gag rules" are rules limiting or even forbidding the raising, consideration, and discussion of particular questions. The most famous "gag rules" emerged in the United States in the mid-1830s. They barred the US House of Representatives from receiving petitions concerning the abolition of slavery and kept slavery off the congressional agenda. But the US Constitution itself had long "gagged" conversations about slavery by that point. The words "slavery" or "slaves" had been strategically avoided in the constitutional text, which nonetheless included provisions tacitly recognizing and protecting the institution of slavery. An iniquitous racial compromise did the "dirty" groundwork believed to be necessary for the ratification of the union and its continued existence. This is perhaps most clearly shown in the 1787 three-fifths compromise clause, which entrenched slavery and the non-personhood of slaves in the text of the Constitution while, or perhaps *because*, it did not name either.[4]

"Gag rules" are sometimes compared to the kind of self-censoring we deploy in everyday conversations to prevent divisive themes from coming up and weakening relationships (Holmes 1995). As such, they are praised for their "civilizing" effects, enabling mutual coexistence. But the analogy is deeply flawed. Self-silencing between neighbors for the purposes of polite conversation does not result in consequential inequalities of power. By contrast, in the political realm, "gagging" risks reproducing an unjust status quo and impairing the mobilization and the accountability necessary for its disruption. It involves controlling the parameters of discussion, setting the agenda that leads to decisions, fixing the context within which such decisions are made, and thereby decisively influencing them. This is why "gagging" inevitably raises thorny questions: Whose interests are ignored, and whose claims go unrecognized, when certain controversial issues are silenced or segregated from public debate? Treating "gagging" as an enabler of "civilized speech" is to ignore how such speech may be parasitical on violence done to others. But just as the analogy is deceptive, it is perhaps equally specious to treat "gagging" as a power of non-decision-making. "Gagging" effectively takes a side in a conflict. It encourages decisions in favor of the status quo, thus further entrenching asymmetries of power and making it more difficult to address related injustices in the future. As neighbors, we can bite our tongues and excuse ourselves. As members of a polity who inevitably exercise power over one another, such willful mutual ignorance, or the repression of unwelcome information, is commonly at somebody's cost. The "gagged" are not just overwritten; they are written out.

"Gagging" is a form of imposed silence about constitutional matters understood to be highly divisive and sometimes posing the risk of conflict and, at the extreme, civil war. The silencing of high-stakes issues has been a trademark of many transitions from authoritarian regimes to democracy. This is the case, for instance, when the parties to the new constitutional settlement make a vow of silence regarding the atrocities of the old regime, something underpinned by the claim that suppressing difficult questions about the past, and even—in some cases—conceding absolution, is necessary to bring about a clean closure and move forward. A case in point is the Pact of Forgetting (Pacto del olvido) underpinning Spain's "pacted" transition to democracy in the 1970s (Resina 2021).

The "pact of forgetting" was agreed on by politicians of all stripes. By "forgetting," they meant a willful disavowal of what people knew but chose not to address, with the aim of leaving the past behind and instead concentrating on their common democratic future. The "pact of forgetting" was an unspoken pact. It constituted a self-bounding of political elites and the citizen body to a collective "disremembering" (*desmemoria*) of the crimes and wrongdoings committed during the Civil War and in Francoist Spain. This was believed to be necessary to build a consensus around the desirability of democracy in the light of all the continuities—or grey zones—that a "pacted" transition implied. The unspoken pact was subsequently given a legal basis by the comprehensive amnesty law (1977) that made it virtually impossible to investigate and prosecute the human rights abuses of the Franco years.

The question of whether the "pact" was necessary to avoid plunging the country into civil strife, or even just to do the groundwork required for the democratic transition, is one that, despite hindsight, remains contentious. What should not be contentious, however, is that the costs of compromising were not equal for everyone involved and that they ended up being somewhat "naturalized" as a result of the pact. This has made it very difficult to mobilize, let alone mobilize successfully, for redress for the injustices and inequalities of power the pact entrenched. It has also made it hard for Spain to face up to and deal with the living legacies of authoritarianism. Given how central the pact is to Spain's democratic settlement, to challenge Spain's collective investment in disremembering is to inevitably raise questions about the legitimacy of a democracy that is at least partly constituted by it.

There is a sense, however, in which the temptation of silencing the past for the sake of the future speaks to the future-oriented nature of democracy. Democracy harbors the promise of self-rule, liberated from the hold of the past, opening up to a collectively made future. If the past is allowed to simply rule us, we cannot rule ourselves. On the flip side, however, if we simply try to rule the past for the sake of ruling it out, as has been done in Spain, the past will still be there ruling us, but it will be accessible only as specters, ghosts, spooks—that is, in ways that preclude any self-reflective, productive engagement. Democracies therefore typically find themselves caught in a double bind. On the one hand, too much remembrance and resentment, too much orientation toward a past that cannot be changed, may prevent subjects from seizing opportunities for transformation in the present. On the other hand, silencing the past by cultivating collective amnesia perpetuates the past's empire while abdicating democratic responsibility for the reproduction of an unjust past. This casts a heavy burden on a *democratic* politics of memory. For the democratic choice is never simply between forgetting or remembering. The only choice genuinely left to democracies is to productively engage the agonistic tension between the two. As P. J. Brendese rightly puts it, a democracy needs to engage in both "remembering to forget and remembering that which others cannot be expected to forget" (2014, 126).

In a telling scene of the documentary *The Silence of Others* (2018), which focuses on the legacy of the "pact of forgetting," Kutxi, one of the victims of torture by the infamous "Billy the Kid," a Spanish police inspector in Francoist Spain, looks out from the window in her apartment and says, "We all wanted to forget."[5] She thereby asserts her own, partial ownership of the national "pact of forgetting" and of the many other silent pacts that unfolded within communities, families, even sometimes within oneself. But in her search to bring perpetrators to justice, she embodies the impossibility of forgetting and asks others—from her co-responsible co-citizens to state institutions—to engage the memories of those who, like her, cannot be asked to forget. People like Kutxi remind us of how the responsibility for silence, though collective, is not distributed equally. It inevitably belongs to some more than others, namely, to those who have actively silenced; to those who have benefited most from the keeping of silence; to those who persevere in their denial and who refuse to face Spain's painful past even in the present; and to the Spanish state and its institutions. Disowning the responsibility for silence offloads the burden of remembrance. As Spain's image of its own past continues to disavow memories like Kutxi's, she is forced to hold on to them and live in a perpetual in-betweenness (Brendese 2014, 107).

Just like "gag rules," constitutional pacts of silence are often shrouded in a counterfeit "neutrality," as if they were a kind of leveling, facilitating a new start or a blank slate. If we collectively leave behind old wounds and unproductive resentments, we all have a chance at a better future. But to say this is to once more elude the questions that need to be asked: Whose power is the silence in aid of? Who is in control of the historical narrative and of constitutional meaning? Whose past has been left behind, whose injustices have been rendered invisible, and who has been given the opportunity to start anew? The power of silencing comes at the cost of the democratic power of making history available to competing narratives, memories, and experiences. Silence shapes agents' memories and beliefs so deeply that it may go unnoticed. It is a power shaping not only agents but also their "democratic" commons. In working on memory, it shapes our ability to understand the present order of things, each other, and ourselves. As Brendese stresses, we risk becoming unknown to ourselves when our identity is built upon such silences and disavowals (2014, 73).

## Silences of Not Determining

However, not every silence in a constitutional settlement is a form of *silencing*. "Gag rules" and the "pact of forgetting" are forms of silencing oriented toward settling something controversial. But silence can be kept or introduced in constitutions to avoid determining. The first, and most radical, way of doing this is by being completely silent about certain matters. While complete silence may prove the best option in some instances, as I will show, there are downsides to it. Namely, the ambiguity of silence leaves it open to contending interpretations: as a simple failure to see or anticipate the issue; as an implicit endorsement of existing unwritten rules; as a willingness to delegate a decision on the issue at hand to future decision-makers; and sometimes even as tacit proscription.[6] Interpretive ambiguity empowers interpreters, and, where the question is deemed one of interpretation, this can mean the courts. However, delegating the decision to the courts may not be ideal, either for reasons of democratic legitimacy or for reducing decision and error costs. If the matter is highly polarizing, and decision costs are high, it can find itself in courts that are themselves ideologically polarized while being unrepresentative and lacking the means to de-escalate the conflict through engaging the parties in negotiation and compromise. Also, if error costs are likely, the court is not a kind of institution that is easily able to gather and process the information, empirical and otherwise, needed to diminish them (Dixon and Ginsburg 2011, 655).

But while the ambiguity associated with keeping absolute silence on certain matters of constitutional relevance can have associated costs, two things should be noticed. First, complete silence may not be as ambiguous (or as complete) as it seems. Second, there is potential constitutional value in ambiguity. I will discuss each of these in turn.

Meaning cannot be attributed to silence irrespective of context. But meaning can often be safely disambiguated by putting silence in context. More specifically, the meaning of constitutional silences must be read against the constitutional culture behind their adoption. If this is accepted, then it can be conceded that, although the adoption of silence does not necessarily generate liberal-democratic constitutionalism, the latter may imply leaving space for silence(s) within constitutions. These silences are compatible with, and can be understood in terms of, liberal-democratic principles.

The case of secession illustrates this well. Secession is a vital matter for any constitutional order and of particular salience in states with sub-units. Yet secession is a matter on which the constitutions of states are often silent. A case in point is the US Constitution. It does not explicitly forbid nor explicitly allow states to secede. Instead, it keeps silent on the matter.

This silence first strikes one as odd, as a baffling omission. And it is. After all, secession is vital for the survival of a constitution: any state or region that wants to secede is a state or region that ceases to accept the constitution's authority. From this, two things follow. First, constitutional silence on secession is very likely to be a deliberate omission (and even more so in federal and multinational states). Second, the recognition of a general right to secede would be "inconsistent with the constitutional order's very character as a constitutional order," as it would make its authority "subject to the disapproval of any self-constituting group," and even the recognition of a specific sub-unit's right to secede, which occurs in some constitutions, represents "a significant compromise of the constitutional order's claims to authority" (Doyle 2018, 900).

Besides this fundamental reason not to explicitly include a right to secession, there are also other, more strategic, reasons why constitutionalizing a right to secession might be problematic. A right to secede can encourage the formation of secession movements, and this can open the way to political strife, even political violence, between those movements and parties opposing the breakup (Sunstein 2001). A rule forbidding secession would fare no better. It would be unlikely to prevent such movements from forming and, where they do emerge, it has the potential to aggravate grievances and secessionist sentiments. Besides this, a prohibition would make it virtually impossible for secessionist parties to negotiate greater levels of self-government or secure independence through constitutional channels.

In the face of these drawbacks, keeping absolute constitutional silence about secession is an attractive option (V. Jackson 2016). For one, it is likely to allow for a more flexible engagement with secessionist forces, if and when they arise, in full knowledge of changing circumstances and their specific demands. But this is only the case, I want to stress, where there are compelling reasons for interpreting a constitutional silence about secession as a silence of (negative) *permission*. Assuming a liberal-democratic framework, this would indeed be its most plausible interpretation and perhaps even the only admissible one, given, on the one hand, the lack of an explicit prohibition, and, on the other hand, that it would be self-contradictory for a liberal-democratic constitution to deny the democratic principle of collective self-determination. Two things follow from this. First, silence is to be read against framing and context, and continuing to hear silence where nearly everyone attending to both would identify a determinative utterance (in this case, to continue to hear no decision either way rather than *prima facie* permission) would be to close one's ears to key cues. Second, when interpreted as a (negative) permission, constitutional silence about secession can be expected to put options on the table, as it encourages the development of constitutional pathways to engage secessionist pressures, especially if backed by a legitimate majority, rather than a narrow focus on the constitution's authority to regulate the secessionist conflict. Constitutional silence means, in this case, an authorization of more space for negotiation and politics.

One can leave silence in a constitution by simply not speaking about something. But there are other ways, too. In the opening chapter of this book, I have shown that it is possible not to speak *by speaking* or, more precisely, by speaking away. A similar dynamic can occur in constitutions. When decision costs at the time of constitution drafting are perceived as high, silence can exercise a functional and positively valuable role in accommodating potentially divisive and/or unresolved points of contention. In other words, instead of simply not saying, one might use multiple meanings or ambiguity not to say anything (too) specific and thus cooperatively maintain things in a state of irresolution.

Despite often being depicted as *one* intentional project of self-rule, constitutional settlements hardly ever express a single project, whose meaning, and whose purpose, is evident and the same for all promisors. Rather, it is often the case that what looks like a single constitution effectively "serves as the common site for a multitude of different, potentially conflicting purposes" (Keenan 1994, 317). That a constitution is not *one* project of self-rule is evident from the multiplicity of conflicting goals, intentions, projects, meanings, and understandings of citizenship that are commonly contained in constitutions. Textually, this multiplicity is sometimes expressed in constitutions that are long and seemingly obsessively detailed, but their "detail" is not a precise elaboration of one project but instead a strategy for both staging and hiding real disagreements. The resulting multiplicity of meanings, with all its contradictions and inconsistencies, resists determination; one is not bound to a *single* form of commonality. Instead, all that is being agreed to is a structure within which it will be possible to share rule with one another and to continue to "act together without knowing whether or what [they] have in common" (M. Ferguson 2012, 27). In the light of the expectation that a constitutional order represents a commitment to something held in common, however, the multiplicity of meanings left in constitutions can be read as a way of unsaying this "common" or at least a way of *not* (or, *not yet*) saying what might be held in common.

Turning now from multiplicity to ambiguity, as we have seen earlier, ambiguity is commonly associated with silence. The specification offered by speech is often contrasted with the ambiguity of silence. But there is, of course, more variability than the binary allows. Ambiguity is the property enjoyed by signs that bear multiple (legitimate) interpretations. Both words and silence are capable of being such signs. For just as we can use words to say, declare, and determine, so we can use words not to say, or at least not to say something expected or anything specific. To put it another way, we can use words to produce a kind of silence, leaving things unsettled, while appearing to do otherwise. However, some may intuitively doubt whether ambiguity, even understood in this fashion, is a useful tool for tackling constitutional problems related to decision costs. Overcoming ambiguity is, after all, often thought to be necessary to resolve a political disputation. However, while some disambiguation might mean that parties do not simply talk past each other, attempts at precisification can bring out deep, substantive disputes. In such situations, the adoption of ambiguous language can offer itself as a way of getting around what could otherwise be intractable conflicts, preventing any constitutional settlement whatsoever.

Besides ambiguity, there are other ways of handling areas of conflict to procure agreement where it is still possible. But in contrast to ambiguity, these alternative paths do not involve silence, since they necessitate a discursive determination that is achieved by moving between abstractness and concreteness. Though they may no longer be species belonging in the genus of silence, they may still need to enlist silence as an aid.

Let me start with abstraction. Abstraction can help parties move beyond particular cases, about which they strongly disagree, to agree on a general principle. But it can also go the other way. Agreement can be sometimes better achieved by moving into greater particularity. This is the case, for instance, where parties are able to agree on particular constitutional outcomes, practices, or even procedures by "bracketing" disagreements of principle. As Cass Sunstein explains, this moving to a lower level of abstraction is distinctive in that "it enlists *silence*, on certain basic questions, as a device for producing convergence despite disagreement, uncertainty, limits of time and capacity, and heterogeneity" (2001, 51; my emphasis). In other words, silence—the silence of selective oversight—is still the critical element here, but now as the midwife of concrete agreements designed to address perceived decision and error costs.

Nonetheless, moving up or down the abstraction scale is not always a route to constitutional agreement. A better option may be leaving certain things explicitly undecided, making it clear that not saying anything about them is a deliberate part of the constitutional design. Complete silence and ambiguity, we have seen, are implicit ways of leaving things in a suspended irresolution, which may be activated by later circumstances or simply left as is. But there are alternative, explicit forms of deferring constitutional issues, most notably "by law" clauses. While enabling constitutions to remain silent on a certain subject, "by law" clauses explicitly deem such a subject to be of (potential) constitutional relevance. They also *explicitly* delegate decision-making on the matter to future decision-makers, by either requiring the legislature to decide on it in the future or else by explicitly empowering the legislature to decide *whether* and *how* to regulate it (Dixon and Ginsburg 2011, 640). The rationale behind the adoption of "by law" clauses is twofold: first, to seek agreement on whether to regulate, where agreement as to how to regulate is impossible or a rushed decision would be prone to serious error costs, and second, to shift decisions on how (and sometimes also whether) to regulate to bodies that have superior information (in both quantity and quality) and whose actions do not require the high thresholds of constitutional amendment. Lower thresholds mean that the stakes are lower for a likely or eventually losing party (Dixon and Ginsburg 2011, 646–47, 656–57).

By being silent about how to regulate a matter, "by law" clauses distinguish themselves from "sunset clauses." "Sunset clauses" provisionally regulate a controversial constitutional matter but with a stipulation that the clauses shall cease to have effect after a specific date. They are traditionally a mechanism designed to ensure that emergency provisions do not become normal, thereby entrenching powers that can adversely impact the enjoyment of our individual and political freedoms. The problem with "provisional regulation" is that it can be renewed on a regular basis, often without much scrutiny of whether it is still necessary or its adverse effects. This can also give them a "stickiness," path dependency, and *status quo* bias that "by law" clauses seek to avoid.[7] "By law" clauses are a distinct combination of not saying and saying: not saying how something should be regulated but saying who should be determining whether and/or how it should be regulated in the future. They introduce silence into the constitution while naming the absence explicitly as something of constitutional relevance as well as designating those responsible for its (possible) future undoing. They thereby avoid some of the uncertainties associated with complete silence, such as its potential ambiguity. Importantly, these are different forms of silence; they perform distinct functions within the constitution (Dixon and Ginsburg 2011, 639–40). Simple silences and ambiguity do not necessarily—or even typically—imply constitutional gaps that need to be filled through delegated legislative action.

## Conclusion

When speaking of constitutions, the emphasis tends to be on constitutions as "declaratory acts of creation" (Foley 2011, 9). To entrench core commitments, and to *decide, determine,* and *resolve* conflicts on how power should be allotted and organized, is what we have been made to believe makes constitutions "constitutions" and gives them their monumental quality. In this chapter, I have argued that this is a reductionist view, as it only highlights half of what constitutions are—and ought to be. For constitutions are effectively as much about what they do *not* say, or do not say determinatively, as about what they say.

I have expounded different reasons why constitutions may need to embrace silence: because it is *necessary* that they do not say, given their normative commitments; because it is *functional* that they do not say to avoid dissensus that might preclude consensus where it is still possible; because it is *not necessary* that they say, as it is said implicitly by constitutional traditions, conventional understandings, and cultural presuppositions; and because it is *desirable* they do not say to avoid decision and error costs that only time, experience, and delegation to legislatures or to political negotiation and accommodation might help reduce. This took us through a multitude of constitutional silences—from the silence of deliberately excluding, and silences of deliberately leaving undecided or in a suspended irresolution, to the silences of the taken for granted and mediation—which make up the fabric of constitutions and give them not so much the herculean quality of monumentality as the protean quality of flexibility and a willingness to embrace the inherent unpredictability and evolving nature of democratic life.

Democratic constitutions need to combine performative and constative elements, the performative insistence on openness with the constative insistence that certain things have to be settled. A more abstract and more entrenched constitutional framework, providing core commitments and rules around which identification can form, can be beneficially combined with more specific provisions, in more routine matters, and with more open-ended allowances in areas in which experience, further information, and leaving options on the table are of the essence. A trend has been noticed recently toward a kind of "flexi-specific" constitutionalism, combining a preference for constitutional specificity with a preference for flexibility. Specificity, or detailed constitutional prescription, is designed in to allow popular majorities to control or even micromanage elite actors by taking many policy choices out of their hands. Flexibility is built in to allow more active constitutional amendment and augmentation by citizens themselves (Versteeg and Zackin 2016). However, besides the risk of such a "flexi-specific" constitutionalism leaving constitutional systems too vulnerable to majoritarian pressures (Ely 1980), it seems to fall into two traps. The first is that of equating saying it well with saying it all. The second is that of equating flexibility with control over processes of constitutional change leading to the constitution saying it *all*, all over again, but just more often (with the constitution becoming, potentially, just another transient ordinary law). And yet, where it is thought that all that the constitution wanted to say has been said (or textualized), constitutional silences are likely to be construed as denials rather than breathing spaces for choices. In other words, constitutional silences can no longer be judiciously planted in constitutions to keep "constitutional conversation open by leaving a number of options on the table" (Tribe 2018, 24, 42).

Fundamental to constitutional adaptability and survival over time, the silences of constitutions, I have argued, are hence also vital for their democraticity. As Michael Foley puts it, they mark "the absence of a definitive constitutional settlement" while they also provide "the means of adjusting to the issues left unresolved in the fabric of the constitution" itself (2011, 10). They move away from the view of the constitution as simply pre-commitment and inter-temporal control to viewing it as a project, thus opening up to the future and allowing the future to (also) make the constitution its own. The silences of constitutions gesture toward an ultimate unrepresentability in texts whose democratic legitimacy depends on representing us not just as builders but as seekers, who may not yet entirely "know how to go on" (Muers 2015a, 335) but who know that to go on they need some abstract, parsimonious constitutional values built in to keep them together in their quest and in their difference.

Democratic politics necessitates "closure, determination, and decision as well as openness, incompletion, and contestation" (Keenan 2003, 135). In this chapter, I have argued that a balance between the two must be struck in the structuring of political order, within constitutions themselves, with constitutional power exercising power over its own powers of determination. To this end, I have turned to different modalities of silence to create space for compromise, adaptation, adjustment, and future political possibility. In the next chapter, I turn from the silence woven into the fabric of constitutions to the challenges citizen silence poses to the electoral and representative institutions constitutions set up.

# 6

## REPRESENTING SILENCE

It's coming from the silence
On the dock of the bay.
. . . . . . . . . . . . . . . . . . . . .
Democracy is coming to the USA.
—Leonard Cohen, "Democracy"

"Let Your Voice Be Heard: Vote!" This often-heard appeal iterates the dominant understanding of representation as being about giving the potentially affected a *presence* in the collective decisions that bind them. This presence is conceived in terms of *voice*. Though strictly speaking voice (*phone*) is the nonlinguistic element enabling speech (*logos*), when people are called upon to express their *voice*, this is taken to mean speech or something akin to it—that is, communicative acts with, or translatable into, linguistic content. From this follows the imperative that informs the voice model of democratic representation: that policy preferences, as determined by interests, values, or both, need to be expressed, or formed into voice, to be communicated *to*, registered *in*, and directive *of* the decision-making process.

In this chapter I argue that the focus on *voice* has three problematic implications. First, it overstates the communicative power of voting and turns representation into a matter of communicative responsiveness. Second, it primes the representative system to maximize responsiveness to well-organized groups with effective voice, while hearing unvoiced signals as silence. Third, it imposes too high a standard on the representation of silence. Against the grain of voice models of political representation, this chapter addresses the question of whether silence can be empowered through representation.

The argument is divided into three steps. I begin by offering a new conceptualization of silence that allows me to dismiss the dominant understanding of silence as the mark of political absence. The notion of silence-as-absence, I argue, is paradoxical in that it perpetuates the very absence it identifies as problematic. I then address the question of whether silence can be used and represented in empowering ways from the perspective of both nonconstructivist and constructivist understandings of political representation. The blank vote, compulsory voting, and the silent majority claim are discussed as attempts to represent silent constituencies. Finally, I assess the risks of domination and displaced involvement in the representation of silence and conclude that taking silence seriously shows the need for a reconstruction and extension of the normative criteria of representation.

Before I outline a new conceptualization of silence, it is worth revisiting how silence has traditionally been treated in democratic theory. Broadly speaking, this has taken two main forms. For some, most notably democratic pluralists, political silence is the norm and represents a form of rational abstention from politics that is essential for the survival of democratic systems, understood as open systems needing to strike a balance between vitality and governability (Dahl 1961; Polsby 1963). Pluralists take silence as physiological and as reflecting either rational indifference or quiescence. Where deemed pathological, silence tends to be blamed on the silent themselves: "Apathetic citizens disenfranchise themselves; active citizens gain influence" (Dahl 1972, 94).

In either form, silence becomes dismissible and eclipsed by responsiveness to voice. The fallacy of this is easily seen, however. Voices making themselves heard through participation and lobbying efforts may provide loud and clear information about their views and interests. But as voice is time- and resource-intensive, voices are far from equal, and it is not necessarily those in greatest need who participate the most in politics. Inequality of participation is pervasive: it excludes many citizens from partisan politics and politics beyond it. It also deprives them of the political language(s) in which their views and interests may be articulated—or indeed *heard* and taken seriously. This includes claims about their own exclusion and the systemic biases responsible for it (Disch 2012).

Cognizant of this, participatory and deliberative democrats stress that participation and deliberation, both conceived as speech-accented activities, must be the democratic norm, and that it is silence that needs explaining. The legitimacy and survival of democracies depends, they insist, on forming silence into voice through commitment to policies promoting, and resulting from, the participatory and deliberative agency of *all* citizens.

This vocal route to empowerment runs up, however, against the "paradox of enablement," submitting the voiceless to a "doubly paradoxical silence" (Olson 2006, 261–63, 113). Having no means to demand entry, they have their voice-empowerment demands articulated by people knowing little about them and sharing in the very understandings of participation and voice responsible for their exclusion. Hence, even if they find access to voice platforms, they may find themselves in places infused with the discursive power dynamics whereby they were silenced in the first instance.

As contrasting as pluralists and participatory democrats may first appear, they overlap in embracing a voice-focused democratic politics according to which "citizens are silent whenever they refuse or are refused the opportunity to speak" (Rollo 2019, 436). Two consequences follow. First, where silence is chosen, it is taken as *a*political or *anti*-political behavior; second, where silence is forced, the proposed solution is to multiply sites for voice empowerment (from vote, to special group influence, to deliberative fora). While there are perfectly good democratic arguments for this solution, it has its drawbacks. It shifts the communicative burden back to citizens, and since voice is resource-intensive, conferring it a monopoly on political presence risks reproducing the rifts of exclusion (Warren 2011).

Paradoxically, therefore, in reading all non-voice as silence and in reading silence as the mark of absence, those seeking to emancipate the silent may be complicit in their silencing. For even where silence is not chosen but suffered as a silencing, treating silence as a "no sign" discharges relevant audiences— most notably, the representative system itself—from their responsibility for silence and for empowering citizens *from* their silent positions.

Re-thinking Silence in Politics

To open up this possibility, we need to resume the conceptualization of silence I presented in the introduction, which moves away from the notion of silence-as-absence, where absence implies the negation of presence, as an actuality or even as potentiality.

Classically conceived as the order of logos, the political order has come down to us as the order of *speech*, the signifier of *meaning*, or more broadly as the order of *voice*, the signifier of *presence*. In the political domain, voice commonly refers to acts of self-expression. The term is used capaciously to capture a whole range of human communication, from speech—that is, a vocalization that signifies something (most notably, the vote, but also verbal acts integral to protesting, petitioning, campaigning, and deliberating)—to action. As the *effect* of voice, political subjecthood is deemed to require "vocal emission" "headed for speech" (Cavarero 2005, 13). Where this is missing, three related absences are postulated: of the *subject of politics*, the speaking subject; of *political voice*, as that which gives us a presence/say in politics; and of *expression, signification*, and *communication*, as that which makes speech political.

The binary economy of the symbolic order of politics is now easily articulated: on the one hand, voice, action, presence; on the other hand, silence, inaction, absence. This is, of course, a problematic binary, leading to the depoliticization, privatization, and marginalization of several political behaviors that cease to register as "political" in representation's vocal register. These include abstention, exit, and even the expression of popular voice through institutionalized channels when no electoral choice is made (the blank vote, for example). It is also a disciplining structure: where chosen rather than forced, political silence is said to imply the renunciation of the right to a voice ("didn't vote, cannot contest").

Contrary to what the voice-silence binary implies, however, the relationship between voice, speech, and silence is anything but simple. Usually viewed as standing in an "either-or relationship," speech and silence, we have seen, can be simultaneously present, with one carrying traces of the other. Michel Foucault reminds us that "there is no binary division to be made between what one says and what one does not say" (1990, 27). That is, silence is a form of control *within* discourse, not a thing outside it. The silences that permeate our speaking are part of a discursive order establishing what can be said, who can speak about it, and what should remain unspoken. The silences we make are ways of navigating, partaking in, and challenging this order from the inside. One can use speech so as not to say—just as one can engage in an articulate silence meant to convey something in context, a silence that is therefore a modality of communication and can speak multivocally.

The multiple functions and uses of silence are generally recognized (e.g., Jaworski 1993), and yet two trends persist in the treatment of silence. First, it continues to be presented as internally undifferentiated—with plural "silences" sliding into one essentialist and totalizing "silence." Second, attempts to "decode" the nature or meaning of silence tend to take a binary approach, assuming silence to be either linking or separating, active or inactive, assenting or dissenting (e.g., Pettit 1994).

One way to avoid these pitfalls, we have seen, is to treat silence as a *signal*—namely, a nonlinguistic form of communication whose meaning is not assumed but interpreted in the broader context of interaction. This approach to silence, I have proposed, is strengthened by distinguishing between two ways in which silence may be produced: by passive omission and active commission (S. Scott 2018, 5; Brito Vieira 2019).

Silence as an act of passive omission is a *not*-doing something, or a *negative* decision, resulting in a neglect, failure, or inability to act. This inability is no muteness but a form of locutionary (self-)exclusion motivated by a resignation to power or the belief that no one will listen. An internalized sense of powerlessness, or a *habitus* of resignation, may develop, which translates into a deep-seated dispositional resistance to action, as is typical of states of alienation experienced at an embodied level as apathy or inertia (McNay 2012). This is how silence is commonly understood in politics, as a silencing or a mark of absence.

Silence as an act of passive *omission* contrasts with silence as an act of *commission*, or a deliberate withholding of speech. This silence is a *doing*: it involves *doing* a non-something out of a *positive* decision *not to* do. It might function like speech, that is, as a non-locutionary speech act whose illocutionary force and perlocutionary effect are gauged against context, and in reference to speech, as "a marked absence occurring in place of an expected [speech] presence" (Acheson 2008, 537). It can contribute to flows of communication or—as we have seen in previous chapters—be used to interrupt and subvert them.

It is often stressed that though silence can act linguistically, as a deliberate withholding of speech, it is the most ambiguous of the linguistic forms. This ambiguity would leave silence particularly vulnerable to neglect and/or misinterpretation—whether unintentional or strategic—and consequently also to misrepresentation (Gray 2019).

Undoubtedly, specific difficulties surround the interpretation of silence, such as the difficulty of distinguishing between silence as no sign and silence as sign, and for silence as sign to convey preferences or opinions. But the implied contrast between the "transparency" of speech and the "opaqueness" of silence, let alone that between vote and silence, is sometimes overstated. It is also problematic in several respects. First, speech is not transparent—even for the speaker. Votes don't speak on their own. They, too, require interpretation. Second, not all silence is ambiguous. Where directives are explicit and signifying conventions strong, the meaning of silence can be distinctive. Think of a wedding ceremony where the congregation is asked whether anyone knows of a lawful impediment to marriage, followed by the phrase "speak now or forever hold your peace." If one hears silence as the response, it can be taken as an illocution of consent.

These domesticated, rule-governed conditions, within which silence speaks clearly, may be hard to replicate in the political domain. Yet it may be possible to empower silent signals to register there through different practices and different institutional choices (Gray 2021). Think, for instance, of electoral systems. Elections where competition is limited—for instance, single-party electoral districts—disenfranchise a large number of voters while they also create no incentive for politicians to pay heed to their silent signals if they abstain or, for that matter, to their voting signals if they cast their ballots strategically. If the goal is to create an incentive for their signals to be recognized, followed up on, and responded to, a proportional electoral system will be preferable. Consider now the potential impact that even minimal changes to electoral institutions and practices of reporting electoral results can have on whether and how the signals of nonvoters register. Electoral results typically represent only the signals of voters. The publication of electoral results, including nonvoter data, is thus an important step for silence to get noticed. While the aggregate signal sent out by abstention numbers may still be relatively blank—it does not discriminate between omissive and commissive silences, and, within the latter, between those expressing tacit approval or forms of disapproval—in some contexts the meaning of the silent signals will be fairly apparent. We know, for instance, that abstention goes up when the number of candidates disputing an election (and their perceived distinctiveness) decreases. When the second round of a presidential election witnesses an especially high rate of abstention, however, as happened in the 2022 French presidential election, it is a reasonable inference to draw that much of this silence expresses a negative opinion on the political landscape and political candidates. Mobilization, notably electoral mobilization, is an effect of feeling represented. By not voting, potential voters are likely to be "saying" one of these things: that the choices on the ballot do not resonate with them, that the choices are equally unacceptable to them, or that they perceive the choices to be all the same / make no difference. Greater clarity on the distribution of these positions can be gained through polling and reaching out to nonvoters after the election. But there must be an incentive for this, which in France was created by the looming competitive legislative elections. As we shall see in the next section, the addition of institutional mechanisms, such as the "none of the above" option, can enable a clearer registration of some silent signals—namely, those that are not just commissive but a way of protest. If nothing else, having nonvoters and those casting blank votes represented in electoral results can show a very different result for an election, one that might help temper claims to a clear electoral mandate. As the French newspaper *Le Monde* explained to its readers the day after the 2022 presidential election, if the blank votes cast by 6.35 percent of those who turned up at voting stations were considered as part of the total, Emmanuel Macron would have been elected not with 58.5 percent of the votes but with 54.7 percent; if "null" votes (2.25 percent) and abstention (28 percent) were added in, Macron would have won with only 38.5 percent of the votes among registered voters. A representation of electoral results that incorporated the signals sent out by nonvoters and blank voters showed the relative fragility of Macron's mandate. (As his left-wing opponent, Jean-Luc Mélenchon, was quick to note in a televised speech, Macron had been "poorly elected," effectively "floating in an ocean of abstention, of blank and null.") Thanks to their numbers and visibility, abstentionists and those casting blank and null votes controlled Macron's access to resources and recognition. His options and his ability to pursue his agenda were constrained by these potential voters, and this explained his need to address abstentionists in his victory speech as well as the need to get to know more about their preferences and to approximate them. They formed a large constituency, whose votes were partly up for grabs and for whom neither Macron nor—in many cases, especially for young people—other political forces seemed to offer (yet) a real option. He could only ignore them at his own peril.

As I have already suggested, relatively minimal institutional mechanisms (which I will discuss further in the next section) can allow for the partial disambiguation of the meaning of the demos's silent signals. I stress partly, because total disambiguation of silence is not only impossible but democratically undesirable. This is because it would imply the denial *both* of the democratic right to silence (Gray 2023, 820) *and* of the primary condition of the exercise of democratic politics, understood as a contest over meaning capable of eliciting transformative claims. The truth is that claims presenting the meaning of the silent signals of abstention as unambiguous or perfectly knowable *as well as* claims setting these signals apart for discounting on account of their illegibility are commonly designed to make such signals (un)available for any use by those claiming to speak in our name.

This is not to say, however, that the meaning of silent signals can never be unequivocally gathered. Long-defined policy, institutional context, and anticipated speech that does not occur can enable silence to take a clear political stand, one that may be seen as providing representation. Take, for instance, the expectations attached to speech-based institutions such as parliaments (from the French word *parler*, meaning to discuss things). Take then a party, Sinn Féin, which, since 1917, has adopted a controversial abstentionist policy whereby it refuses to take the parliamentary seats to which it is elected. Sinn Féin's refusal to lend its voice to adopt or reject policy in the UK Parliament is a *commissive* act—a staged *resistance* to sitting and speaking in a foreign legislature that Sinn Féin sees as an instrument of oppression over the Irish people. As Susan Dovi rightly points out, for those understanding the presence conferred by representation strictly in terms of voice, vote, and decision-making, Sinn Féin's strategy seems irrational, even self-defeating, especially where decisions at Westminster directly affect its constituency, as was the case with Brexit (2020, 563). But for the Sinn Féin members of Parliament, actively abstaining—refusing to be an Irish nationalist voice at Westminster—is the only way in which to honor the mandate on which they see themselves as being elected. To resist British rule over Northern Ireland from *within* the institution that holds supreme legal authority in the United Kingdom would be to recognize that institution's legitimacy and its sovereignty over a part of Ireland. Taking their seats in Parliament, in their view, would sanction Westminster as a political venue in which to legislate on Irish interests. By contrast, making their constituency absent by "withholding words and disengaging from representative bodies" is their "way to represent" by seeking to frustrate extant political configurations (Dovi 2020, 563). The efficacy of Sinn Féin's policy may be disputed, but its meaning is not lost on the represented constituency or on relevant audiences in the United Kingdom.

To insist unqualifiedly on the "opaqueness" of silence is not only conducive to its *prima facie* discounting as a mode of representation. It also places the burden of communication entirely on silence while discounting what else might explain its failed, refused, or distorted uptake. Yet, as we have seen, silences as acts of omission are effects rather than causes, the condition of being acted upon rather than acting. For this reason, they are also frequently deemed to be, and discounted as, no signs. However, I have submitted that as indicators of socially and politically inflected inabilities, they are signs. What is more, they are signs that signal powerfully the interdependence between, on the one hand, the experience of being listened to, in consequence of acts of representation that constitute one, one's interests, and one's aspirations as such and such, and, on the other hand, the *ability* to express oneself and act politically.

The represented can speak, but they can be systemically failed by the lack of the political work of representation necessary for them to identify politically and join together around specific political demands. This type of silencing is all too common within our representative systems, and it is often explained by structural, systemic biases. The examples abound, but one will suffice. According to a 2017 study by Pew, 82 percent of Americans favor paid maternity leave. The policy is now gathering bipartisan support, but for years systemic biases—including the overrepresentation of business interests and the underrepresentation of women in Congress—kept it off the policy agenda, as if the public did not really care for it. To understand silence, we need therefore not look only at signals that are not emitted, or only weakly so, but also at why some voices—however clear—do not register.

Equipped with this more nuanced understanding of the diverse nature of silence and its (il)legibility, I now explore whether silence can be represented in democratic politics and, if so, how.

Re-presenting Silence

Voice—I have argued—is integral to how we think of political representation. It is both normatively presupposed *by* and expected *from* it. Voice-based communication, understood as an array of acts with linguistic content (expressions, assertions, arguments, opinions, preferences), is traditionally placed at the *input* and *output* ends of representational relationships.

This is especially salient in the "transmission belt" view of representation, which treats representation as the medium through which preferences, interests, and values are communicated from a place where they are present (civil society, public opinion) to a place from which they would otherwise be absent (state institutions, policy) (Manza and Cook 2002, 639). From this perspective, representation occurs when communicative responsiveness is observed: that is, where the expressed preexisting preferences of the represented register in and direct the positions and policy decisions (the "authoritative voice") of their representatives.

As a voice-based model of representation, the transmission-belt model reads silence as an *absence*—that is, as the refusal or denial of political self-expression undercutting representation *qua* vocal register. Silence gets in the way of representation, because it hinders a constituency's self-organization (by making group coordination impractical, if not impossible) as well as preference formation, expression, and advancement. If representation is synonymous with responsiveness to voice, representing a silent constituency is a *non sequitur*: "In a meaningful democracy, the people's voice must be loud and clear: clear so that policy makers understand citizen concerns and loud so that they have an incentive to pay attention to what is said" (Verba, Schlozman, and Brady 1995, 1). Should voice be replaced with silence, representation would go blank.

The specter of "blankness" activates fears of domination and displaced involvement. Responsiveness to constituents' interests, I submit, is a key normative commitment of representation, and usurpation is representation's constitutive attribute. Hence, it is fitting that domination and displaced involvement should be the two normative concerns against which I will be assessing the representation of silence in the remainder of this chapter. Closely interdependent, they have two different criteria in mind: in the case of *domination*, that political action is responsive to citizens and their interests (Brito Vieira 2017; Fossen 2019), and in the case of *displaced involvement*, that whatever political action is taken, it also happens *through* the involvement or mobilization of the represented (Markell 2008; Disch 2011).

Bearing in mind this distinction, it is easily seen that where representation is taken to mean responsiveness, concerns about displacing involvement are demoted to a secondary level. Concerns about domination remain paramount, though, because where too many are silent, non-domination is dependent on voting citizens' interests being representative of the interests of the silent. This is why the assumption that silence means either indifference or assent is necessary for democratic pluralists to dismiss the necessity of wider citizen involvement to avoid domination through minority rule. Yet, given the structural relationship between economic and political power, such concerns are not so easily dismissed. Empirical studies show that "vocal" citizens are unlike most "silent" counterparts in their socioeconomic status, and this difference is very likely to ground a difference in the interests seeking representation (Schlozman, Verba, and Brady 2010; Verba, Schlozman, and Brady 1995).

But the more fundamental reason why silence is deemed unrepresentable in a transmission-belt model of representation is the model's overstatement of the communicative quality of voting and the unnecessarily high standard this sets on the possibility of representing silence. This model regards votes as sufficient to inform elected representatives of, and constrain them to, voter preferences. Yet votes in themselves are very poor at telling representatives what voters want, which is why representatives seeking to establish and shape what constituents will reward in the next election gather information by other means: polls, focus groups, and the like. That we should continue to refer to the vote as "voice," when it effectively replaces voice by "compressing multivocality into a single communicative act, designed to exclude qualification or nuance from the expression of preferences," attests to the normative and ideological appeal of voice models (Coleman 2013, 12). However, just like the silences of omission and commission, votes too are relatively ambiguous. They only explicitly refer to a party or candidate, being silent about specific policies or pieces of legislation. Votes may not even reflect a positive preference for the "chosen" party or candidate but instead apathetic habituation, hegemony, social pressure, resignation to the paucity of electoral choice (that is, hold your nose and pick), or simply tactical voting, protest voting, or negative partisanship ("anyone but X"). In sum, votes are signals, and as signals they are far from establishing a mandate or a positive representative relationship.

## Enfranchising Silence

Once one brings both vote and silence under the category of "signal," the difference between the two becomes one of degree rather than kind, as do the challenges they pose to representation. Their treatment as "signals" also highlights that the purported weakness of silence-as-signal owes as much to the ambiguity of silence as to the cost-free manner in which "silence" can be ignored by a representative system designed to respond to those who are *more likely* to vote and/or *more likely* to voice, by organizing and contacting representatives directly to strengthen signals about the content and intensity of their views (Bartels 2016).

Hence, the question follows: Can silent signals be enfranchised in such a system? With its focus on vote, the transmission-belt model fails to register silent signals, most notably those of abstention. For silence to pull levers within it, the model needs to integrate silence through the only register it recognizes: the vote. The blank vote and the compulsory vote are two ways in which this might be secured. I take them in turn.

### The Blank Vote

One way of enfranchising silence is to separate it out as an act of *commission* and channel it into the electoral system by institutionalizing the blank vote on the ballot. Giving voters a "none of the above" option might empower what would otherwise be a relatively powerless exit into abstention by rendering silence's communicative content explicit and allowing protest to register *within* the electoral system. Furthermore, in showing the level of political discontent, the blank vote may increase the representative system's proactive responsiveness in order to forestall exit and incentivize new political forces to emerge, seeking out those who feel unrepresented.

Implicitly relying on the distinction between *commission* and *omission*, campaigners for the blank vote compare it positively with abstention. Abstention is easily depicted as political inaction and demeaned as free-riding on the representative system by lazy, disengaged, or apathetic voters. But the blank vote should not be discounted as political inaction nor regarded as action whose communicative content must be interpreted by the representative system. The blank vote is not a silent vote, as it is also sometimes deceptively known. One can see why it might be deemed "silent," though. Where voting is regarded as the key form of political voice, and political voice is equated with a positive choice for one of the political forces competing for our representation, the blank vote emerges as silent because it refuses to speak in the ways anticipated. The blank vote is a vote *not to* vote, *not to* exercise a voice binding one to any of the representative relations on offer. But precisely because it voices disidentification with the options provided—and perhaps even with the system providing them—its expressive nature is conspicuous.

Yet even if the blank vote helps the silence of *commission* to be separated out from the silence of *omission*, and even if it enables dissatisfaction with the representative system to be signaled clearly, to count as empowerment it must not simply be expressive but linked to consequences. The blank vote, which is normally deemed invalid, must therefore be formally admitted, reported, and taken into account when determining vote shares and the allocation of seats. Real representation for blank votes is a growing demand. After the financial crisis, for instance, "none of the above" parties formed in Spain (Escaños en Blanco / Ciudadanos en Blanco), campaigning for changes to the electoral law linking blank votes to electoral results. They also proposed to symbolically represent those ignored or frustrated by the representative system through the election of blank/empty seats (which they achieved, at a local level, in Catalonia) marking citizen voice exclusion beyond elections.

If the blank vote ceases to be simply expressive or its vote share increases, then difficult issues arise, from questions about trade-offs between voting blank and risking electing one's least favorite option to what happens in the unlikely scenario that the blank vote gets the greatest share of votes or becomes the main opposition party. The second round of France's 2017 presidential election indicated the risks presented by such scenarios, with an estimated 9 percent of votes cast being blank or spoiled but only counting toward the turnout. Elsewhere, as in Colombia, however, the blank vote can be of great consequence: a win for the blank vote in two-round elections triggers a reelection, where none of the candidates who initially ran is allowed to participate. This can wipe out the entire political status quo. Yet this is a high-risk gamble: should the blank vote come second, it means a win for the first candidate (in congressional elections); should it come first, the "blank vote" camp needs to create lists and choose its own candidate (in presidential elections). This presents a challenge. The blank vote is a *negative* vote signaling dissatisfaction with the choices available but not necessarily pointing toward choices of its own.

Radical scenarios aside, the question of whether the blank vote can empower the silence of abstention by disambiguating it calls for further consideration. The blank vote is more determinate than abstention, in that abstainers might not think all parties are equally bad. If, for instance, the incumbent party is likely to be reelected, abstention can express satisfaction; where the electoral result is open or perceived as such, abstention can express the understanding that all options are equally acceptable. By contrast, the "none of the above" vote is a protest vote, showing frustration with the available options.

The "none of the above" vote can thus partly disambiguate abstention and give more teeth to systemic disaffection, but it cannot represent all abstainers, not even among the disaffected. Survey data show that abstainers are more likely to be dissatisfied with the state of democracy than voters. Disadvantage is a major predictor of abstention: the more socially and economically marginalized, the less likely one is to vote or to participate in other ways (Brennan and Hill 2014, 146–47). The profile of blank voters differs, however, from the profile of abstainers: blank voters are well educated and politically sophisticated (Superti 2015). It is thus unlikely that the two constituencies should converge. They may, of course, occasionally align over protest about problems cutting across the representative system, such as perceived widespread corruption. While neither might feel represented by the options on the ballot, they are unlikely to be represented by the same alternative option, should this emerge from the pressure of the blank vote. Hence, the blank vote might clarify, confer visibility, and demand response to *some* of the silence generated by the representative system. But if incentivized to seek out blank voters, the system might reinforce rather than erase preexisting biases in favor of the educated and the politically knowledgeable.

## Compulsory Voting

This skewing effect might seem easily solved by integrating abstention into the electoral system through compulsory voting.[1] After all, domination haunts those silently exiting the system: nonvoters are typically among the less well-off and, in renouncing their modicum of voting power, they risk having their interests overridden by those voting. Could compelling them to vote defend them from domination through indifference to, unwarranted interpretation of, or even manipulation of the weak signals provided by their silence?

Before addressing these questions, a preliminary note is necessary. Compulsory voting is sometimes said to compel voice by denying the possibility of exit. However, while compulsory voting seeks to draw positive choices from voters, it need not violate the right to silence entirely. All that compulsory voting requires is turnout. Once voters turn up, they are free to spoil the vote, abstain, or choose the "none of the above" option, if given.

What changes then? If voters are forced to go to the polls but do not express a partisan preference, the silence of abstention would seem to become *commissive*: deliberate, more informative, and harder to dismiss. But this is too quick. A failure to express a preference can then still be *omissive*: not a deliberate expression of dissatisfaction with the options but a reflection of voter limitations in accessing or processing electoral information (Driscoll and Nelson 2014). It is sometimes claimed that even a registered preference not to voice conveys "vitally important information to politicians, and other voters," since "it communicates that there is a constituency whose votes are up for grabs and that unavailable alternatives need forming" (Brennan and Hill 2014, 142). Yet given that the non-registration of preference may be *omissive* or *commissive*, it remains uncertain how much more information one is effectively getting. This is not to say that things are not further disambiguated. In place of abstention signaling approval, we might now have a formal vote. Some abstention might turn into explicit protest through, for instance, intentional spoiling of the vote or "none of the above" votes (if the option exists). But invalid votes—blank or accidentally spoiled—are still likely to be cast by the politically unknowledgeable, uninterested, untrusting, and disaffected (Singh 2019). Their votes will mix elements of commission and omission, and where they are meant as protest, this might now—confusingly—include protest against compulsory voting itself.

There are, however, potential benefits in terms of domination and even involvement. As citizens with lower incomes and education levels are required to vote in higher numbers, inequities in turnout are ironed out, and parties may have incentives to reach out and invest in their political socialization. Additionally, as the voting population becomes more representative of the general population, the probability of the electoral signal being distorted to the advantage of the well-off is likely to decrease. But the benefits may prove elusive. If many among the forced voters lack interest, knowledge, and sophistication, and if political sophistication is a precondition for choosing the party closest to one's political preferences and holding it to account, then forcing unsophisticated voters to cast a vote may undermine the representative function of elections and leave them as unrepresented as before (Jakee and Sun 2016).

It could be objected that political sophistication is endogenous and will increase with the incentives created by repeated mandatory electoral participation. Yet the evidence on this is inconclusive (Carreras 2016). What is more, compulsory voting has been found to have no impact on accountability and a negative impact on preference correspondence (Dassonneville, Hooghe, and Miller 2017). This finding may have less to do with voters' choice than with the supply side of representation. Compulsory voting increases the adoption of programmatic vote-seeking strategies, involving noncontingent policy bundles aimed at large groups rather than subgroups (Singh 2019). It may also encourage a focus on the politically sophisticated—seen as more likely to switch their vote in response to policy changes—and on a strategy of persuasion rather than mobilization (Singh 2019). Thus, for most of those previously exiting silently into abstention who are now forced to turn out, compulsory voting may produce some indirect responsiveness by preventing wider distortions of the electoral signal but not necessarily foster the formation of and mobilization around their interests. In sum, while domination may decrease, involvement may remain largely untouched.

This takes me to a final and more fundamental objection to compulsory voting as a way to avoid powerless exit into silence: in order for voting to empower, the option of exit must be real and effective. *Ceteris paribus*, silently exiting to another party offers a stronger signal than silent exit to abstention, since the latter reduces one's customary party's vote share without increasing the voter share of a competing party. It also offers—especially where the party exited in protest becomes vulnerable to electoral competitors—a better chance that the party will reach out to seek information and enhance responsiveness by changing policy. But protest voting is demanding, strategic, and risky. Hence, abstention may prove a more palatable (if less effective) strategy for many dissatisfied voters. What is more, for voters on either extreme of the political spectrum with a strong distaste for centrist parties but wanting to signal dissatisfaction to their preferred party, or for voters wanting to send a signal of dissatisfaction to the entire political-party system, abstention may well be the only adequate option.

A compulsory system will push for the normalization of oppositional silence. Invalid votes still contribute to voter turnout, while poll abstention adversely impacts it and—potentially—the legitimacy of an election. When "internalized," the act whereby one suspends one's cooperation with the political system (by refusing to register a choice or spoiling the vote) is also the act whereby one complies with it (by going to the polls). Refusal to choose lends itself to being interpreted as a failure to act or as a reformist act making demands *from within* the representative system, rather than repudiating its authority and calling for its serious restructuring.

The right to exit the formal representative system thus constitutes not only a *freedom from* but also a *freedom to* make politics by removing oneself from politics *as is*. This removal need not denote unreflective political inaction, just as voting need not denote reflective participation. It can be a reflexive reaction to concerns of private and general interest, such as a broadly uncompetitive and unrepresentative political system in which voting might have ceased to be empowering for many.

To conclude, the transmission-belt model of representation is constitutively incapable of accommodating silence, especially omissive silence. Because it makes presence primary and representation derivative, it formulates the problem posited by silence as how to reflect within representative institutions a presence that may otherwise be obscured by abstention. What it misses is that the question is not simply one of disambiguating a preexisting presence but producing that presence (that is, preferences, interests, identities, constituencies) in the first place (Disch 2011). Some problems of information and ambiguity affecting commissive silence may be mitigated by implementing positive abstention mechanisms, such as the blank vote, and providing political clout to "easy, low-cost and actionable" options for silent exit (Warren 2011, 699), such as protest voting. But to mandate 100 percent voter turnout fails to produce the incentives to constitute and mobilize constituencies among those trapped in omissive silence while potentially forcing more distorting signs into the representative system.

## Enacting Silence

With its normative and ideological emphasis on representing voice through the ballot, the transmission-belt model of representation struggles with silence. It overstates the ambiguity of silent signals while understating the ambiguity of voting in asserting a coherent mandate. What the model misses is that just as silence is never just a cause but also an effect of representative exclusions, voice is not just echoed in the representative system but primarily enacted and spoken for by it.

In this respect, the issues surrounding the representation of silence are not so different from those surrounding the representation of expressed votes or, indeed, political representation *tout court*. However, focusing on silence brings these issues to the fore while it also uncovers silencing effects owing to the discursive bias in representation. In this section, I show how the latter manifests itself in constructivist views of representation. While I argue that they offer a more promising way to empower citizens from their silent positions, I reconstruct and expand criteria of legitimate representation to more effectively ward off dangers of domination and displaced involvement.

On a constructivist view, preferences, interests, and identities are *constituted* through processes of representation rather than being *objects* of representation prior to such processes (Saward 2010; see also Brito Vieira and Runciman 2008; Disch 2011, 2015; Montanaro 2012). What is true of preferences, interests, and identities is also true of the groups sustaining them. Groups are not simply given, prior *to* or independently *of*, representation, but they are (at least partly) brought about by being represented *as such* (Brito Vieira 2015). In bringing group members into a meaningful relationship with one another and with out-groups, representative claims generate a distinctive self- and collective understanding of who they are and what they want. This forms them *into* and mobilizes them *as* a group. As Lisa Disch puts it, political representation "aims, then, not to reproduce a state of affairs but to produce an effect: to call forth a constituency by depicting it as a collective with a shared aim" (2011, 207).

If representation is constitutive, then there is necessarily an element of usurpation involved in it (Brito Vieira 2015). This is not simply because authority to enact a group must be seized before it can be gained, as the authorizing subject—the group—might be nonexistent, undefined, or incapable prior to its representation. It is also, more generally, because a representative claim always appropriates the voice—or, indeed, the silence—of the represented.

To speak of appropriated voice is not to posit an original—immediate, authentic, self-created—voice that is then appropriated. It is rather to argue that any voice arising from representation is *produced*—a precarious, contested appropriation, calling for recognition and validation by the represented. It would thus be a mistake to equate this *constitutive* usurpation—a necessary and productive element of representation, inviting the represented into a relationship—with displaced involvement, the deviant pathology identified by my normative criteria for assessing representation. While one can evolve into the other, the latter occurs when representation loses its necessary relational quality and slides into a mere speaking and acting *in the place of.*

This danger is more pervasive than is acknowledged (Fossen 2019, 834). For while it may seem that speaking *about*—that is, *representing* or portraying the group as being like this or that—raises fewer concerns of displaced involvement than speaking and acting *for*, in practice, the distinction is hard to draw, with both types of "speaking" intertwining closely and widely in the construction of representative claims (Alcoff 1991, 9). Furthermore, to speak *about* is to create for the represented a public self in the presence of others. This impacts how audiences engage the represented and provides the latter with a means of self-understanding and self-description that may empower (or, indeed, disempower) reflexive self-constitution and effective talk-back.

The identification of domination as my second criterion for assessing the legitimacy of representation may seem inadequate—if not wholly contradictory—within a constructivist view of representation (Disch 2011). I defined domination as lack of responsiveness to the represented and their interests. *Responsiveness, authorization,* and *accountability* constitute the normative triumvirate of the transmission-belt model of representation, with its focus on questions of control rather than involvement. Responsiveness, in particular, is its nub: the model hinges on representatives being responsive to the represented and on the represented being able to hold representatives accountable for what the latter say or do in their name (Dahl 1972, 1). This, in turn, requires previous authorization, insofar as the most fundamental form of accountability—"the possibility that authorization may be withdrawn or contested" (Schweber 2016, 393)—is taken to depend on it.

Taking a constructivist position, I submit, involves redefining rather than abandoning these criteria. In the transmission-belt model, responsiveness implies *correspondence* between citizens' preferences—given prior to, and independently of, representation—and representatives' actions or policies (Sabl 2015). But if voters' preferences are endogenous to political representation, responsiveness to existing preferences is a circular criterion of representation, assessing representatives by criteria partly of their own making (Disch 2011).

While the objection holds, it does not follow that we can do without the criterion of responsiveness, if taken in the reconstructed sense I advance here. Domination, I argue, occurs when the *normative* (not ontological and temporal, as is assumed in the transmission-belt model) *priority* of the represented and their interests is violated. To represent is to act on behalf of the represented and in their name—not that of the representative. This does not imply that the interests of the represented precede representation or that the representative must follow the represented's views of their interests. It does imply, however, that representatives must orient themselves to the represented and their interests, and that where they deviate from what the represented believe to be in their interest, they must engage the challenge and give reasons to the represented to broker their interests in what is proposed (Pitkin 1967, 213; Brito Vieira 2017, 28–29; Fossen 2019, 834–35). This requirement of "response" demands an "openness to being interpellated by another's address" (interpellation being here irreducible to voice) (Athanasiou 2017, 244) and is predicated on the acknowledgment of the *contestability* of claims to represent.

By the same token, *authorization*, understood as process, has an important place in constructivist accounts. If representation is "not *just* there, a thing" (Saward 2010, 13), but a relationship of giving-voice-to whereby represented and representative are mutually constituted, the emphasis must move from *authorization* as the act establishing representation to *uptake* and *acceptance* by those subject to representative claims (151–53). Authori*zing* becomes thus a retrospective and ongoing process, so that even where authorization is formally or informally pre-given, what remains critical from a constructivist perspective is that the procurement of such authorization "does not render null and void all the attendant problems of speaking for others" (Alcoff 1991, 10). Equally, and of salience to my argument, "the power to confer such authorization, and to have power over the designated representative," may be "rarely present in instances where one is spoken for" (10), demonstrating the problems of inferring an assenting constituency from silence.[2]

Before I examine claims to represent silent constituencies using these criteria, it is important to stress the discursive bias of the particular constructivist understanding of representation I adopt in my analysis of such claims, representation as a matter of claims-making (Saward 2010). In the claims-making view, claims are constitutive of representation. That someone is a representative, or a constituent, is a consequence of claims-making.

Makers of representations "call forth" constituencies by making claims *about* themselves and their constituencies and offering these claims to the would-be audiences or constituencies for approval or disapproval. In what follows, my analysis focuses on two distinct aspects of claims-making: claims *about* silent constituencies, casting them in particular ways, and claims that someone should be regarded as a representative of a silent constituency. These claims can, of course, be separated: one can make representations of someone or something without claiming to be their representative. But since constituency and representative are mutually constituted, how one constitutes a constituency and how one constitutes oneself as its representative are closely interdependent.

Adopting a claims-making framework is not without challenges, given the framework's discursive bias.[3] To focus on claims is to focus on *speech* acts as the way to represent and create political presence. Here, I want to qualify this assumption. Silence, too, can be a mode of representation rather than just something to be represented. As demonstrated by Sinn Féin, it is possible to make representational claims silently. That a representational claim need not be voiced to be articulated is, again, shown by athletes refusing to sing national anthems because they do not believe them to represent their communities. But their silence might still look like a signal, or a way of speaking, that relies on language for the translation of representations into propositions or claims that constituencies may approve or disapprove. There is, however, a more distinctive way in which silence can act as a mode of representation: where it refuses to act like speech and explicitly departs from claim-centered modes of representation.

To appreciate this possibility properly, it is important to note that the notion of representative *claim* presupposes a particular political subject—a public speaker, a rhetor—and a discursive form of political subjectivity or agency. When feminist groups like the Women in Black perform silence as their mode of dissent, they contest a gendered order identifying political action and political agonism with speech, and speech, particularly public speaking, with power, citizenship, and authority. Their use of silence is thus no mere "background" to claims-making or even mere bodily speech act. It represents—not by saying, but by demonstrating—war victims and women *as* silenced. It refuses complicity in the discourses responsible for their depoliticization and subordination and reclaims the agency of silence to interpellate them (Athanasiou 2017, 231). It also prefigures a new politics, "breaking the linguistic and representational structure" of politics as we know it (245). One might see a radical departure from representational politics in their enactment of a political subjecthood not exclusively reliant on transforming representations into claims, propositions, or demands (253). But there is another way to see it: as a critique of the treatment of the represented as essentialized objects of representation within a one-sided model of representational politics focused on claiming but hardly suited for genuine responsiveness. Yet listening for, and being responsive to, citizen silences pregnant with political meaning is one—perhaps *the*—main task of representation.

## Claiming a Silent Majority

I can now turn to the analysis of a specific and widespread linguistic claim about silence: the claim to represent an alleged "silent majority."[4] Silent majority claims have a long history, starting with Richard Nixon, who famously used it to co-opt a socially conservative electorate in silencing antiwar protesters and the 1960s civil rights movement. Thus, in some contexts, the phrase works as a shorthand for a racialized identity embraced by working-class whites, especially Republican voters. But claims to represent the silent majority have been made on both the right and the left of the political spectrum, and the claim's meaning has been both produced and re-signified in the process. The claim has been used, for example, to mobilize racial minorities around exclusion from majority rule; during the 1960s, Black Power groups presented themselves as the actual silenced majority in major cities like Chicago. Yet the idea was also used to resist the Black militants' self-characterization: the NAACP leader at the time, Roy Wilkins, urged those he saw as the true Black majority, "the silent middle," to resist the capture of the African American political agenda by Black militants prioritizing racial issues over crime (Fortner 2015). After the 2008 global financial crisis deepened inequality, Ed Miliband, then the leader of the Labour party in the United Kingdom, positioned himself as the spokesman for a law-abiding silent majority. Populists on both right and left have followed suit (Mudde and Kaltwasser 2017).

There is a genealogy to be teased out of these multiple appeals to the "silent majority" and their changing contextual significance. But here I want to focus on why claims about a silent majority enjoy such political purchase in democracies and examine possible implications of these claims for representational dynamics.

The political appeal of the claim may be obvious: it raises concerns about minority tyranny. But there is more to its appeal than first meets the eye.

First is the moral pull of majoritarianism in a context where representative democracy has become associated with rule of the majority. Second is a culturally specific understanding of silence that bolsters the fiction of the majority as *the* people, understood as an entity with one voice and at one with itself. I begin with majoritarianism.

Majoritarianism's moral pull hinges on two premises: the equality of voters *qua* speaking citizens who must have an equal "say" in decisions affecting them *and* the fiction that the majority is *the* people (Rosenblum 2008, 52). The latter, in particular (and as Tocqueville predicted), foregrounds the recurrence of the silent majority trope in democratic politics. When parties competing for our representation "fail to obtain [the majority] from the voters, they will say it lies with those who abstained from voting, and if it still eludes them, they will say it lies with those who are denied the right to vote" (Tocqueville 2011, 275).

In speaking about a "silent majority," one is not only representing the constituency as a numerical majority but also, and critically, as silent. There are two distinct ways in which the silent majority can be deemed a majority and in which silence might be deemed its expression. Put in broadly Hobbesian terms, the claim might be that it is *one voice* being silenced or a multitude of *different voices* being silenced, each (individual or group voice) in its own way, adding up to a numerical majority. The distinction underwrites contrasting conceptions of the represented: as a unity without parts or as a whole comprising parts, respectively.

Much of the clout of the "silent majority" claim lies precisely in projecting its silence as a collective silence, muting *the* sovereign will and thus sustaining the fiction of the people-*as*-one. This is a fiction fraught with dangers of holism: totalizing claims to a "silent majority" are no different from totalizing claims to the "voice of the majority." Just as *the* mandated voice of the people can be constructed out of an aggregation of information-poor ballots, so can the ambiguity of silent signals be made to be heard as a unison, blank authorization.

This is not to say, however, that the claims are entirely interchangeable. There is a specificity to claims about a "silent" majority, immersed as they are in cultural norms and givens, that strengthens the fiction of the people-*as*-one. This is most notably the case with the understanding of silence as the "Other" of voice, with this "Other" referring to either a *lack* (of speech, constituting absence) or a *beyond* (speech, conveying full presence).

It is as a figure of absence—and thus powerlessness—that silence is first heard in claims about a "silent majority." This absence could be blamed on the silent: a numerical majority that does not vocalize itself is likely to set off a spiraling of silence whereby active minority voices become amplified (Noelle-Neumann 1993). But constituencies are formed and mobilized by framing a conflict. Hence the silent majority is evoked as "silenced" (by elites, privileged and/or noisy minorities) rather than simply or even necessarily "silent."

This is just a first layer of meaning, however. The white canvas is a metaphor commonly used for silence. This is because it is empty, blank, but also because it is a receptive surface, responsive to shifts in color, light, and structure. Silence is not unlike it in that it is "available for various projections of meaning because no meaning or definition can 'match' the notion of silence" (Loevlie 2003, 9). It thus lends itself to be used as an empty signifier—indeed, one could argue, as *the* empty signifier *par excellence* (Laclau 2005). This gives it a protean quality. It can open up to protect and accommodate difference. It can absorb different particular grievances and demands. It can establish an equivalence between these demands negatively, through the projection of a shared antagonistic position. It can also neutralize differences among demands in the process.

To appreciate this, we need to turn from silence as an empty container, waiting to be filled, to silence as full presence. For silence is not just capable of *receiving* meaning. It is also capable of *giving* meaning, without pinning it down to particular signifieds. The enduring appeal of silence as a *beyond* lies precisely in its alleged capacity to provide a quasi-mythical meaning to the inexpressible: "all those experiences, insights, institutions, feelings, states 'whereof one cannot speak'" (Loevlie 2003, 11; Sontag 2009). Silence brings these into a relation of equivalence, allowing for a potential "universal identification in difference to take place" (Saldaña-Portillo 2003, 196). As this happens, silence becomes an "incommensurable universal signifier," forming a collective subject that becomes hegemonic, but at the risk of any difference within silence becoming "dangerously close to losing all specificity" (196).

The effect is reinforced by how we are primed to hear silence. Where speech is seen as differentiating, silence is seen as internally undifferentiated and "beyond all the distinction speech can make" (Muers 2004, 11). As such, voice stands for distinctive individual political judgments, which, once transformed into votes, are aggregated and counted in. Silence, by contrast, is perceived as undifferentiated or, at best, as binarily discursive. This reflects itself in the tendency to resolve silence into reductive binary meanings—"yes" or "no," assent or dissent, and so on—and in the call for referenda to enable majorities purportedly silenced by normal politics to express themselves. Forced to operate in this narrow way, "silence" acquires an acclamatory character, which returns a "clumped" effect (Schwartzberg 2010, 453).

This analysis of how our culturally given understandings of silence work themselves into claims to represent an alleged "silent majority" shows how such claims may attract a diverse following by preserving their ambiguity, while leaving the represented at the mercy of "elite minorities with privileged access to technologies and institutions of claim-making" (Saward 2006, 304) and displacing involvement by "silenc[ing] the constituencies or audiences that they may in part constitute by evoking" (Saward 2010, 55). Let me explain.

A key tenet of constructivist accounts of political representation is that representation is *relational:* it must *presuppose* and *support* agency and judgment on the parts of representatives (as makers of claims) and the represented (as those challenged to take them up) alike (Pitkin 1967, 155). Those claiming to represent a silent constituency can enhance their agency at the expense of the represented by playing with the equivocal meaning of silence to mobilize resentment while *willfully* reading a constituency out of the evoked silence in ways that foreclose agonistic engagement and only empower preestablished views. This precludes responsiveness, including responsiveness to the potentially agonistic nature of silence itself. But if domination is a concern, so is the risk of impairing the agency of the represented. To take the consequences of constructivism seriously, one needs to see the represented's capacity for action and judgment as (partly) constituted in terms of the claim made (Enroth 2017). Claims about a "silent majority" can be challenging in this respect, as they ask constituents to judge, decide, and act under a particular self-image rendering them as people who must be spoken *for.*

Another way that claims may disallow talk-back is by immunizing themselves against *contestation*. Claims to represent must put the representatives at some risk (Enroth 2017). Yet where unaccompanied by a specification of interests, policies, and reforms, claims about purported silent majorities leave the represented without a focus of accountability. In addition, where such claims cast the silent as dutiful, judicious citizens, expressing themselves only through proper electoral channels, they de-authorize verbal objection and seek to induce a spiral of silence whereby opponents (cast as unreasonable and as minoritarian) may be silenced or become less willing to express dissent. While attempts at foreclosing objection are part and parcel of claims-making and can only be addressed at the system level through confrontation with competing claims, the silent majority claim, especially where the reference group is large, disallows contestation on its own terms.

It trades on the ambiguous and unverifiable nature of the evoked silence to resist falsification. As Tocqueville noted, it is not uncommon for those with a precarious or uncertain electoral win to bolster their legitimacy by claiming the support of a majority still "out there" (2011).

These are risks, not inevitabilities. Claims are not good or bad. They must be assessed not in the abstract but in their particular performance. Take, for instance, the meaning and effects of the descriptions under which the represented are asked to act. The claim may be the same, but these meanings and effects may change radically depending on who makes the claim and how the representative relationship is posited by the claim and enacted. Consider a Black Power leader in Chicago pursuing a seat in city government by representing Black citizens as the real silenced majority in the city while seeking to reinforce their agency and political efficacy by community organizing, engaging political education programs, and building multiracial and ethnic coalitions grounded in class solidarity. The leader's social positioning and efforts to promote relationships with—and between—the represented, which may enable the causes of silence to be identified and spoken of, and discrepancies in accounts of causes and solutions to be interpellated avert fears of domination and displacement. By contrast, consider Donald J. Trump's claim to represent the silent majority of Americans in the 2016 US presidential election. Combined with assertions such as "I am your voice," "I alone can fix it," and "I will restore law and order," the claim displaces the judgment of the represented by positing the speaker as the sole knowledgeable, authoritative, and empowered subject. It also uses evasiveness ("fix *it*") to deprive the spoken *for* of a focus of accountability while positioning them as passive followers to be "championed for from afar" (Alcoff 1991, 24).

In emphasizing the constitutive dimension of representation, constructivists foreground its importance in mobilizing and challenging different forms of exclusion that result in effectively silenced constituencies. Unauthorized bids for support challenging marginalized constituencies to accept them will always be necessary to bootstrap a "productive form of antagonism" out of antagonisms that are currently muted or even "largely silent, pre-rational and unarticulated" (McNay 2012, 240). However, with their almost exclusive focus on uptake and systemic reflexivity, constructivists can lack part of the normative vocabulary necessary to engage such claims critically.[5]

Even under conditions of pluralism, publicity, and reflexivity, to infer a presence or "passive authorization" from silence (non-objection) (Saward 2010, 175n; Runciman 2007) is deeply problematic. It downplays the fact that the "agonist[ic] capacity to engage contestatory activity speaks of being in a position of relative power," as Lois McNay puts it, "not in a position of relative powerlessness where such a process of contestation may be experienced as profoundly alienating" (2012). It also deemphasizes the fact that agents are empowered to judge and object not only by systemic conditions of reflexivity through competitive claims-making (Disch 2011) but also by how they are constituted by claims to represent. Yet, where silence is taken as univocal rather than potentially agonistic, where it is taken for an absence rather than a potential presence, and where the silenced are addressed as non-agents rather than as actual or potential speakers who are currently unheard (Muers 2004, 44), their agency is undercut.

This brings me back to my extended notion of responsiveness. In arguing that representatives should show an openness to being interpellated by the silenced's address, I am not assuming that this is because the silenced's speech is simply found, necessarily emancipatory, or reflective of their "true" interests. Nor am I suggesting that silent constituencies should be left to speak for themselves and be listened to rather than represented. This would mistakenly assume their voice—and their capacity for voice—as a given rather than a constructed position. The point is, rather, that one's ability to speak is contingent on the experience of being listened to. Hence, only representation involving *generative listening*—a listening that pays heed to while actively drawing out—and that speaks *with* and *to*, rather than simply *about* and *for*, can be constitutive of subjects that may come to voice, challenge, and subvert (Alcoff 1991, 23; Spivak 1988).

While only representative claims-making performed in this way may activate and empower effectively silenced constituencies, one must be cautious. The representative system is responsible for extensive silencing effects, since it is constitutive *of* and constituted *by* many of the exclusions underwriting them (Devenney 2019). While these exclusions may have become naturalized by treating silence as assenting, prophylactic, or negligible—or indeed by offloading responsibility for silence onto citizens—they have a "presence," "history," and "form" (Rich 2013, 17). This is productive of systemic institutional and structural processes (for example, the underrepresentation of women, or campaign financing privileging big-money donors) whereby certain claims and claimants are allowed and taken up, others are shut down, and still other claims, while taking shape, struggle to gain traction. Unless constructivists engage the notion of structural injustice (I. Young 2011, 52), they will remain unable to scrutinize and potentially challenge the background conditions—including constitutive representations of race, gender, and class—preventing the inclusion and empowerment of many through representation.

## Conclusion

"Voice" has a primary position in our accounts of representative democracy, though most citizens are unvocal most of the time—some chronically so—and the chief mechanism for "voice," the vote, is an abridged speech act of equivocal interpretation at best. This chapter has advanced a novel and broader conceptualization of silence to counter the exclusionary effects of conceiving representation as a register of vocal expression. In particular, it has argued that speech and silence are not opposites, but they are also not the same; neither silence nor vote is necessarily, or straightforwardly, meaningful. They function at best as *signals* soliciting engagement by a representative system earning its legitimacy from giving-voice-to. Hence, though the chapter has assessed representation from the perspective of silence, many of its conclusions apply to representation *tout court*.

Taking silence as the site of a potential presence, rather than meaningless absence, is the first step in enabling its representation. I have stressed the importance of distinguishing between *commissive* and *omissive* silences, silences of dissent and silences of powerlessness, before we assess models of representation—non-constructivist and constructivist—for their ability to engage them. While I have shown that the transmission-belt model of representation could, to some extent, accommodate commissive silences, in assuming exogenous capacity for preference formation, it struggled with omissive silences. Constructivist models of representation proved more promising in this respect. Taking representation as constitutive of our capacity to articulate identities and preferences and mobilize around them, the model shifts the burden of voice from citizens to the representational relationship between representatives and represented. However, with their focus on claims-making, constructivists have a blind spot for commissive silence and active, generative listening as means of representing, and they lack part of the normative vocabulary required to set apart genuine cases of representation from the mere inference of constituencies from silence.

While prior scholars have focused on claim-acceptance and systemic conditions of reflexivity under which acceptance can reflect robust political judgment, here I have argued for a broadened notion of responsiveness—as openness to interpellation, vocal and nonvocal, grounded on the acknowledgment of the fragility and contestability of all claims to represent and an understanding of the represented's capacity for action and judgment as dependent on how they are constituted in terms of the claims made. These may be read as a shift back from system-level to claim-level criteria of representation, but that conclusion is unwarranted. Although it is important not to bypass the claim level, the focus remains on legitimacy produced by the conditions secured at system level rather than legitimacy produced within discrete claims to represent. What my broadened notion of responsiveness does is to put reflexivity at the service of an answerability acknowledging the priority—*logical* and *normative*—of the represented as bearers of interests and as potential or actual speakers. As to my notion of displaced involvement, it draws attention to how involvement is ultimately distributed by the representative system itself.

For all their focus on the system, constructivists struggle to account for its displacing effects: the constituencies that are never formed, the cleavages never articulated, the minorities and supermajorities persistently muted, the claims illocutionarily and perlocutionarily disabled, including those made in the name of entities that cannot speak for themselves—like nature, the focus of the last chapter of this book. Conceived as constitutive, representational claims can present themselves as almost free from determination. Yet representative systems share responsibility in the formation and distribution of power positions, opportunities, and resources. If systemic reflexivity is to be a sufficiently trenchant criterion of representation, it must go beyond mobilizing challenges and objections to claims made. It must generate and mobilize awareness of structural oppression, disruptive claims, and reform.

# 7

## THE SILENCE OF NATURE

A silent death is an endless word.
—Yasunari Kawabata, "Silence"

The previous chapter focused on the complexities of representing silence in the political domain. The silence under analysis there was that purportedly emanating from human constituencies comprising actual or potential speakers. But what of nonhuman constituencies? Are they, unlike the examined human constituencies, effectively mute or necessarily silent? What would such a silence mean for their representation in the political domain and for our democratic politics? These are the main questions I pursue in this final chapter.

Given the power we collectively hold over the social, political, legal, and economic structures affecting nonhuman constituencies, the structural limitation of anthropogenic power—allowing the survival and well-being of other entities to be considered alongside our own—requires an overcoming of the "nonpolitical status of nonhumans" (Dolgert 2012, 264). This implies the extension of the meaning of politics so that it addresses not only how human beings ought to live with one another but also how they ought to live with nonhuman beings and things.

However, putting ourselves in a political community with nonhuman beings and things presents a challenge. Political agency entails the capacity to act in concert with others. To do so, we must engage with the question of how we should act, which requires reflexive and deliberative abilities seemingly absent in nonhuman constituencies. If political relationality depends on such abilities, then the possibility of an interspecies politics might seem dim, as the abovementioned abilities are speech-based.

Is Nature Mute?

On the question of whether nonhuman constituencies speak or are silent, there are two opposing camps. On the one hand, there are those who argue that nature is not just silent but effectively mute, that is, constitutively incapable of speech (see, e.g., Vogel 2006 and Dienstag 2021). On the other hand, there are those who claim that nature does speak and that the trouble is that we won't listen (see, e.g., Friskics 2001). Driving the disagreement are different understandings of "speech" and what speech counts as political. Those arguing that nonhuman constituencies are incapable of speech refer to conventional symbolic language and, specifically, to reasoned speech, spoken deliberation, or speech as a linguistic capacity characterized by historicity and communicative reciprocity. Accordingly, they maintain that we cannot speak *with* nature but only *about* and *for* it. This means that our relationship with nature is "necessarily representative" (Dienstag 2021, 628). Those arguing that nonhuman constituencies speak extend the concept of speech to include nonsymbolic communicative faculties. They maintain that it is our disavowal of nonhuman constituencies' self-speaking, not nature's lack of communicative abilities, that reduces the latter to an object of representation.

The disagreement is pregnant with political consequences. While both camps acknowledge the necessity of some form of democratic inclusion of nonhuman constituencies, they differ regarding the shape this might take. Those who see nonhuman constituencies as mute oppose their enfranchisement. Nevertheless, they acknowledge the need for their inclusion in the class of the represented on the grounds that all those affected by a political decision ought, at least indirectly, to have a say in its making. They argue that the political agency of nonhuman constituencies is dependent on trustee representation by human stewards responsible for promoting nonhuman constituencies' interests in legislative, deliberative, or regulatory bodies (Eckersley 2000, 2004, 2011; Dobson 1996; Donoso 2017; Cochrane 2016; Garner 2016). Those who take nonhuman constituencies as self-speaking counter that democratic inclusion is not solely, or even primarily, about interest promotion but about agency, or about agents who are acknowledged as political equals and allowed to participate in decision-making. They deem nonhuman constituencies capable of self-representation or making positive inputs into the democratic process. As such, some in this camp argue that, at least in certain cases, nonhuman constituencies should be entitled to participatory rights (e.g., in the case of domesticated animals; see Donaldson and Kymlicka 2011). The majority, however, make lesser claims. They argue for representatives who behave as delegates rather than trustees facilitating nonhuman constituencies' political agency by translating and entering their inputs or signals into the political process (Friskics 2001; a moderate version of this position can be found among deliberative democrats, such as Romero and Dryzek 2021). While this camp's aim is to transform politics into an interspecies affair, the first camp insists that the domain of politics is strictly human: "Nature is silent; we—you and I, the ones who can talk—have to decide what standards should guide our practices, because there's no one else who can" (Vogel 2015, 170; see also Dienstag 2021, 631).

Despite the considerable differences separating both camps, there is agreement that nonhuman constituencies' political presence entails representation, necessarily or to some degree. Yet it is doubtful that nonhuman constituencies can authorize or revoke representatives, let alone monitor, assent to, or dissent from the representation made on their behalf.[1] This places represented nonhuman beings and things in an unequal power relation, fraught with the potential for ventriloquism (Vogel 2015, 190–94).

Ventriloquizing Nature

By "ventriloquism" I mean a form of domination entailing the representative's projection of their own voice, interests, or wishes onto the represented under the pretense that they are that of the represented. Interestingly, both those taking "nature" as self-speaking and those taking it as "mute" respond to the risk of ventriloquism in a similar way: namely, by establishing a bedrock of representation or seeking to check their representation against representation-independent realities. These realities differ in the two cases—nature's objective interests versus nature's communications—but their role and effect are alike. Those taking nature to be mute look to assuage concerns about ventriloquism by holding to the notion of objective interests, that is, interests they characterize as independent of the represented's thoughts, wants, or wishes (Pitkin 1967, 159, 61) and as interests about which the represented need not have a say, or be able to communicate, as they refer to more or less obvious basic needs (Donoso 2017). Those taking nature to be self-speaking seek to dispel ventriloquism by letting nature have its say. All that is required by non-ventriloquizing representation is that "we give our full attention to the address of the beings and things we meet, engage them as self-speaking presences, and respond to their claims wholeheartedly and without reserve" (Friskics 2001, 395–96). One of the most significant problems with both solutions to ventriloquism is that they conceal the constitutive nature of representation. In other words, they cast representation as a matter of advancing preexisting "things"—namely, objective interests or nature's claims—while in truth, representation is integral to their constitution.

To speak of nature's interests as "objective" is to portray them as pre-political—as things dictated by facts about "nature's nature" that are reliably identifiable by some authority, namely, scientific experts. The combination of a value-free, representational view of science as a provider of facts to political actors and a view of political representation as a technical activity that involves responding to scientists tends to impermeabilize both scientific and political claims to accountability (Disch 2016, 626). More than decontesting scientific claims, however, it keeps out of sight the political questions that remain open and contested: Which claims are relevant to the representation of entities like "the environment"? Those concerning the welfare of human individuals? Or those concerning the welfare of ecosystems? Although the expectation is often that the good of one is the good of the other, they can come into conflict with one another. For instance, measures necessary to combat global warming may threaten the economic growth of developing countries, and the political decision is what to do in the face of this dilemma. Overstated versions of "nature's" communicative or political agency have similarly depoliticizing effects. The portrayal of the communicative interaction between human and nonhuman constituencies as simply a matter of listening, attending, or responding to nature's "signals" (species extinction, drought, climate change, flowers blooming and insect eggs hatching earlier, oceans rising and warming, and so on) downplays the complexity of such interactions. Just as voters' signals need articulation by being represented as such and such, "signals" received from nature require interpretation to say something, and their interpretation often comes up against limitations in our self-conceptions, sensibility, knowledge, and representative thinking as well as our biases and self-interests.

## From Signals to Claims

What is more, *political* meaning is not something that can be simply extracted from a "signal": it needs construing. This implies agenda-setting, priming, framing, formulation of lines of conflict, and constituency building and mobilizing through representative claims about states of affairs in the world and about how we ought to act collectively about them—and why (Disch 2011; Saward 2010).

A perfect illustration of this can be found in Rachel Carson's trailblazing book *Silent Spring* (1962). This is the book that makes silence *the* signal of a looming human-induced environmental crisis, one that Carson argues is being dangerously ignored. *Silent Spring* asks a simple but consequential question: What if spring were no longer heralded by the sound of singing birds? With this question, the demise of birdsong is posited as both a symptom and a symbol of a menace that is no less insidious than the more familiar menace Carson evokes to emotionally prime her readers: the radioactive fallout spread by atomic explosions. In her "Fable for Tomorrow," Carson introduces her readers to a similar "grim specter," making the world turn strange in an unnamed "town in the heart of America" (1962, 21). Un-naming allows the town to be nowhere—a no-place and yet also everywhere, a here-place: your town, my town, our towns, as we are all brought together as potentially affected constituencies. She lists a cascade of signals—all of which are witnessed by individual readers—that, when brought together, add up to something bigger and produce an apocalyptic figuration: vegetation browning and withering, adults and children succumbing to unexplained afflictions and enigmatic deaths. Anxiety about what might have been (and what might still be) lost is activated, with readers introduced to the ominous quiet of a world "deserted by all living things" (R. Carson 1962, 22). Now that the readers' attention is gained, they are open to focus on the causes of the catastrophe, ready to claim and exercise a right to know. Carson's aim is that of "breaking silence" through the use of scientific insight and synthesis. However, as a representative of silenced constituencies, nonhuman and human, she tries not to act as the scientific expert educating readers from outside and above. Instead, she "place[s] herself squarely" among the constituency she is seeking to constitute and mobilize, namely, "people trying to sort through the conflicting evidence of experts and officials" (Harris 2000, 142). The first lines of conflict are drawn: the public against collusion between the scientific establishment, the chemical industry, and the "political machinations behind organized campaigns to defeat inconvenient scientific knowledge in the public forum" (Ceccarelli 2011, 216). These collusions encouraged the growing use of pesticides and herbicides in agricultural and home settings, promoting chemicals as miracle aids. However, while the promoters wanted the debate closed, Carson frames it as open and positions the public as a major stakeholder.

My point is that several steps are required to saturate a signal with political significance, with even more being required to provide orientation to political action. In Carson's case, orientation is provided through an imaginative structure that opens a novel perspective and possibility. Pesticides epitomized man's desire to exert ever-greater control over nature and a hubristic view of the capacities of science. What started as a war against mosquitoes had locked man into a war against himself. To come back from this, it was necessary to regulate the chemical industry, but this alone was insufficient. A bigger shift was required: from traditional science to a holistic ecology, foregrounding our entanglements with the environment. For those needing to see what ecologically entangled subjects might look like, Carson offers a microscopic vision, leading into a vast network of fluid and hybrid relations troubling the assumed separation between humans and their environment. She produces enlarged, long-living images of chemicals traversing from the ecology of the natural world to the "ecology of the world within our bodies," "from the moment of conception until death" (R. Carson 1962, 189, 15). This encourages her readers to open their eyes to the dangers they incur as chemicals work themselves into the fabric of their bodies, acting as silent killers, "creating sleeping cancer cells, cells in which an irreversible malignancy will slumber long and undetected" (233). Carson thus politicizes cancer, recasting it from a shameful hidden affliction to an industrially induced disease.

My reason for delving into Carson's scientist-activist work is to show that while signals must play a role in the political representation of nonhuman constituencies, this role must be set against everything else representation needs to do for signals to represent something and lend it political force. As Carson put it, the representation of silenced nonhuman and human constituencies is a privilege and a duty (Carson in Lear 2009, 328), a privilege and a duty that "cannot be allocated, assigned, or portioned to any community other than the *humanopolis*" (Dienstag 2021, 631). This is why it is so important to distinguish among signals, addresses, and claims and what they can do. A sign is "something which stands for something in some respect or capacity" (Peirce 1955). Natural signs are sensations or perceptions causally linked to what the sign signifies. As things that indicate something, signals convey information, but they require "reading" to represent something, to be understood. This "reading" can be more or less straightforward, and reading of natural signs can on many occasions be far more straightforward than "reading," for instance, the meaning of someone's vote. As legal scholar Christopher Stone (1972) rightly stressed, it is relatively easy for my yellowing lawn to signal to me that it would be in its interests to be watered. But in most cases, more is necessary to articulate a natural sign's meaning. Take, for instance, Carson's "silence." The perceived silence points to a real and observable phenomenon. This phenomenon is an indicator of something—notably, a decline in bird populations. But, as we have seen, the meaning lying behind this surface meaning needs to be disclosed by a conscious, skilled interpreter. It is Carson's "semiotic elaboration" on readers' perceptions, "draw[ing] together the local and the global," that—combined with her scientific knowledge—causally binds together the perceived silence "with human actions in ways that are sometimes readily apparent and sometimes barely perceptible" (Whitehouse 2015, 55, 56). A form of communication between birds, the birdsong and its disappearance are not meant to communicate anything to us. This distinguishes this first type of natural signal from animals' gestures and vocalizations that establish or seek to establish "a relation, anticipate a reception, appeal for a response" (Menely 2015, 19). This "seeking" may be intentional (such as when my cat meows for food) or follow from the fact that we commune with the animal in some way, in this case that we share a creaturely voice that can call out, cry, and clamor (as in the groan of an animal in pain or distress). In either case, the signal may be called an address or even a claim (of injury, in this case), in the general sense, of something that asks for a response. Such claims are different, however, from claims asserting something to be the case, to be desirable/undesirable, wrong/right—to be *due*. The latter fall under a narrower understanding of claiming, where to claim is to say something that may elicit contestation, dissent, or even rejection and is therefore always in need of justification. While it is true that in practice there is more continuity between *aesthesis* (sensuous perception), *phone* (creaturely voice), and *logos* (meaning both discourse and reason), natural and instituted signs, creaturely voice and human speech, than is normally recognized within a logocentric perspective, it is equally important to acknowledge that normative claims—such as rights claims, for instance—are "neither simply an intrinsic condition of nature nor a contingent matter of state recognition" but a "communicative transaction" between signals, interpellations, and the claims humans make about them (Menely 2015, 13; see also Hawhee 2017, 170). These claims cannot and do not simply follow from signals or interpellations, since ultimately it is we who "have to decide what standards should guide our practices, because there's no one self who can" (Vogel 2016, 170). The problem that arises when signal, address, and claim are treated interchangeably is that this is blanked out, and purported "claims of the nonhuman world" risk being treated as "absolute, like those of a monarch," leaving "no room for competing claims, nor for justification" (149).

In pointing toward this difference, I in no way mean to exclude signals or addresses from the political representation of nonhuman constituencies. In effect, the latter could not proceed legitimately without continuously engaging both. If representation is not just about protecting interests but about acknowledging and distributing agency, it must account for and be responsive to nonhuman constituencies' multiple forms of embodied agency, whether they are communicative or not. In a sense, this openness is partly baked into the very notion of advocacy, as the advocate is she who adds a voice, who is "called upon by another's voice to speak for others *in his or her own voice*" (Menely 2015, 1; my emphasis). This foregrounds representation as needing to remain constitutively open to signals and voices that are refused uptake—that are currently silenced—but it also makes it clear that representation is not simply about expanding nonhuman nature's voice but about adding a new one: our own. Responsiveness, as I defined it in the previous chapter, is all the more important when any effort to speak about or for nonhuman constituencies runs against the epistemic impairments caused by a history of dominative relations. And so is the recognition that we may ultimately speak in our own voice when we speak for the Othered. A position of humility is thus commendable, where we acknowledge and take account of the Other without assuming their interests or perspectives (I. Young 1997, 71). Humility also implies critical engagement with the belief that what is human—and what is political—is distinctive and clear-cut. The casting of "nature" as inert, law-bound, and agency-less is the foil against which the political domain defined itself. Shaped as the domain of speech, freedom, and agency, the political domain forced out alternative forms of agential doing, being, and becoming and their subjects, leaving them unacknowledged and uncared-for in the articulation of the common and its management. Consider, for instance, passionate expression—the voice (*phone*)—that nonhuman and human animals share and that is integral to human speech as signifying voice, which rhetoric scholars are rightly foregrounding as a medium of "transactional, cross-species partnerships" (Hawhee 2017, 170). The ability to engage creaturely voice, as something that signifies in and by itself, is critical in constituting nonhuman nature—namely, animals—as a political and rhetorical constituency.[2] Another medium of transactional, cross-species partnerships is our embodied and material agency, which is in many ways similar to, dependent on, and co-constituted by that of nonhuman beings and things and even the nonliving (Haraway 2016; Latour 1999). If our bodies have agentic properties, and if agency springs from bodily interaction between the human and the nonhuman, the dualism (mute) "material reality" / (speech-based) "human ingenuity" surfaces as an artifact of "particular projects and politics" (T. Mitchell 2002, 33), occluding the human and the nonhuman "dissimilar ways of worlding together" (Anker 2022, 179). But while ecological democracy must acknowledge that the nonhuman material world figures centrally in the constitution of our agency, it would be hasty to move from the acknowledgment of these dependencies and interconnectedness to taking "actants" (Bennett 2005, 446) for actors, conflating the agency of the one with the other so that one would wrongly place normative claims on the plane of things and entrust ecological democracy to a "material politics," whose chief aim is to bring forth the ways in which "things" display "normative capacities ... to activate and mobilize publics" (Marres 2012, 33).

Representing Nature

Activation, mobilization, and participation depend on representation as the process of making, accepting, or rejecting representative claims, both descriptive and normative. Nonhuman nature needs representation precisely because it cannot instruct anyone to act for it and therefore risks being left out of decision-making that vitally affects its interests and prospects. Proposals for "nature's" representation abound, from Robyn Eckersley's "political trusteeship" (2004, 120) through to Andrew Dobson's "proxy representation" (1996) and Alfonso Donoso's "objective-interests representation" (2017). Many other examples could be cited. But I want to explore an alternative route for thinking about nonhuman constituencies' representation that embraces a more constructivist understanding of it.

Briefly put, what distinguishes a constructivist view is its emphasis on representation's performative dynamics. Constructivists maintain that constituencies, their interests, and their preferences are not given prior to or apart from representation but are shaped in the process of being represented (Disch 2011; Saward 2010; Brito Vieira and Runciman 2008). In spelling out the details of what the political representation of nonhuman beings and things might look like from a constructivist perspective, I take inspiration from a perhaps unlikely source, the philosopher Thomas Hobbes.[3] I will be interpreting his theory of representation rather freely, however, overhauling some of its elements when necessary (Brito Vieira 2009; Brito Vieira and Runciman 2008).

There is something inherently self-defeating in attempting to bring nonhuman nature into political community with us by requiring from it the same competences that have been historically responsible for its political exclusion, namely, reflective cognitive and linguistic abilities. The problem is not whether nonhuman nature possesses language or communicative abilities but rather that the definition of the human and the political around those abilities has led to the denial of nonhuman nature's intrinsic worth and to its exclusion from being part of and participant in what is common. Can we bring nonhuman nature into political communion with us without falling into the trap of just seeing us in it and politics everywhere? From a Hobbesian perspective, the absence or only partial presence of communicative abilities is not a problem, since indirect political agency can still be exercised via representation. All manner of "things," Hobbes tells us, are capable "of being represented by Fiction," and he goes on to list a series of examples, including humans with no (or limited) use of reason, objects, and purely imaginary entities (Hobbes 1996, 113). Despite being unable to represent themselves, all these entities can acquire the capacity to speak and act—and to do so in very consequential ways—as long as someone is authorized to act in their name. But how can this be if these things are themselves incapable of authorizing a representative? Hobbes's answer is straightforward: a third party can authorize on their behalf as long as it stands in the right kind of relationship to the being or thing in need of representation. By this he means ownership, governorship, or some other form of dominion. To appreciate what this might look like, consider Hobbes's example of a bridge. A bridge is a "thing" constitutively incapable of speaking or acting on its own. But the entity owning the bridge and responsible for its upkeep and repair can appoint a representative for the bridge—an overseer, charged "to procure [the bridge's] maintenance" in the way she sees fit (113).

There are several reasons why Hobbes's account of representation may be useful in thinking through the representation of nonhuman beings and things. First, Hobbes sees representation as an active force shaping the represented and their interests. Second, he takes representation to be a matter of social or legal attribution. As such, he does not need to enter disputes about what kind of "thing" the represented needs to be, or about what "competences" it needs to have, to be able to exercise (indirect political) agency and be a participant in what is common. Third, and relatedly, he believes representation to be possible even where the represented have neither the capacity to authorize nor the capacity to revoke a representative. Fourth, Hobbes takes representation as a form of responsible stewardship. As we have seen, he premises the capacity to authorize on dominion, which is problematic when applied to nonhuman nature, as it evokes a view of it as existing purely for our purposes. However, he conceives representation as a duty or a way of fulfilling the distinctively human responsibility for providing for the needs and well-being of beings and things over whom we hold power, thus structuring between us and them a relation that is more than merely instrumental. Finally, the Hobbesian framework has great built-in flexibility, enabling different forms of distributing agency to nonhuman nature. Through it, nonhuman beings and things can exercise indirect political agency in legislative, deliberative, and regulatory bodies via representatives (official advocates, ombudspersons, and so on) authorized by the state. Although Hobbes saw representation by fiction to require the authorization of the state or civil law, one could extend it to environmental organizations, animal-rights groups, environmental movements, and activists either formally authorized by their members (in case they have an organizational structure) or informally authorized by their followers and institutional interlocutors (in case they don't) to speak for nonhumans. Representation by fiction can also be used to grant the legal status of personhood to nonhuman nature and enable it to be a rights-holder.

Before I turn to Hobbesian legal personhood and the possibilities it opens, I need to stress a limitation of Hobbes's model of representation for entities who are not self-speaking and cannot act on their own. It is still primarily focused on the representation of the needs and interests of nonspeaking beings and things for the sake of securing their flourishing or welfare. It thus does not sufficiently break away from the caretaker model of representation, which tends to treat representatives as stewards, managing the represented for their best interests, and the represented as inert and mute objects. This objectification means that the agency of the represented is presumed absent or, at best, insufficiently accounted for in the process of representing. As such, although nonhuman beings and things may gain (indirect) political agency through representation, and although Hobbes's materialism acknowledges material agency as widely distributed, the representative relationship can seem to bypass the represented's prior agency (communicative and/or material), leaving little room for any "independence, difference and self-directedness" on their part, which can make it impossible to represent it adequately and to provide representation to conflicts of interest (Plumwood 1993, 16).

This requires correction, and I advance some possibilities below. But there is, nonetheless, undoubted power in Hobbes's performative theory of representation (Fleming 2019).[4] To see why this is the case, it is helpful to distinguish between two different understandings of personhood: personhood as an intrinsic property and personhood as a performative conception (List and Pettit 2011, 171). In the first case, personhood is solely dependent on inner properties and the makeup of an entity; in the second case, personhood is solely dependent on the entity's ability to act in the manner of a person. As I pointed out, Hobbes holds a distinctively performative understanding of personhood whereby personhood depends exclusively on entities' capacity to perform the role of persons. Entities that are not persons (naturally speaking) can be persons in law as long as they can speak and act through authorized representatives. They thereby become capable of performing in a system of mutual obligations by holding the reciprocal power to make claims (in the narrow sense I defined above) and address the claims of others (List and Pettit 2011, 174). As persons in law, nonhuman beings and things are able to hold not just obligations but also rights: they can own themselves, enter contracts, and seek redress for their rights when those rights are violated.

Christopher Stone was walking in Hobbes's footsteps when, more than fifty years ago, he raised the possibility of treating nonhuman entities (forests, oceans, rivers, and other so-called natural objects in the environment, and perhaps even the natural environment as a whole) as subjects and legal persons endowed with a right to flourish and be protected by human guardians seeking legal redress if their rights were violated (1972). What might have seemed science fiction then has become a feature of our world, especially in postcolonial countries where Indigenous people seek to protect their lands. The best-known example is the 2017 act of parliament in New Zealand that granted the whole Whanganui River rights as an independent entity in a settlement between the government and the Māori people. Guardians were appointed to speak and act on behalf of the river and enforce its rights. Other cases have followed suit.

Operating in the fictional mode of "as if," representation can stretch the bounds of imagination and restructure reality in ways that disrupt taken-for-granted divisions between human and nonhuman, persons and things, real and fictive (Brito Vieira 2020a). But it is not without problems.

The first problem is ventriloquism. This is a risk inherent in all representation, but—as Hobbes himself stressed—it is especially present where the entities represented cannot speak for themselves or at least cannot speak in ways that can be understood directly and require human mediation. By this he meant God and "the people," but we could easily add nonhuman beings and things. A question can thus be posed: Who is it that speaks when the representative speaks? Representatives accrue power by hiding behind the pretense that they are mere conveyors of words and instructions handed down or passed on to them by the represented. They thereby acquire a unique aura of authority and a potentially absolute, arbitrary—because it places itself beyond scrutiny—power. The antidote to this is the reflexivity of the representative system, by which I mean that the system must enable us to see representation for what it is: fallible attempts to speak on the represented's behalf. We are the real speakers, advancing claims about and for nonhuman beings and things—namely, claims about their present condition and how we ought to act to secure their flourishing. Although some may have a special claim to speak for them—professional ecologists, environmental campaigners, and Indigenous peoples being cases in point—their claims about and for nonhuman natural constituencies need justification so that they may be held accountable to one another as well as to the media, the general public, and so on. Given the structurally unequal position in which nonhuman nature finds itself—because it cannot question or revoke any representative it is assigned or who chooses to speak for it—the risk is high that nonhuman nature's interests are ventriloquized by, and made subservient to, those who purport to represent them. As such, it is vital that no one representative has a monopoly over its representation, as this would facilitate environmental domination, understood as the state of "being subject to insufficiently checked or unlimited power" and of being "treated as a mere instrument for the profit or power of another without regard to one's own well-being" (Krause 2020, 446). This is best avoided where the representative system comprises multiple representatives who examine one another's claims to represent and check them for problems. Going back to the example of the Whanganui River, the advancement of its interests, health, and well-being has been entrusted to the Te Pou Tupua, an office comprising two people, or two guardians, one nominated by the iwi (the Whanganui River tribes) and one nominated by a government minister.

When considering the representation of the nonspeaking, the question that immediately poses itself is how representatives for nonhuman nature will be appointed.[5] Where the focus is political representation, this question cannot be asked apart from a second one: How are these representatives going to relate to—and, just as importantly, compete with—the representatives of conventional human constituencies? One could treat nonhuman nature as just another constituency, to be represented within the political process alongside everyone else. Trustees for nonhuman nature could be elected if, for instance, a certain number of reserved seats were set aside for nonhuman nature's representatives. One would still need to decide who could run for those seats and who could vote for the candidates, but the advantage of the electoral model is that it seems to place the interests of human and nonhuman constituencies on an equal level.

But this leveling out is deceptive (Brito Vieira and Runciman 2008, 187). Only representatives of human constituencies are answerable to constituents who, being members of the franchise, can actually vote and thereby dissent from their chosen course of action. Given the key role that dissent plays in the exercise of control over any form of representation, it is hard to see how treating nonhuman constituencies like any other constituency would not result in their marginalization. Unlike human constituencies, which belong to both the class of the enfranchised and that of the represented, they cannot hold their representatives accountable nor (de-)authorize their decisions in time.

It is true that this might not be as relevant as it seems, insofar as representation can also be regarded in terms of mere coincidence between the interests voiced by representatives and the interests of the represented supported by processes of surrogate accountability. For instance, one could argue that scientific knowledge about nonhuman nature and identification with it (for instance, in the case of Indigenous peoples who conceive themselves as *of* nature or activists internalizing nature's interests as their own) could support greater coincidence. To think of this as a matter of coincidence, however, is to misconceive the process: what is happening here is a co-constitution of interests and identities through cultural and political work. Equally, the fact remains that representative thinking across species faces considerable limitations. Nonhuman nature's interests are not limited to the overlap they may have with human interests, and nonhuman nature could never actually say "no" to what is being proposed as an area of contention or overlap. Furthermore, where seats have been reserved for the representation of nonhuman natural constituencies, representatives of human constituents may think that they no longer need to be concerned with the representation of nonhuman interests. Since the former's seats will always be fewer than the latter's, this can leave nonhuman interests marginalized and ultimately unrepresented. This only changes if "nature's interests come to be internalized by a sufficient number of people with sufficient leverage in the political system for nature's interests to secure the protection that they deserve" (Goodin 1996, 844). However, given the co-constitution of interests through claims-making, claims-making by representatives who self-conceive as representatives *for* traditional constituencies (as opposed to nonhuman ones) may be an obstacle to internalization. This is all to say that nonhuman constituencies, even when placed in the class of the represented and thus represented alongside traditional human constituencies, remain in a political relationship of structural inequality.

In the dynamics of representative politics, it therefore seems that nonhuman nature is always in a position of structural vulnerability and disadvantage if it has to compete on equal terms (Brito Vieira and Runciman 2008, 187). It is therefore reasonable to think that the representation of nonhuman nature might need special protection. This points in the direction of constitutional protections and/or the appointment of officers entrusted with special powers designed to ensure that representative officers pursue environmental welfare. Constitutional protections can take multiple forms, from the recognition of nature or natural entities as having rights or legal personhood to directive principles requiring the state to promote environmental values. The latter range "from general obligations to protect the environment to more specific obligations to protect certain natural resources or pursue certain policy objectives" (Weis 2018, 846). While constitutional rights provisions allocate institutional responsibilities for giving effect to environmental protections to courts, directive principles allocate them to political branches, especially the legislative. While legislatures may be "better positioned than courts to respond to social needs and values, particularly where this requires making complex and contentious decisions about resource allocation and trade-offs between competing social welfare priorities," there is a danger that such conflicts between competing priorities will always be resolved to the detriment of environmental values (Weis 2018, 859). Besides constitutional protections, another mechanism for institutionalizing the environmental representation of nonhuman nature is environmental ombudspersons with far-reaching powers to speak and act authoritatively on its behalf. An ombudsperson is an independent institution, outside the representative state branches, whose function is to influence them in their actions and secure their conformity to environmental norms. The ombudsperson's powers can be defined more or less extensively. It can be tasked with ensuring articulation between different dimensions of government departments' environmental planning and management and can have powers to carry out information campaigns, *ex officio* investigations, and reactive inquiries in response to citizens' complaints. It can act as a parliamentary commissioner, ensuring that the environment and its interests are always considered and, as much as possible, safeguarded in legislation. Besides reviewing legislative proposals, it can also take the initiative to recommend legislative action when required. Despite having potentially far-reaching power, the ombudsperson merely issues recommendations, which may or may not be followed by the relevant authorities.

One does not have to be unduly skeptical about the political efficacy of ombudspersons to wonder what their real impact might be (Brito Vieira and Runciman 2008, 188–89). An ombudsperson is normally nominated by and formally accountable to elected officials—a democratically elected parliament, for example—since those whom they represent cannot consent. As I have argued previously, any form of political representation must set its claims not simply against nonrepresentation but against rival forms of representation. Airing environmental interests is hardly enough, as it does not give those interests a force that can compete with that of traditional constituencies when there is a conflict. As such, any ombudsperson's effectiveness in the delivery of its formal role will depend on more informal ties. It will need to look outside for support and recognition from those regarded as nature's advocates and from the general public, which might translate into political clout. The ombudsperson alone can do very little, but the combination of different layers of representation might have more power. Nonetheless, they would have to get hold of the public imagination before they could get hold of politics.

A different set of difficulties surrounding the political representation of the environment derives from trusteeship itself (Brito Vieira and Runciman 2008, 190–91). As Hobbes stressed, the representation of entities who cannot authorize their own representatives depends on two conditions. First, there needs to be a clear sense of who has the right to appoint a representative, and this is usually someone with a particular claim over the represented. Second, those appointing the representative need to be willing to stand back and let the representative perform their role. Both conditions are hard to meet when what is at stake is the political representation of such entities as "the environment." The entity is so large that it is hard for anyone to assert a particular claim over its representation. Those who do have particular claims—for example, environmental organizations with a track record of taking environmental interests seriously—will always be suspected of some partiality. Even where the represented entity is more clearly delimited (as in the case of the Whanganui River) and those having particular claims to represent it are relatively clearly identifiable (such as the Māori people), the power to appoint representatives will still lie with the state, and the state may be unlikely to give representatives the powers they need to represent effectively. For instance, even where a river is legally recognized as a living being and a legal person, it may not be given rights to the water that flows in its banks.

This takes me to my final point: the potential and limitations of legal personhood. Legal personhood has the power to establish nonhuman natural beings and things as subjects rather than simply objects of law. Through it, rivers like the Whanganui can be recognized as indivisible and living beings, endowed with the right to exist, flourish, and thrive and to demand restoration if they are damaged, even if the action causing the damage is not illegal. The recognition of the river as a subject of law, and a holder of rights, confers on it a worth independent of its use value for us. The actioning of these rights depends—as we have seen, following Hobbes—on authorized representatives acting on the river's behalf. Even if the river cannot object to their action, it can be protected from ventriloquism by being assigned more than one guardian (in the case of the Whanganui River, one from the crown and the other from the Whanganui iwi, the peoples of the river), with none being allowed to speak or act singularly on the river's behalf. Furthermore, legal personhood, where giving the person self-ownership, has the potential to condition private property by the rights of the ecosystems that cross it. But for all its "legal-operational" and "socio-psychic" potential, the extension of legal personhood and rights to nature is not without its detractors (Stone 1972, 458). Many worry that the master's tools—namely, the very system of law that structures and protects property rights and capitalism—will never be able to dismantle the master's house and, indeed, that any mask assigned by law will inevitably conceal, assimilate, and disfigure the singularity and living materiality of the represented (Esposito 2012, 8–9). To this, objections of a more practical nature can be added. Corporations are the Goliaths of legal personhood; nonhuman nature, its David. Without being adequately financially resourced (through sizeable trust funds and other mechanisms), without mechanisms preventing the capture of nature's guardians by corporate interests, without a differentiated assignment of rights to natural persons and legal persons and between legal persons themselves (namely, corporations and environmental legal persons) establishing their hierarchy, and without making sure that our responsibilities do not get simply devolved to nonhuman nature on account of its personhood, the battle is lost before it starts. Additionally, rights talk, given that rights are designed to protect interests, may encourage viewing our relationship with nonhuman nature as a battle of interests. This is misguided because, as Val Plumwood comments, rather than "just another interest group or another speaker," nonhuman nature must be taken as "the condition for all our interests and for all our speech" (1995, 142).

These practical objections carry considerable weight. They point toward ways in which political representation and legal devices can be hamstrung or limited. But the anti-legalistic and anti-representational stance underpinning some of them unduly discounts what Hobbes saw as representation's generative potential, its capacity to alter and fundamentally reorganize social and political relations, to which we could add its capacity to "animate, and be reinvigorated by, emancipatory struggles" (Gündoğdu 2021, 571; see also Brito Vieira 2020a, 2009). Take, for instance, how representation's plasticity can be too easily neglected by those in the materialist camp. The political implication of the porosity and entanglements between nature and culture, the nonhuman and the human, they sometimes argue, is that it no longer makes sense to politically represent and thereby seek to "preserve a nature that is defined by being not human" (Purdy 2015, para. 6.6). This conclusion is overstated, however: it is not clear why the acknowledgment of human-nonhuman entanglements and the abandonment of a romantic notion of nature as pristine need overrule the representation of entities like "wild nature" or "wild animals" as necessarily depoliticizing. As has been noted, this can remain a "thoroughly political strategy," where it advances "an environmentalist strategy for resisting the logic of mastering the planet" (Thaler 2022, 106n38).

Ecological Denial as Effect

There is a question, however, about whether this logic is resistible from within a representative system seemingly unable to reckon with human to human, let alone human to nonhuman, entanglements—or to address major areas of mass production and mass consumption in which these entanglements are mostly at stake. Environmental injustice intersects with many other forms of structural injustice (racial, gender-based, and so on). This means that some humans "share the same expendable condition as nature" and are given the (silent) status of nature, not because they stand naturally closer to nature but because their own powerlessness and exclusion produce that closeness (Plumwood 1995, 139; 1993, 32). Where they are kept at the representative system's doors, the representation of nature is "hollowed" of its potential avant-garde agents.

The impetus for ecological change is sometimes thought to come from "ecological reflexivity," with deliberative democracy believed to be the right institutional setting for achieving it (Schlosberg 2007, 192; Dryzek 1995, 2000). The reasoning here is that environmental problems are highly complex and demand the "wisdom of the crowd"—knowledge claims, interpretations of nature, listening for nature's signals and ensuring their representation by proxy, and the like—to arrive at informed, reflexive decisions (Schlosberg 2007). Ecological reflexivity is a critique of "authoritarian environmentalism," relying on centralized, technocratic solutions to environmental problems and an affirmation of democracy as better able to detect, adapt to, and correct those problems. "Democracy" here means deliberative democracy, showing the capacity to support the involvement, recognition, and representation of "nature" as a silenced constituency in integrated opinion-formation and decision-making processes.

What seems to be missing from this account of reflexivity is the understanding that "ecological denial" may be structured into our democratic representative systems (Plumwood 1995, 134). One of the strengths of democracy seems to be its capacity for problem-identification, adaptation, and correction (see Plumwood 1995; see also Brito Vieira 2021). But this capacity is severely hampered where the representative system insulates itself against "representations of the ecological crisis, refracted through the lives and experiences of a diverse range of stakeholders" (Thaler 2022, 147).

To put it bluntly, representative democracies silence the ecological crisis on account of structural biases and structural inequalities (across race, gender, class, nation, and land; between humans and nonhumans; between current and future generations) driving the miscounting of the rights, needs, capabilities, and well-being of the most-affected constituencies. Given the entanglements between environmental and human exploitation, the politics of ecological conflict hinges on "distributing exposure to undesirable things" (Beck 1995, 9). While some ecological undesirables are evenly spread across the population, many "impact differentially in terms mediated by privilege" (Plumwood 1995, 138). What this means is that structures of power molded by political and economic systems leave some extremely vulnerable to climate change and the toxicity of ecosystems while empowering others to redistribute harms down and insulate themselves from their worst effects. The latter also tend to hold the power to produce environmental harm, as they are "likely overall to be creating the most pollution and [ . . . ] have the strongest economic stake in maintaining forms of accumulation which exploit nature" (Plumwood 1995, 138). This has at least two political implications. First, since the formal representative system favors the wealthy in its decision-making, its decisions are likely to be positively responsive to the pursuit of particular forms of accumulation, production, and consumption while discounting the signs and costs—financially tangible and financially intangible—of environmental degradation. Second, constituencies disproportionally affected by these costs are already marginalized within the system—and increasingly so, given rising inequalities—and claims-making around lines of ecological conflict is unlikely from inside that system. As such, either the most affected self-represent, engaging in climate activism, or their claims go unarticulated. What is more, not all articulatory practices will constitute them as a progressive force, especially if they give them no reason to believe that the costs of tackling climate change will not fall massively on their shoulders despite the fact that they are less liable. As Carson hinted, collective action on climate depends on the recognition of our "toxic connectedness," of differences in "the toxic load we create and distribute," and of the economic and political regimes that implicate us in its production (Shotwell 2016, 83). Neither a shared condition nor coinciding interests form political actors, however. Only political representation does: it alone creates groups by representing them as such and such, by putting them into a meaningful relationship with one another (and others). Representation is necessary to provide frameworks against which it becomes possible to form new political identities, recognize common grievances, generate ties between each other (human and human, human and nonhuman), and to side for or against other constituencies to drive effective ecological change.

It is also for this reason that we should resist facile explanations for ecological and other democratic failures as a matter of ignorance, lack of concern, or reckless disregard for others (see, e.g., Achen and Bartels 2016). To understand citizens' actions and omissions, we need to inquire into the relationship between political actors, institutions, and constituencies. The average citizen's relative apathy in the face of a climate-changed world is not a cause but an outcome: namely, it is a "constituency effect" of a far-reaching failure of politics (Disch 2021, 30–33). The scale of the problem is such that individual actors inevitably feel powerless. Representations of a risky and highly uncertain future are disorienting. The sense that the dice have already been thrown, and the future is thus sealed, means that there is little reason to act or care. Yet collective action is necessary, and it depends on coordination and orientation. Still, politics is failing on both accounts. It remains too narrow, too captured, and too uninspired to imagine ways out or incite in citizens "a desire for being and living otherwise" (Thaler 2022, 3). Since "imagination and action depend on each other," since "action [is] facilitated through imagination" and "imagination stirred by action," it is no wonder most of us find ourselves stuck (52). Hence the slow-burning climate denialism, not in the sense of "literal" denial (of something happening or being true) or in the sense of "interpretive" denial (where facts are accepted but their meaning disputed), though both still exist, but in the sense of "implicatory" denial, where information is not disputed but "the psychological, political or moral implications" that should follow are, in a way, suspended or only marginally acted upon (Cohen 2001, 8).

The concept of "socially organized denial" has been advanced to explain the workings of "implicatory denial" in relation to climate change (Norgaard 2011, 58). Climate denial, we are told, is best understood not as an individual failure to do or say but as something socially produced and consisting in the active—albeit hardly ever deliberate or conscious—"organization of [troubling] information about global warming, in such a way that it remains outside the sphere of everyday reality" (60). In this context, "outside" does not mean unspoken but confined to the realm of small talk, rather than driving consequential political conversation.

Denial as mere negation is always unfeasible, as the very act of denying something implies that this something is never totally gone (Cohen 2001, 22). This is why it takes effort—a strenuous effort, even—to deny, to resist the moral and political implications of our climate-changed world. Although we know that this world is already upon us, most of us back off from accepting its consequences. We struggle to relinquish our carbon-fed capitalist freedoms and feed on stories of "green" growth, technological breakthroughs, or space colonization to keep to the ordinary ongoingness of our existence despite knowing better. A no-futures future, a future not enlivened by progress as we have come to understand it, is unthinkable, so we try hard not to think. In writing this, my intent is not to undo the work of this chapter by individualizing or moralizing a responsibility that can only be widely and unevenly shared. Far from it. The scale of the problem is too large for that, and the power of individual actions too little to make the necessary difference. Faced with this mismatch, we are left with two options: to give up or to delude ourselves that small steps will be sufficient. The explanation and solution for the predicament in which we find ourselves is one and the same: politics. Faced with our politics' short-termism, narrow-mindedness, and interest-boundness, faced with our representative system's closures, our temptation may well be to sign off. But to put a future in our no-futures future, we need to put pressure on the ideological closures of the present to make room for an ecological democracy in which the representation of the nonhuman world and the participation of the constituencies most affected by climate are *likely* to be effective. Taking politics into our hands may be our only hope for reconnecting society around the promise of engaging with the nonhuman world in new ways—ways that will represent a shock to the system. The possibility of collective agency needs to be assumed and acted upon to be created. We depend on it to avoid the endless word of silent death.

## CONCLUSION

As scholars and citizens, we tend to see democratic agency in terms of voice, with silence understood as the meta-figure of its negation. Thus understood, silence is singular and flat, the litany of the *un-* that democracy had better undo: the *un*articulated, the *un*speakable, the *un*voiced, the *un*named, the *un*remembered, the *un*-hearable, the *un*accounted for.

It is undeniable that silence can be passive omission, a not-doing or not-being something, enforced through a series of impairments and subversions of our capacity for political action. Silencings can prevent political action from taking place and, even where it does occur, can ensure that it does not mean or do what was intended as well as make certain that its effects are lost and its demands deprived of normative or practical purchase. Silence might thus just be an effect, the effect of the exercise of power, using control over communication and information flows, speaking hierarchies, and institutional mechanisms for representing popular voice to immobilize the capacity for dissent and to buttress the tacit accommodations that sustain relations of domination and oppression. It can also be an effect that no longer needs enforcing by specific agents and whose blame cannot be apportioned, a speech-related injustice in which we all unwittingly partake to the degree that it is built into our social processes, institutions, and structures.

To see silence as effect rather than cause is vital for challenging the pathologization of silence as nothing more than self-interested individual choice and for politicizing previously neutralized areas of social and political action. As such, in this book I have foregrounded the importance of asking and researching why citizens "might 'not do' or 'not be' potential things," so that politics may be inscribed and—indeed—implicated again in silences that do not represent a power to hold back but a politically constituted impotence (S. Scott 2018, 4). This, as I have shown, is the case with nonhuman constituencies whose political speechlessness is an effect of our definition and constitution of the political and whom we continue to ventriloquize by attributing to them a transparent voice—or having their signals "speak for themselves." Or indeed by simply speaking and acting instead of them, thus closing off the possibility of any relation or conflict of interest. The same pattern recurs in totalizing claims to a purported "silent majority," which, instead of listening for and seeking to be responsive to citizen silences and helping realize the potential of their voices, try to silence them and make them speak univocally.

Against the blanket assumption that all silence means apathy or political disengagement, I have argued that to choose silence, either consciously or unconsciously, is not necessarily to choose political passivity over action. Nor does the practice of silence incontrovertibly reflect a lack of interest or care for politics or the world we share with others. Even where withdrawal into silence represents a failure to act politically, even where it expresses a drive to stay away from known injustices or complex problems of collective action, the silence produced around these issues is still something that needs to be actively, if not necessarily consciously, borne, not least because injustices and problems of collective action cannot simply be wished away. Their ignoring, non-discussion, or barely superficial addressing requires an ongoing investment of the self and, often, the cooperation of others. Taken as a phenomenon that is socially created and socially sustained, omissive silences raise questions of social responsibility. They also—more than anything else—raise questions of political responsibility: for failures to clarify lines of conflict, for failures to structure choice meaningfully, for failures to open up alternatives and define possibilities for political action. All of this results in the non-mobilization or the demobilization of constituencies; it induces their *un*-acting and co-opts them into reproducing a state of silence and powerlessness.

This book has shown silence to be sometimes what it was always thought to be: the site of the *un-*. It has argued that silenc*ing* is an insidious form of structural injustice and, moreover, one about which we are too often complacent. But it has also shown that silence can *be* and, most importantly, *do* much else. My intent in writing the book has been to go beyond the speaker/silence(d) binary to pluralize our understanding of silence and foreground the dearth of interest in the potential of silence as a form of politics, one that might be recommended from a democratic perspective.

Democratic theory takes speech as the norm, in the sense of its being both the most common and the most desirable. However, the notion that democratic citizenship is regularly exercised in a speech mode flies in the face of reality. There are very few occasions in which we, as citizens, find ourselves articulating political opinions or verbally passing political judgments. Silence is in this sense the norm, speech the exception—but for this reason it also remains "unmarked" and largely undetected by democratic theory's radar. The belief that silence is politically unnoteworthy and has no place in the "repertoire of good democratic practice" (MacKenzie and Moore 2020, 432) is exactly what this book has sought to refute through its analysis of the workings of silence in different spheres of democracy as a way of life and as a form of government.

For all its importance as a legitimating ground of democracy, citizens' discursive engagement—let alone their idealized engagement in sustained, reasoned discussion of public affairs—commands a disproportionate and oftentimes acritical attention in democratic theory, with the "talking cure" being prescribed indiscriminately to all ailments of democracy. Also, for this reason, we have a pressing need for a democratic theory of silence, where silence is no longer passively defined by the absence of speech but comes into view as a modality of democratic action and interaction in its own right (Brekhus 1998). This book has sought to contribute to this theory and create an appetite for further study.

That silence is a key constituent part of politics—and of democratic politics at that—should be apparent even if one embraces the dominant, talk-centric view of democracy. Between speech and silence there is a mutuality: the ability to make silence belongs to those who can speak, just as the ability to speak belongs to those who can keep silent. If the legitimacy of democracy depends on discursive practices of civic engagement and self-disclosure, then the right to silence must be democracy's bedrock: speech cannot be free, I have shown, if it does not include the capacity for self-limitation.

A prerequisite of democratic speech, silence is also a requirement of its everyday implementation, insofar that listening, silence, and speech are interdependent. There is no space for speech or political dialogue, let alone compromise or transformation, in a democratic culture that knows "how to speak but not how to listen" (Fiumara 1990, 27). As Susan Bickford emphasizes, and as I have shown in my discussion of democracy-promoting and democracy-hindering conversational silences in chapter 3, a genuinely listening silence, which listens to and for others (even or especially in their silences), enables us to *be with* someone else across difference, while dominative speech or excessive verbiage "fill[s] up the space between us and keep[s] from actually hearing [and working on] our distance from one another" (1996, 154). For a communicative democracy, holding back speech to actively listen to others in their expression but also in their difference is as essential as the equality of speakers (as well as being essential to this equality). In other words, such a democracy must preserve a listening space that makes common without assuming communality or expecting consensus.[1]

It is thus perhaps a symptom of democratic culture's hubris about speech that we, as democrats, should value speech and downgrade silence; take speech as reason or logical argument and silence as dumbness; see speech as a medium for building and fostering relations and underestimate silence as a way of relating and experiencing a relationship with others. Rather than the site of unreflectiveness or the condition of those who have nothing to say, silence, as we have seen, can be an active and reflective way of engaging politically and advancing fundamental democratic values, whether that be by defamiliarizing us from the speech we habitually take for granted or as plainly evident (and thus silencing) and that way creating the context in which new claims can be heard; refusing to play one's ascribed part in the polis for the sake of a more just division of parts in the future; intentionally moderating one's speaking part or the influence exercised by one's voice to give way to others and foreground their influence in the political process, thereby enacting equity, equality, and reciprocity; enacting forms of individual and collective subjectivation that deviate from the sovereigntist model of the self-speaking, self-transparent, agent who has control over their actions and the responses they generate; or creating constitutional abeyances and gaps that defer to and invite future political action.

If all of this is true and necessary to recognize, it is equally important to note that the book has not limited itself to recovering silence as an equally relevant, but overlooked, "other side" of speech. Instead, it has argued that speech and silence are not simply complementary but co-constitutive and coextensive, both alike and *un*like. Certainly, there is silence that is articulate, that says something in context and is a kind of speech. However, there is also silence that resists articulation, determination, signification, and verbal meaning. So there is silence that is a sign but, significantly, there is also silence that is produced so as *not* to be a sign—and silence that is embodied action in the world offering a resistance to its linguistic reinscription. Such silences are responsible, therefore, for forms of political action and political sociality distinct from those grounded in speech or speechlike silent acts.

In bringing out commissive silence as a complex mode of political action, I have challenged an idea that governs much work on democracy as a deliberative system: that speech is the sole "doer" of politics, that it is exhaustive of the *proper* modes of political engagement. The preeminence conferred on speech is responsible for the denigration of silence as apolitical or antipolitical. The resulting casting of silence as an "outsider" to civic engagement and political participation is, in turn, liable for the alignment of silence with quietism, a term haunted by its negative association with passivity, complicity, acquiescence, and withdrawal from the world. This is silence as deserting politics, fellow citizens, and all manner of care for "worldly things," things that in Ella Myers's felicitous formulation constitute "common and contentious object[s] of concern" around which citizens mobilize (2013, 14).

Pushing back against this, I have shown silent political action to be ubiquitous and complex. As a practice, silence blends seeming opposites—disengagement and engagement, *un*acting and acting, nonparticipation and participation, absence and presence—while effectively cutting across them to both negotiate existing conditions of political existence and transform them.

Given my interest in the political work of silence, I have paid a considerable amount of attention to both omissive and commissive silences, but given my intention of adding silence to the repertoire of good democratic practice, I have brought out the work of silences that are consciously and reflectively chosen, that constitute a positive action of nonperformance, including those that constitute a public performative act. These silences, I have shown, are distinctively agential. Rather than doing *nothing*, they distinguish themselves by marking the *doing* or the *being* of a non-something and by being the site of much political action besides. They are actively chosen, positive performances of nonperformance that are conscious, reflexive, and demanding, requiring skilled and discerning enactment.

Such commissive silences do not just do a non-something. They also do something *in* and *with* the silence. They abstain from speech, for example, to give way to others' speaking; they hold back from exercising influence or decisive voice to bolster the influence of others or make their voice decisive; they withhold constitutional determination to open space for politics; they publicly perform silence to enact and protest inaudibility. This "something" is a capacious category, and the contradictory nature of its affordances underpins the unsettled role of silence in democracy. The book has acknowledged the ambivalence of this "something" while seeking to provide theoretical resources for distinguishing silences that are omissive from silences that are commissive, silences that are disempowering from silences that are empowering, empowered silences that are democracy-promoting from silences (both disempowered and empowered) that undermine core democratic norms.

Among the silences whose democratic potential I have explored here were silences of unsaying, protesting, resisting, refusing, boycotting, paying heed, bearing witness, being present, gathering together differently, and enacting new, more democratic forms of political agency. In some cases, we saw silence staged as a form of political activism claiming a share in power; in other cases, silence was engaged covertly as a form of resistance to power but also as a resource for self-reinvention and the creation of community. We saw instances of silence reclaiming for itself the visibility and agency of voice, cases of silence acting as a linguistic form and articulating a message. But we also saw cases where silence deliberately cultivated imprecision, indetermination, ambiguity, opacity—simply put, silence that resisted the demand for meaning.

This resistance was sometimes used as a tactic to escape power, or at least gain the freedom to act around it and in its interstices. But it was also deployed as a means of opposition to ideological speech, its closures and its exclusions. While there is a tendency to conflate empowered silence with silence that acts as a signal, we have seen that silence is politically powerful not only when it recaptures the power of speech but also when it suspends, outplays, or thwarts it. To be more specific, we saw silence being used to discontinue taken-for-granted meanings predicated on ideologies of oppositionality; to suspend the discursive field determining the subject positions from which claims can be made; to break down the communal terms by which people are held in relation to one another; and to interrogate the remainders created by the use of ideals of unity and generality to enforce less (self-)questioning speech communities. The keeping of silence was, in all these cases, intent on reopening and sustaining a discursive space that had been closed down. To this end, silence refrained from becoming itself a sign immediately overlaid with a caption—that is, a sign shutting down the reopened discursive space with its new hegemonic meaning.

As Roland Barthes warned, "to oppose dogmatic speech, one must not produce equally dogmatic silence" (2005, 28). In politics, dogmatic silence means silence placing itself beyond speech, silence that is permanent, absolute, an end in itself. This type of silence is profoundly undemocratic. Hence, while a literal, blunt silence can be a temporary but radical political act necessary to create a split within hegemonic common sense and enact a breakdown in communication, it cannot be the endgame: it must always gesture *toward* and prepare *for* the possibility of resuming the exchange.

We commonly understand self-assertion and control as core elements of political agency. In turn, these capacities seem to require voice, understood as authoritative and effective "speaking" that can solicit a response to one's reasons, concerns, interests, preferences, and claims. Thus understood, the point of political agency is to impose "one's own will, even against opposition" (Weber 1978, 38), to influence collective decision-making by exercising a degree of control over decision-makers' access to resources and recognition (Gray 2023, 821). We have seen that, in certain circumstances, silent political agency can exercise this kind of power over, and the associated power to influence, what gets done in a political community. But I hope to have shown that a democratic theory of silence would be greatly impoverished by focusing exclusively on the contentious struggle over power relations without examining the ways in which silent political agency supports and produces cooperative and prefigurative democratic politics more generally.

While it is vital to empower democracy-promoting silences, it is equally important to note that power and empowerment are different things. An action can enact power and yet not be empowering, in the sense of giving some/body power *over* or even *to*. Silent political agency is sometimes a power over our power of utterance, often deployed in order to abate it. Admittedly, this exertion of power over power can sometimes be empowering in the above sense. As we have seen in chapter 1, since the subject is an effect of speech, the unsaying of one's self-naming may be a way of *un*acting essentialist views of identity and of establishing the conditions of possibility for alternative subjectivities that are born out of a process of continuous articulation, dis-articulation, and rearticulation. But, in other cases, the power that silence exerts over the power of speech is not meant to empower the subject exerting it. Instead, it constitutes a self-imposed moderating power intent on more equitably distributing voice and influence across the political community. To put it clearly, by choosing silence, an agent may be exercising power over their own ability to exercise authoritative and effective voice, to command, prescribe, commit, define, or determine. Their choice of silence may then constitute a reflective decision to exercise less control than they could have over democratic processes.

Where commissive silences partially abdicate power over what gets done, they may seem to be failings of agency. And yet they may well be the reverse: powerfully affirmative of one's *democratic* agency. For while democratic political agency implies a degree of influence or control over what gets done, it also implies knowing when to refrain from exercising that agency. The book has offered multiple examples of this. Silences about disagreements of principle can be a constructive force in reaching constitutional agreements while also going a long way to create mutual respect and reciprocity between the disagreeing parties. Self-imposed restrictions of voice or vote may empower the most affected to exercise effective influence over collective decisions. Silences may defer to the future, thus conveying a sense of epistemic humility in acknowledging that it may not yet be the moment to act and lock in commitments given uncertainty or limits of time, experience, and capacity. To borrow Dennis Thompson's apt phrase, it is via the silences they leave in constitutions that present sovereigns seek to "represent future sovereigns by acting as trustees of the democratic process," which they leave open to them (2005, 248). In all these cases, silence is a means to relinquish (a degree of) control with the aim of distributing it in more equitable ways in both the present and the future.

While some silences exert an undemocratic power by limiting accountability, contestation, and revisability, silences like the ones listed above enact an acceptance of the open, contingent, and uncertain character of democratic politics. This acceptance is not to be confused with passivity. Here as elsewhere, a passive receptivity would preclude relationality. Similarly, a relationality limited to what falls under words, bound as they are to preexisting concepts and settled contexts, could preclude receptiveness. Genuine receptiveness implies the need to be active and is responsible for a series of effects that we saw commissive silences producing: rupturing contexts, effecting conceptual suspension, and moderating authorized verbalizations for the sake of verbalizations yet to be, to mention a few. An active, reflexive silence can be politically enabling. It can enact a careful orientation toward one another and toward worldly things that are thus allowed to have an effect on us, to interpellate us, to challenge us. As something holding people in a relation of presence and attention to each other and to aspects of their common world, silence is a "yielding which binds and joins" (Dauenhauer 1979, 438). Political action transforming the conditions of the possible is impossible without such a silence.

# NOTES

## INTRODUCTION

1. Some conceptualizations of silence inspired by the disability literature risk leaving it so undefined that the concept lacks distinctiveness and has limited empirical traction. See, for instance, the conceptualization of silence as simply the "presence (of embodied action)" (Rollo 2019, 438).
2. "Silence"—the word and the concept—is used several times in the poem, which constitutes a thorough study of silence in all its complexity. Also, almost all reviews of the book have "silence" in their title and engage "silence" as the main concept through which the poem is to be read.
3. While the poem starts with deafness *to* and silence *before* authority as forms of resistance, as the poem unfolds, silence's capacity to hold opposites in tension—resistance, refusal, defiance, but also complacency and complicity—comes to the fore.
4. "Our country woke up next morning and refused to hear soldiers" (Kaminsky 2009, 14).
5. See the Oxford English Dictionary, s.v. "silence," https://www.oed.com/dictionary/silence_n.
6. Big Mijo's silent dance protest can be viewed here: https://www.youtube.com/watch?v=tF-5ySMAR6A.

## CHAPTER I

1. The full interview with Riggs can be viewed here: https://www.youtube.com/watch?v=wGgtVpjcqak.
2. Famously, an ad run by Pat Buchanan's 1992 campaign against George Bush accused Bush of funding pornographic films with tax dollars.
3. This "bending and blending" is not free from the risk of recapture. As bell hooks notes in her essay on Jennie Livingston's film *Paris Is Burning* (1990), the scenes of Black men appearing in drag are both "progressive and reactionary." While they oppose "a heterosexist representation of black manhood," the idea/ideal of womanness and femininity on display "is totally personified by whiteness," so that the impending but never quite visible figure in the film is that of the "white male patriarch" and a "ruling class culture and power elite" (hooks 1992, 149, 147, 148, 150).
4. Roland Barthes explains this clearly in relation to how one might answer journalists' questions about one's sexuality: "[T]o give imprecise answers to precise questions: this imprecision of the answer, even if it is perceived as a weakness, is an indirect way of demystifying the question" (2005, 107).
5. This possibility may not be immediately apparent, given the strong ontological and metaphysical premises that seem to be attached to apophasis in the theological realm, where it appears to point toward the limitations of language to comprehend or express what is ultimately real. But the obstacle is not insurmountable, since even within

theology, there have been attempts at the apophatic framing of a "God without Being" (Marion 2012).

6. Nicholas of Cusa's (1401–1464) notion of *coincidentia oppositorum* is especially relevant here. For a helpful discussion, see Bond 1997, 22.

7. Bobbie Johnson, "Privacy No Longer a Social Norm, Says Facebook Founder," *Guardian*, January 11, 2010, https://www.theguardian.com/technology/2010/jan/11/facebook-privacy.

8. Privacy can be understood in terms of access and/or control. As Julie Inness puts it, "Privacy may work by separating a realm of the agent's life from the access of others, or it may work by providing the agent with control over a realm of her life" (1992, 23).

## CHAPTER 2

1. Miranda v. Arizona, 384 US 436 (1966). In 1966, many of the safeguards now in place to ensure that police questioning is conducted without oppression or improper inducement were not in place, including electronic recording of custodial interrogations.

2. *Miranda*, 384 US at 436.

3. In this respect, however, claiming a First Amendment right to silence rather than the Fifth Amendment right against self-incrimination would probably be more effective.

4. This contrasts with the situation in the United Kingdom, where the choice of silence can contribute to proof of guilt, and thus suspects may feel an added pressure to speak or "volunteer" information because they have been warned that negative inferences can be made from unexplained silence.

5. Moran v. Burbine, 475 US 412, 426 (1986).

6. Berghuis v. Thompkins, 560 US 370 (2010), and Salinas v. Texas, 570 US 178 (2013).

7. And this is on top of the fact that empirical evidence shows that very few people assert their right to silence, and almost no one invokes it (again) after a waiver.

8. In effect, the requirement that one explicitly and unambiguously claim one's right to silence is symptomatic of a feeling of discomfort associated with those doing silence without verbally claiming it (Strauss 2008–9, 792).

9. West Virginia State Board of Education v. Barnette, 319 US 624 (1943), and Wooley v. Maynard, 430 US 705 (1977).

10. *Barnette*, 319 US, and *Maynard*, 430 US at 714.

11. *Barnette*, 319 US at 631, 633, 637.

12. *Barnette*, 319 US at 646.

13. This point is made by Justice Rehnquist in his dissent in *Maynard*, 430 US at 722.

14. *Barnette*, 319 US at 633.

15. Chicot v. Canada (Indian Affairs and Northern Development), 2008 FC 3, 129–30.

16. Pettit sees three benefits accruing from enfranchising silence: the "silent" citizen's active presence in the conversation of the community; the "silent" citizen's active participation in the generation of interpersonal consensus; and, finally, the "silent" citizen's capacity to participate actively in the regulation or control of another's behavior (1994).

17. Here I will not engage critically with these justifications, but for a critique of the notion of a "free market of ideas," please see chapter 3.

18. Consequentialist speech theories, suggesting that speech is protected when it advances specific individual or social interests such as democracy, truth, or autonomy, are not the only type of justification given for free speech protection. Larry Alexander

and others point to the inadequacy of such theories, proposing that instead of focusing "on the *effects* of regulations on messages intended and received" we turn to "the regulator's *purpose* in regulating" (Alexander 2003, 53). Once we focus on the "why question," "[f]reedom of expression is implicated whenever an activity is suppressed or penalized for the purpose of preventing a message from being received" (41).

19. Spence v. Washington, 418 US 405 (1974); my emphasis.

20. The overturning of binaries was, of course, fully in keeping with the Zen tendency to dissolve dualities.

21. This is one of the reasons why classifying *4'33"* as a work of conceptual art might have been rejected by Cage. Cage stresses the thought process going into the conceptualization of the piece but also its unintentionality. Conceptual art places agency, consciousness, and intention at the center of artistic production.

22. See Kostelanetz 1988, 12.

23. To make my argument, I do not need to directly address the question of what kind of artwork *4'33"* is. Those interested in the question of what art form the piece belongs to have given various answers, including a literary work (Saw 2005, 469–70n8), performance art (Davies 1997, 461), conceptual art, as a specific form of performance art (Dodd 2018), and music (Seymour 2013). However, for all their differences, these commentators agree that there is a creative and artistic intention behind *4'33"*.

CHAPTER 3

1. Here is the link to the blog post: https://renieddolodge.co.uk/why-im-no-longer-talking-to-white-people-about-race/. The blog post text can also be found in the preface of Eddo-Lodge's 2017 Bloomsbury book. As she explains, "I've turned 'Why I'm No Longer Talking to White People About Race' into a book—paradoxically—to continue the conversation" (xv).

2. Judith Butler, "The Compass of Mourning," *London Review of Books*, October 19, 2023. While my argument is general in scope, Butler's focus in the piece is the difficulty of speaking about and to violence in the context of the 2023 conflict in Israel and Gaza.

CHAPTER 4

1. Atwood speaking to the *Guardian* on August 3, 2018; see Beaumont and Holpuch 2018.

2. Where conceptual efforts have been undertaken, they have not challenged the equation of silence with repression but unpicked the latter's mechanisms and the kind of wrong it constitutes (see, e.g., Hornsby and Langton 1998).

3. Belinda A. Stillion Southard offers a thorough examination of the Sentinels' rhetorical acts of mimesis emulating and parodying Wilson's rhetorical presidency (2011).

4. See "Who Are Women in Black?" on the Women in Black website, https://womeninblack.org/about-women-in-black/.

5. See "Not in Our Name: The Women in Black," Remembering Srebrenica, https://srebrenica.org.uk/what-happened/not-in-our-name-the-women-in-black.

6. "Not in Our Name: The Women in Black," Remembering Srebrenica.

7. This control extended to the excessive expression of grief in mourning commonly associated with women. Organized ritual was expected to bring it under control. Plutarch, commenting on Solon's funerary laws, stresses how women's mourning

was subjected "to a law which did away with disorder and licence." This association of women's "sound" with "noise" or the "uncontrolled outflow of sound" marking their otherness is integral to the ideology of gender (see A. Carson 1995).

8. See "Not in Our Name: The Women in Black," Remembering Srebrenica.

9. For instance, at least two Democratic representatives refused to participate in the minute of silence held on the House floor for the victims of a mass shooting in Las Vegas in 2017 that killed 58 people and wounded 489.

10. Public support increased even as violence against suffragists increased (in the form of incarceration, forced feeding, and the like), especially after America entered the First World War and they were labeled "traitors" or internal enemies.

11. On the communal aspects of Quaker silence, see also K. Ferguson 2003.

CHAPTER 5

1. For notorious exceptions, see Loughlin 2018 and Tribe 2018.

2. "A life without speech and without action," Arendt writes, "is literally dead to the world; it has ceased to be a human life because it is no longer lived among men" (1958, 176).

3. This constitutional silence also applies to territory (see Doyle 2018).

4. The 1787 Three-Fifths Compromise between the free and slave states established that the enslaved Black people of southern states would be legally considered three-fifths of the total population of persons. This was meant to settle the question of how states with different populations should be represented in Congress.

5. "Kutxi" is a nickname for Felisa Echegoyen and "Billy the Kid" for Antonio González Pacheco.

6. "Rules of construction" are sometimes inserted in constitutions to avoid reading "silence" as negation. Take, for instance, the Ninth Amendment of the US Constitution, which states, "The enumeration in the Constitution, of certain rights, should not be construed to deny or disparage others retained by the people." That is, lists are not to be taken as exhaustive, such that silence about a particular right—that is, the fact that it is not listed—would be construed as denying that right.

7. Sunsetting normally refers to a piece of emergency legislation that tries to strike a balance between the extraordinary measures needed to respond to a crisis and existing rules and standards. Recently, they have been associated with emergency legislation introduced in the wake of the terrorist attack of September 11 (for instance, the infamous Patriot Act included a sunset clause scheduled to be triggered at the end of 2005) and COVID-19 legislation. In the United Kingdom, for instance, section 89 of the Coronavirus Act states that most of the provisions will expire after two years.

CHAPTER 6

1. For a contrasting assessment of the sort of compulsory voting proposal I am discussing here, see Gray 2021b.

2. I thank Sean Gray for this formulation.

3. Michael Saward gives a role to images and symbols in claims-making (2010, 16), but the emphasis is on words and figurative language.

4. Discursive and visual representations can combine to establish the reality of a silent majority, as in the 1969 United States Information Agency propaganda film *The Silent Majority*.

5. Disch partly makes up for this deficit with her notion of "responsibility" (2012, 608).

CHAPTER 7

1. For the view that domesticated animals may be able to authorize and deauthorize their representatives, see Donaldson 2020, 723.

2. See, for example, Tobias Menely's study (2015) of eighteenth-century British philosophers and poet-advocates who, in turning their attention to animals' vocal and gestural communication, helped construct a shared normative and affective horizon leading up to the passing of the Cruel Treatment of Cattle Act in 1822 (also known as Martin's Act), the first piece of animal welfare legislation in the United Kingdom.

3. For an earlier attempt to model the political representation of nonhuman nature inspired by my work on Hobbes, see M. Brown 2017.

4. I would like to thank Sean Fleming for sharing with me his unpublished paper "Rivers Are People Too? On Legal Personhood for Nature." We would eventually work on the paper together, and our discussions have brought much clarity to my discussion of Hobbes on personhood in this chapter.

5. My argument here follows along the lines of the argument I have advanced with David Runciman for the representation of future generations; see Brito Vieira and Runciman 2008.

CONCLUSION

1. For the distinction between deliberative and communicative democracy, see I. Young 1996, 120.

# REFERENCES

Achen, Christopher, and Larry Bartels. 2016. *Democracy for Realists: Why Elections Do Not Produce Responsive Government*. Princeton, NJ: Princeton University Press.

Acheson, Kris. 2008. "Silence as Gesture: Rethinking the Nature of Communicative Silences." *Communication Theory* 18:535–55.

Adams, Tony. 2010. "Paradoxes of Sexuality, Gay Identity and the Closet." *Symbolic Interaction* 33:234–56.

Agamben, Giorgio. 1999. *Potentialities: Collected Essays in Philosophy*. Translated and edited by Daniel Heller-Roazen. Stanford, CA: Stanford University Press.

———. 2000. *Means Without End: Notes on Politics*. Translated by Vincenzo Binetti and Cesare Casarino. Minneapolis: University of Minnesota Press.

Alcoff, Linda. 1991. "The Problem of Speaking for Others." *Cultural Critique* 20:5–32.

———. 2000. "On Judging Epistemic Credibility: Is Social Identity Relevant?" In *Women of Color and Philosophy: A Critical Reader*, edited by Naomi Zack, 236–62. Hoboken, NJ: Wiley.

Alexander, Larry. 2003. "Freedom of Expression as Human Right." In *Protecting Human Rights: Instruments and Institutions*, edited by Tom Campbell, 39–79. Oxford: Oxford University Press.

American Memory. n.d. "Tactics and Techniques of the National Woman's Party Suffrage Campaign." Washington, DC: Library of Congress. https://www.loc.gov/static/collections/women-of-protest/images/tactics.pdf.

Anderson, José F. 2009. "Freedom of Association, the Communist Party, and the Hollywood Ten: The Forgotten First Amendment Legacy of Charles Hamilton Houston." *McGeorge Law Review* 40:25–54.

Anker, Elisabeth. 2022. *Ugly Freedoms*. Durham, NC: Duke University Press.

Arendt, Hannah. 1958. *The Human Condition*. Chicago: University of Chicago Press.

———. 2006. *On Revolution*. New York: Penguin. Orig. pub. 1963.

Aristotle. 1996. *The Politics and the Constitution of Athens*. Edited by Stephen Everson. Cambridge: Cambridge University Press.

Armijo, Enrique. 2018. "The Freedom of Non-speech." *Constitutional Commentary* 34:291–329.

Asenbaum, Hans. 2018. "Anonymity and Democracy: Absence as Presence in the Public Sphere." *American Political Science Review* 112:459–72.

Athanasiou, Athena. 2005. "Reflections on the Politics of Mourning: Feminist Ethics and Politics in the Age of Empire." *Historein* 5:40–57.

———. 2017. *Agonistic Mourning*. Edinburgh: Edinburgh University Press.

———. 2021. "Mourning's Work and the Work of Mourning: Thinking Agonism and Aporia Together." In "Mourning Work: Death and Democracy During a Pandemic," edited by D. W. McIvor, J. Hooker, A. Atkins, et al. Special issue, *Contemporary Political Theory* 20:165–99.

Austin, J. L. 1976. *How to Do Things with Words*. Oxford: Oxford University Press.

Ayala, Saray, and Nadya Vasilyeva. 2016. "Responsibility for Silence." *Journal of Social Philosophy* 47:256–72.

Bachrach, Peter, and Morton S. Baratz. 1962. "Two Faces of Power." *American Political Science Review* 56:947–52.
———. 1970. *Power and Poverty: Theory and Practice*. New York: Oxford University Press.
Bargu, Banu. 2022. "The Silent Exception: The Politics of Sacrifice, Martyrs and Migrants." *Law, Culture and the Humanities* 18:290–317.
Barry, Brian. 1974. "Review Article: Exit, Voice, and Loyalty." *British Journal of Political Science* 4:79–107.
Bartels, Larry. 2016. *Unequal Democracy*. Princeton, NJ: Princeton University Press.
Barthes, Roland. 2005. *The Neutral: Lectures at the Collège de France (1977–1978)*. New York: Columbia University Press.
Bataille, George. 1985. *Visions of Excess: Selected Writings, 1927–1939*. Manchester: Manchester University Press.
Batiste, Stephanie L. 2014. "Affect-ive moves: Space, Violence, and the Body in *Rize*'s Krump Dancing." In *The Oxford Handbook of Dance and the Popular Screen*, edited by Melissa Blanco Borelli, 199–224. Oxford: Oxford University Press.
Batman, Michael E. 1992. "Shared Cooperative Activity." *Philosophical Review* 2:327–41.
Beaumont, Peter, and Amanda Holpuch. "How *The Handmaid's Tale* Dressed Protests Around the World." *Guardian*, August 3, 2018.
Beausoleil, Emily. 2017. "Responsibility as Responsiveness: Enacting a Dispositional Ethics of Encounter." *Political Theory* 45:291–318.
Beck, Ulrich. 1995. *Ecological Enlightenment*. Atlantic Highlands, NJ: Humanities Press.
Bejan, Teresa M. 2017. *Mere Civility: Disagreement and the Limits of Toleration*. Cambridge, MA: Harvard University Press.
———. 2019. "What Quakers Can Teach Us About the Politics of Pronouns." *New York Times*, November 16.
———. 2023. "Hobbes and Hats." *American Political Science Review* 117:1188–201.
———. 2024. "Hobbes Against Hate Speech." *British Journal for the History of Philosophy* 32:247–67.
Bell, Catherine. 1992. *Ritual Theory, Ritual Practice*. Oxford: Oxford University Press.
Bennett, Jane. 2005. "The Agency of Assemblages and the North American Blackout." *Public Culture* 17:445–65.
Bernal, Angélica Maria. 2017. *Beyond Origins: Rethinking Founding in a Time of Constitutional Democracy*. New York: Oxford University Press.
Bickford, Susan. 1996. *The Dissonance of Democracy: Listening, Conflict, and Citizenship*. Ithaca, NY: Cornell University Press.
———. 2011. "Emotion Talk and Political Judgment." *Journal of Politics* 73:1025–37.
Bindeman, Steven. 2017. *Silence in Philosophy, Literature, and Art*. Leiden: Brill.
Blasi, Vincent, and Seana Shiffrin. 2004. "The Story of *West Virginia State Board of Education v. Barnette*: The Pledge of Allegiance and Freedom of Thought." In *Constitutional Law Stories*, edited by Michael Dorf, 433–75. New York: Foundation Press.
Blocher, Joseph. 2012. "Rights To and Not To." *Columbia Law Review* 100:761–816.
Block de Behar, Lisa. 1995. *The Rhetoric of Silence and Other Selected Writings*. Berlin: Mouton De Gruyter.
Bond, H. Lawrence. 1997. "Introduction." In *Nicholas of Cusa: Selected Spiritual Writings*, edited by H. Lawrence Bond, 3–84. New York: Paulist.
Braaten, Carl A. 1967. *A History of Christian Thought from Its Judaic and Hellenistic Origins to Existentialism*. New York: Simon & Schuster.
Brekhus, Wayne. 1998. "A Sociology of the Unmarked: Redirecting Our Focus." *Sociological Theory* 16:34–51.
Brendese, P. J. 2014. *The Power of Memory in Democratic Politics*. New York: University of Rochester Press.

Brennan, Jason, and Lisa Hill. 2014. *Compulsory Voting*. Cambridge: Cambridge University Press.
Brito Vieira, Mónica. 2009. *The Elements of Representation in Hobbes*. Leiden: Brill.
———. 2015. "Founders and Re-founders: Struggles of Self-Authorized Representation." *Constellations* 22:500–513.
———. 2017. "Performative Imaginaries: Pitkin Versus Hobbes on Political Representation." In *Reclaiming Representation*, edited by Mónica Brito Vieira, 25–49. New York: Routledge.
———. 2020a. "Making Up and Making Real." *Global Intellectual History* 5:310–28.
———. 2020b. "Representing Silence in Politics." *American Political Science Review* 114:976–88.
———. 2021. "The Great Wall of Silence: Voice-Silence Dynamics in Authoritarian Regimes." *Critical Review of International Social and Political Philosophy* 24:368–91.
Brito Vieira, Mónica, et al. 2019. "Silent Agency." In "The Nature of Silence and Its Democratic Possibilities." Critical exchange, *Contemporary Political Theory* 18:441–45.
Brito Vieira, Mónica, and David Runciman. 2008. *Representation*. Cambridge: Polity Press.
Brooks, Peter. 2000. *Troubling Confessions*. Chicago: University of Chicago Press.
Brown, Mark. 2017. "Speaking for Nature: Hobbes, Latour, and the Democratic Representation of Nonhumans." *Science and Technology Studies* 31:31–51.
Brown, Wendy. 1996. "In the 'Folds of Our Own Discourse': The Pleasures and Freedoms of Silence." *University of Chicago Law School Roundtable* 3:185–97.
———. 2005. "In the 'Folds of Our Own Discourse': The Pleasures and Freedoms of Silence." In *Edgework: Critical Essays on Knowledge and Politics*, 83–97. Princeton, NJ: Princeton University Press.
Brummett, Barry. 1980. "Towards a Theory of Silence as a Political Strategy." *Quarterly Journal of Speech* 66:289–303.
Butler, Judith. 2004. *Precarious Life: The Powers of Mourning and Violence*. London: Verso.
———. 2011. "Bodies in Alliance and the Politics of the Street." *Transversal*, October. https://transversal.at/transversal/1011/butler/en.
———. 2014. "Performing the Political." Lecture given at the First Supper Symposium, Oslo, Norway, May 12, http://www.thefirstsuppersymposium.org/images/texts/Oslo_Judith%20Butler.pdf.
———. 2015a. *Notes Toward a Performative Theory of Assembly*. Cambridge, MA: Harvard University Press.
———. 2015b. "Theatrical Machines." *Differences: A Journal of Feminist Cultural Studies* 26:24–42.
———. 2015c. "What's Wrong With 'All Lives Matter'?" Interview by George Yancy. *New York Times*, January 12.
Cage, John. 1961. *Silence: Lectures and Writings by John Cage*. Middletown, CT: Wesleyan University Press.
———. 1970. "Defense of Satie." In *John Cage*, edited by Richard Kostelanetz, 77–84. New York: Praeger.
Cage, John, and Joan Retallack. 2012. *Music: John Cage en conversación con Joan Retallack*. Translated by Sebastián Jatz Rawicz. Santiago: Metales Pesados.
Carreras, Miguel. 2016. "Compulsory Voting and Political Engagement (Beyond the Ballot Box)." *Electoral Studies* 43:158–68.
Carson, Anne. 1995. "The Gender of Sound." In *Glass, Irony and God*, 120–21. New York: New Directions.

Carson, Rachel. 1962. *Silent Spring*. New York: Houghton Mifflin.
Cavarero, Adriana. 2005. *For More than One Voice: Towards a Philosophy of Vocal Expression*. Stanford, CA: Stanford University Press.
Ceccarelli, Leah. 2011. "Manufactured Scientific Controversy: Science, Rhetoric, and Public Debate." *Rhetoric and Public Affairs* 14:195–228.
Chapman, Mary. 2014. *Making Noise, Making News: Suffrage Print Culture and U.S. Modernism*. Oxford: Oxford University Press.
Clair, Robin. 1998. *Organizing Silence: A World of Possibilities*. Albany: State University of New York Press.
Cobussen, Marcel. 2003. "Ethics and/in/as Silence." *Ephemera* 3:277–85.
Cochrane, Alasdair. 2016. "Labour Rights for Animals." In *The Political Turn in Animal Ethics*, edited by Robert Garner and Siobhan O'Sullivan, 15–31. Lanham, MD: Rowman & Littlefield.
Cohen, Stanley. 2001. *States of Denial: Knowing About Atrocities and Suffering*. Cambridge: Polity Press.
Coleman, Stephen. 2013. *How Voters Feel*. Cambridge: Cambridge University Press.
Colley, Linda. 2014. "Empires of Writing: Britain, America and Constitutions, 1776–1848." *Law and History Review* 32:237–66.
Connor, Steven. 2019. *Giving Way: Thoughts on Unappreciated Dispositions*. Stanford, CA: Stanford University Press.
Constable, Marianne. 2005. *Just Silences: The Limits and Possibilities of Modern Law*. Princeton, NJ: Princeton University Press.
Constant, Benjamin. 1988. *Political Writings*. Edited by Biancamaria Fontana. Cambridge: Cambridge University Press.
Dahl, Robert A. 1961. *Who Governs?* New Haven, CT: Yale University Press.
———. 1972. *Democracy in the United States*. 2nd ed. New York: Houghton Mifflin.
———. 1998. *On Democracy*. New Haven, CT: Yale University Press.
Dassonneville, Ruth, Mark Hooghe, and Peter Miller. 2017. "The Impact of Compulsory Voting on Inequality and the Equality of Vote." *West European Politics* 40:621–44.
Dauenhauer, Bernard. 1973. "On Silence." *Research in Phenomenology* 3:9–27.
———. 1979. "Discourse, Silence, and Tradition." *Review of Metaphysics* 32:437–51.
———. 1980. *Silence: The Phenomenon and Its Ontological Significance*. Bloomington: Indiana University Press.
Davies, Stephen. 1997. "John Cage's 4'33'': Is It Music?" *Australasian Journal of Philosophy* 75:448–62.
Davis, Ryan, and R. Finlayson. 2022. "Public Reasoning Together: Gender and Political Deliberation." *Journal of Politics* 84:1556–69.
Decena, Carlos Ulises. 2011. *Tacit Subjects: Belonging and Same-Sex Desire Among Dominican Immigrant Men*. Durham, NC: Duke University Press.
Derrida, Jacques. 1978. *Writing and Difference*. Translated by Alan Bass. Chicago: University of Chicago Press. Orig. pub. 1967.
———. 1986. "Declarations of Independence." Translated by Tom Keenan and Tom Pepper. *New Political Science* 7:7–15. Orig. pub. 1984.
Devenney, Mark. 2019. "The Improper Politics of Representation." In *The Constructivist Turn in Political Representation*, edited by Lisa Disch, Mathijs van de Sande, and Nadia Urbinati, 224–38. Edinburgh: Edinburgh University Press.
Dewey, John. 1934. *Art as Experience*. New York: Minton, Balch.
Dhawan, Nikita. 2007. *Impossible Speech: On the Politics of Silence and Violence*. Sankt Augustin: Academia Verlag.
DiAngelo, Robin. 2020. "Nothing to Add: A Challenge to White Silence in Racial Discussions." *Understanding and Dismantling Privilege* 2:1–15.

Dienstag, Joshua Foa. 2021. "Dignity, Difference and the Representation of Nature." *Political Theory* 49:613–36.
Disch, Lisa. 2011. "Towards a Mobilization Conception of Representation." *American Political Science Review* 105:100–114.
———. 2012. "Democratic Representation and the Constituency Paradox." *Perspectives on Politics* 10:599–616.
———. 2015. "The Constructivist Turn in Democratic Representation: A Normative Dead-End?" *Constellations* 22:487–99.
———. 2016. "Ecological Democracy and the Co-participation of Things." In *The Oxford Handbook of Environmental Political Theory*, edited by Teena Gabrielson, Cheryl Hall, John M. Meyer, and David Schlosberg, 624–40. Oxford: Oxford University Press.
———. 2021. *Making Constituencies: Representation as Mobilization in Mass Democracy*. Chicago: University of Chicago Press.
Dixon, Rosalind, and Tom Ginsburg. 2011. "Deciding Not to Decide: Deferral in Constitutional Design." *International Journal of Constitutional Law* 9:636–72.
Dobson, Andrew. 1996. "Representative Democracy and the Environment." In *Democracy and the Environment*, edited by William M. Lafferty and James Meadowcroft, 124–39. Cheltenham, UK: Edward Elgar.
Dodd, Julian. 2018. "What 4'33" Is." *Australasian Journal of Philosophy* 96:629–41.
Dolar, Mladen. 2006. *A Voice and Nothing More*. Cambridge, MA: MIT Press.
Dolgert, Stefan. 2012. "Sacrificing Justice: Suffering Animals, the Oresteia, and the Masks of Consent." *Political Theory* 40:263–89.
Donaldson, Sue. 2020. "Agora: Animal Citizens and the Democratic Challenge." *Social Theory and Practice* 46:709–35.
Donaldson, Sue, and Will Kymlicka. 2011. *Zoopolis: A Political Theory of Animal Rights*. Oxford: Oxford University Press.
Donoso, Alfonso. 2017. "Representing Non-Human Interests." *Environmental Values* 26:607–28.
Dovi, Suzanne. 2020. "What's Missing? A Typology of Political Absence." *Journal of Politics* 82:559–71.
Doyle, Oran. 2018. "The Silent Constitution of Territory." *International Journal of Constitutional Law* 16:887–903.
Driscoll, Amanda, and Michael J. Nelson. 2014. "Ignorance or Opposition?" *Political Research Quarterly* 67:547–61.
Dryzek, John S. 1995. "Political and Ecological Communication." *Environmental Politics* 4:13–30.
———. 2000. *Deliberative Democracy and Beyond: Liberals, Critics, Contestations*. Oxford: Oxford University Press.
Du Bois, W. E. B. 1911. "Forward Backward." *Crisis*, October, 243–44.
———. 1915. "Woman Suffrage." *Crisis*, April, 285.
Dufourmantelle, Anne. 2021. *In Defense of Secrets*. Translated by Lindsay Turner. New York: Fordham University Press.
Duncan, Patti. 2004. *Tell This Silence: Asian American Writers and the Politics of Speech*. Iowa City: University of Iowa Press.
Eckersley, Robyn. 2000. "Deliberative Democracy, Ecological Representation and Risk: Towards a Democracy of the Affected." In *Democratic Innovation: Deliberation, Representation and Association*, edited by Michael Saward, 117–32. London: Routledge.
———. 2004. *The Green State: Rethinking Democracy and Sovereignty*. Cambridge, MA: MIT Press.

———. 2011. "Representing Nature." In *The Future of Representative Democracy*, edited by Sonia Alonso, John Keane, and Wolfgang Merkel, 236–57. Cambridge: Cambridge University Press.

Eddo-Lodge, Renni. 2017. *Why I'm No Longer Talking to White People About Race*. London: Bloomsbury.

Eisgruber, Christopher L. 2001. *Constitutional Self-Government*. Cambridge, MA: Harvard University Press.

Eliasoph, Nina. 1998. *Avoiding Politics: How Americans Produce Apathy in Everyday Life*. Cambridge: Cambridge University Press.

Elster, Jon. 2009. *Alexis de Tocqueville, the First Social Scientist*. Cambridge: Cambridge University Press.

Ely, John Hart. 1980. *Democracy and Distrust: A Theory of Judicial Review*. Cambridge, MA: Harvard University Press.

Emerson, Ralph Waldo. 2010. *Essays*. Vol. 3 of *The Works of Ralph Waldo Emerson*. 2nd ser. New York: Liberty Fund. Orig. pub. 1844.

Enroth, Henrik. 2017. "The Construction of What? From Weak to Strong Constructivism in the Study of Political Representation." Unpublished paper.

Esposito, Roberto. 2012. *Third Person: Politics of Life and Philosophy of the Impersonal*. Cambridge: Polity Press.

Ferguson, Kennan. 2003. "Silence: A Politics." *Contemporary Political Theory* 2:49–65.

Ferguson, Michaele. 2012. *Sharing Democracy*. Oxford: Oxford University Press.

Festenstein, Matthew. 2018. "Self-Censorship for Democrats." *European Journal of Political Theory* 17:324–42.

———. 2023. "The Ethics and Politics of Self-Censorship." In *The Routledge Handbook of Philosophy and Media Ethics*, edited by Carl Fox and Joe Saunders. London: Routledge.

Finnegan, Margaret. 1999. *Selling Suffrage: Consumer Culture and Votes for Women*. New York: Columbia University Press.

Fiumara, Gemma Corradi. 1990. *The Other Side of Language: A Philosophy of Listening*. Translated by Charles Lambert. London: Routledge.

Fleming, Sean. 2019. "Rivers Are People Too? On Legal Personhood for Nature." Political Theory Seminar, Oxford, November 1.

Foley, Michael. 2011. *The Silence of Constitutions: Gaps, "Abeyances" and Political Temperament in the Maintenance of Government*. London: Routledge.

Ford, Linda. 1991. *Iron-Jawed Angels: The Suffrage Militancy of the National Women's Party, 1912–1920*. Lanham, MD: University Press of America.

Fortner, Michael. 2015. *Black Silent Majority*. Cambridge, MA: Harvard University Press.

Fossen, Thomas. 2019. "Constructivism and the Logic of Political Representation." *American Political Science Review* 113:824–37.

Foucault, Michel. 1990. *The History of Sexuality, Volume I*. New York: Pantheon Books.

Frank, Jason. 2010. *Constituent Moments: Enacting the People in Postrevolutionary America*. Durham, NC: Duke University Press.

Franke, William. 2015. "Learned Ignorance: The Apophatic Tradition of Cultivating the Virtue of Unknowing." In *Routledge International Handbook of Ignorance Studies*, edited by Matthias Gross and Linsey McGoey, 26–35. Milton Park, UK: Routledge.

Freeden, Michael. 2022. *Concealed Silences and Inaudible Voices in Political Thinking*. Oxford: Oxford University Press.

Fricker, Miranda. 2007. *Epistemic Injustice: Power and the Ethics of Knowing*. Oxford: Oxford University Press.

Friskics, Scott. 2001. "Dialogical Relations with Nature." *Environmental Ethics* 23:391–410.

Fumagalli, Corrado. 2021. "Counterspeech and Ordinary Citizens: How? When?" *Political Theory* 49:1021–47.

Fung, Archon. 2004. "Deliberation's Darker Side: Six Questions for Iris Marion Young and Jane Mansbridge." *National Civic Review* 93:47–54.
Garner, Robert. 2016. "Animals, Politics and Democracy." In *The Political Turn in Animal Ethics*, edited by Robert Garner and Siobhan O'Sullivan, 103–18. Lanham, MD: Rowman & Littlefield.
Gauthier, X. 1981. "Is There Such a Thing as Women's Writing?" In *New French Feminisms*, edited by Elaine Marks and Isabelle de Courtivron, 161–64. New York: Schocken Books.
Gaventa, John. 1980. *Power and Powerlessness*. Urbana: University of Illinois Press.
Gerber, Megan. 2018. "The Powerful Silence of the March for Our Lives." *Atlantic*, March 25.
Glenn, Cheryl. 2004. *Unspoken: A Rhetoric of Silence*. Carbondale: Southern Illinois University Press.
Glenn, Cheryl, and Krista Ratcliffe, eds. 2011. *Silence and Listening as Rhetorical Arts*. Carbondale: Southern Illinois University Press.
Glennon, Lynda M. 1983. "Synthesism: A Case of Feminist Methodology." In *Beyond Method: Strategies for Social Research*, edited by Gareth Morgan, 260–71. Beverly Hills, CA: Sage.
Goffman, Erving. 1956. *The Presentation of Self in Everyday Life*. Edinburgh: University of Edinburgh.
Goodin, Robert. 1996. "Enfranchising the Earth, and Its Alternatives." *Political Studies* 44:835–49.
Gray, Sean. 2015. "Mapping Silent Citizenship: How Democratic Theory Hears Citizens' Silence and Why It Matters." *Citizenship Studies* 19:473–91.
———. 2019. "Interpreting Silence: A Note of Caution." *Contemporary Political Theory* 18:431–33.
———. 2021. "Silence and Democratic Institutional Design." *Critical Review of International Social and Political Philosophy* 24:330–45.
———. 2023. "Towards a Democratic Theory of Silence." *Political Studies* 7:815–34.
Green, Jeffrey Edward. 2010. *The Eyes of the People: Democracy in an Age of Spectatorship*. Oxford: Oxford University Press.
Griffiths, Paul. 1981. *John Cage*. Oxford: Oxford University Press.
Guillaume, Xavier. 2018. "How to Do Things with Silence: Rethinking the Centrality of Speech to the Securitization Framework." *Security Dialogue* 49:476–92.
Guillaume, Xavier, and Elisabeth Schweiger. 2019. "Silence as Doing." In *Political Silence: Meanings, Functions and Ambiguity*, edited by Sophia Dingli and Thomas N. Cooke, 96–111. London: Routledge.
Gündoğdu, Ayten. 2021. "At the Margins of Personhood: Rethinking Law and Life Beyond the Impasses of Biopolitics." *Constellations* 28:570–87.
Guzmán, Joshua Javier. 2015. "Silence ≠ Death: On Not-Not Coming Out." *Criticism* 57:145–49.
Haines, Christian. 2017. "The Impersonal Is Political: Adrienne Rich's *The Dream of a Common Language*, Feminism, and the Art of Biopolitics." *Cultural Critique* 96:178–215.
Hall, Robert L. 1985. "Language and Freedom: An Analysis of the Demonic in Kierkegaard's *The Concept of Anxiety*." In *International Kierkegaard Commentary*, vol. 8, *The Concept of Anxiety*, edited by Robert L. Perkins, 153–66. Macon, GA: Mercer University Press.
Halley, Janet. 1991. "Equivocation and the Legal Conflict over Religious Identity in Early Modern England." *Yale Journal of Law and the Humanities* 3:33–52.
Hamilton, Lawrence. 2014. *Freedom Is Power: Liberty Through Political Representation*. Cambridge: Cambridge University Press.

Haraway, Donna. 2016. *Staying with the Trouble: Making Kin in the Chthulucene*. Durham, NC: Duke University Press.
Hardon, Anita, and Deborah Posel. 2012. "Secrecy as Embodied Practice: Beyond the Confessional Imperative." *Culture, Health and Sexuality* 14:S1–S13.
Harris, Randy. 2000. "Other-Worlds in *Silent Spring*." In *And No Birds Sing: Rhetorical Analyses of Rachel Carson's "Silent Spring,"* edited by Craig Waddell, 126–56. Carbondale: Southern Illinois University Press.
Havel, Václav. 1985. *The Power of the Powerless: Citizens Against the State in Central-Eastern Europe*, edited by John Keane. Armonk, NY: M. E. Sharpe.
Hawhee, Debra. 2017. *Rhetoric in Tooth and Claw: Animals, Language, Sensation*. Chicago: University of Chicago Press.
Higginbotham, Evelyn Brooks. 1993. *Righteous Discontent: The Women's Movement in the Black Baptist Church, 1880–1920*. Cambridge, MA: Harvard University Press.
Hill, Shonagh. 2019. *Women and Embodied Mythmaking in Irish Theatre*. Cambridge: Cambridge University Press.
Hirschman, Albert O. 1970. *Exit, Voice, and Loyalty: Responses to Decline in Firms, Organizations, and States*. Cambridge, MA: Harvard University Press.
Hobbes, Thomas. 1996. *Leviathan*. Edited by Richard Tuck. Cambridge: Cambridge University Press.
Hoekstra, Kinch. 2012. "Hobbesian Equality." In *Hobbes Today: Insights for the 21st Century*, ed. Sharon Lloyd, 76–112. Cambridge: Cambridge University Press.
Holmes, Stephen. 1995. *Passions and Constraint: On the Liberal Theory of Democracy*. Chicago: University of Chicago Press.
Honig, Bonnie. 1991. "Declarations of Independence: Arendt and Derrida on the Problem of Founding a Republic." *American Political Science Review* 85:97–113.
———. 2021. *A Feminist Theory of Refusal*. Cambridge, MA: Harvard University Press.
hooks, bell. 1989. *Talking Back: Thinking Feminist, Thinking Black*. Boston: South End Press.
———. 1992. "Is Paris Burning?" In *Black Looks: Race and Representation*, 145–56. Boston: South End Press.
Hornsby, Jennifer, and Rae Langton. 1998. "Free Speech and Illocution." *Legal Theory* 4:21–37.
Horton, John. 2011. "Self-Censoring." *Res Publica* 17:91–106.
Horwitz, Paul. 2010. "Anonymity, Signaling, and Silence as Speech." In *Speech and Silence in American Law*, edited by Austin Sarat, 172–89. Cambridge: Cambridge University Press.
Huntington, Samuel. 1975. "The United States." In *The Crisis of Democracy*, edited by Michel Crozier, Samuel Huntington, and Joji Watanuki, 59–119. New York: New York University Press.
Huxley, Aldous. 1931. "The Rest Is Silence." In *Music at Night and Other Essays*, 17–20. London: Chatto and Windus.
Ikuta, Jennie C. 2020. *Contesting Conformity: Democracy and the Paradox of Political Belonging*. Oxford: Oxford University Press.
Inness, Julie. 1992. *Privacy, Intimacy and Isolation*. New York: Oxford University Press.
Irigaray, Luce. 2011. "How Can We Meet the Other?" In *Otherness: A Multilateral Perspective*, edited by Susan Yi Sencindiver, Maria Beville, and Marie Lauritzen, 107–220. Frankfurt: Peter Lang.
Irwin, Inez Haynes. 1921. *The Story of the Woman's Party*. New York: Harcourt Brace.
Jackson, John. 2009. "Re-Conceptualizing the Right of Silence as an Effective Fair Trial Standard." *International and Comparative Law Quarterly* 58:835–61.

Jackson, Vicki C. 2016. "Secession, Transnational Precedents, and Constitutional Silences." In *Nullification and Secession in Modern Constitutional Thought*, edited by Sanford Levinson, 314–42. Lawrence: University Press of Kansas.

Jakee, Keith, and Guang-Zhen Sun. 2006. "Is Compulsory Voting More Democratic?" *Public Choice* 129:61–75.

Jaworski, Adam. 1993. *The Power of Silence: Social and Pragmatic Perspectives*. Newbury Park, CA: Sage.

Jefferson, Mark. 1983. "What Is Wrong with Sentimentality?" *Mind* 92:519–29.

Johnson, James Weldon. 1995. *The Selected Writings of James Weldon Johnson*. Vol. 1, *The "New York Age" Editorials (1914–1923)*, edited by Sondra Katryn Wilson. New York: Oxford University Press.

Jung, Carl. 1940. *The Integration of the Personality*. Translated by Stanley M. Dell. London: Kegan Paul.

Jung, Theo. 2019. "Silence as a Mode of Political Communication: Negotiating Expectations." *Contemporary Political Theory* 18:425–31.

———. 2021. "Mind the Gaps: Silences, Political Communication, and the Role of Expectations." *Critical Review of International Social and Political Philosophy* 24:296–315.

Jungkunz, Vincent. 2011. "Dismantling Whiteness: Silent Yielding and the Potentiality of Political Suicide." *Contemporary Political Theory* 10:3–20.

———. 2012. "The Promise of Democratic Silences." *New Political Science* 34:127–50.

———. 2013. "Deliberate Silences." *Journal of Public Deliberation* 9:1–32.

Kahn, Douglas. 1997. "John Cage: Silence and Silencing." *Musical Quarterly* 81:556–98.

Kalamaras, George. 1994. *Reclaiming the Tacit Dimension: Symbolic Form in the Rhetoric of Silence*. Albany: State University of New York Press.

Kalin, Alan. 1978. "The Right of Ideological Nonassociation." *California Law Review* 66:767–808.

Kaminsky, Ilya. 2009. *Deaf Republic: Poems*. Graywolf Press.

Katz, Daniel, and Floyd H. Allport. 1931. *Student Attitudes*. Syracuse, NY: Craftsman.

Keenan, Alan. 1994. "Promises, Promises: The Abyss of Freedom and the Loss of the Political in the Work of Hannah Arendt." *Political Theory* 22:297–322.

———. 2003. *Democracy in Question: Democratic Openness in a Time of Political Closure*. Stanford, CA: Stanford University Press.

Keller, Catherine. 2005. *God and Power: Counter-Apocalyptic Journeys*. Augsburg: Augsburg Books.

———. 2008. "The Apophasis of Gender: A Fourfold Unsaying of Feminist Theology." *Journal of the American Academy of Religion* 76:905–33.

Khatchadourian, Haig. 2015. *How to Do Things with Silence*. Boston: De Gruyter.

Kirkpatrick, Jennet. 2019. "Resistant Exit." *Contemporary Political Theory* 18:135–57.

Kostelanetz, Richard. 1988. *Conversing with Cage*. New York: Limelight Editions.

Kramer, Elizabeth. 2020. "A Tense New Classical Work Bottles the Feeling of a Police Stop." *Deceptive Cadence*, National Public Radio, November 24. https://www.npr.org/sections/deceptivecadence/2020/11/24/936756472/a-tense-new-classical-work-bottles-the-feeling-of-a-police-stop.

Krause, Sharon. 2011. "Bodies in Action: Corporeal Agency and Democratic Politics." *Political Theory* 39:299–324.

———. 2015. *Freedom Beyond Sovereignty: Reconstructing Liberal Individualism*. Chicago: University of Chicago Press.

———. 2020. "Environmental Domination." *Political Theory* 48:443–68.

Kukla, Rebecca. 2014. "Performative Force, Convention, and Discursive Injustice." *Hypatia* 29:440–57.

Kurzon, Dennis. 1998. *Discourse of Silence*. Amsterdam: John Benjamins.

Laclau, Ernesto. 2005. *On Populist Reason*. London: Verso.
Langton, Rae. 1993. "Speech Acts and Unspeakable Acts." *Philosophy and Public Affairs* 22:293–330.
———. 2018. "Blocking as Counter-Speech." In *New Work on Speech Acts*, edited by Daniel Fogal, Daniel W. Harris, and Matt Moss, 144–64. Oxford: Oxford University Press.
Latour, Bruno. 1999. *Pandora's Hope: Essays on the Reality of Science Studies*. Cambridge, MA: Harvard University Press.
Lawrence, Charles R., III. 1993. "If He Hollers Let Him Go: Regulating Racist Speech on Campus." In *Words That Wound: Critical Race Theory, Assaultive Speech and the First Amendment*, edited by Mari Matsuda, Charles R. Lawrence III, Richard Delgado, and Kimberlé Crenshaw, 53–88. Boulder: Westview Press.
Lear, Lea. 2009. *Rachel Carson: Witness for Nature*. Boston: Mariner Books.
Leiter, Brian. 2017. "Justifying Academic Freedom: Mill and Marcuse Revisited." In *Moral Puzzles and Legal Perplexities*, edited by Heidi Hurd, 113–33. Cambridge: Cambridge University Press.
Lepora, Chiara, and Robert E. Goodin. 2013. *On Complicity and Compromise*. Oxford: Oxford University Press.
Lepoutre, Maxime. 2017. "Hate Speech in Public Discourse: A Pessimistic Defense of Counter-Speech." *Social Theory and Practice* 43:851–85.
Lichau, Karsten. 2014. "'Noise' or 'Silence'? Listening to Sacred Sound in 20th-Century Europe." In *Exploring the Senses: South Asian and European Perspectives on Rituals and Performativity*, edited by Axel Michaels and Christoph Wolf, 145–64. New Delhi: Routledge.
List, Christian, and Philip Pettit. 2011. *Group Agency: The Possibility, Design, and Status of Corporate Agents*. Oxford: Oxford University Press.
Loevlie, Elisabeth. 2003. *Literary Silences in Pascal, Rousseau, and Beckett*. Oxford: Oxford University Press.
Loraux, Nicole. 1986. *The Invention of Athens: The Funeral Oration in the Classical City*. Translated by Alan Sheridan. Cambridge, MA: Harvard University Press.
Lorde, Audre. 1984. "The Transformation of Silence into Language and Action." In *Sister Outsider: Essays and Speeches*, 40–44. New York: Crossing Press.
———. 1995. *The Black Unicorn: Poems*. New York: W. W. Norton.
Loughlin, Martin. 2018. "The Silences of Constitutions." *International Journal of Constitutional Law* 16:922–35.
Luckyj, Christina. 1993. "'A Moving Rhetoricke': Women's Silences and Renaissance Texts." *Renaissance Drama* 24:33–56.
Lukes, Steven. 1974. *Power: A Radical View*. London: Macmillan.
MacKenzie, Michael, and Alfred Moore. 2020. "Democratic Non-Participation." *Polity* 52:430–59.
Maitra, Ishani. 2009. "Silencing Speech." *Canadian Journal of Philosophy* 39:309–38.
———. 2012. "Subordinating Speech." In *Speech and Harm: Controversies over Free Speech*, edited by Ishani Maitra and Mary Kate McGowan, 94–120. Oxford: Oxford University Press.
Manza, Jeff, and Fay L. Cook. 2002. "A Democratic Polity?" *American Politics Research* 30:630–67.
Marcuse, Herbert. 1965. "Repressive Tolerance." In Robert Wolff, Barrington Moore Jr., and Herbert Marcuse, *A Critique of Pure Tolerance*, 81–119. Boston: Beacon Press.
Marion, Jean-Luc. 2012. *God Without Being*. Chicago: University of Chicago Press.
Markell, Patchen. 2008. "The Insufficiency of Non-Domination." *Political Theory* 36:9–36.

———. 2014. "The Moment Has Passed: Power After Arendt." In *Radical Future Pasts: Untimely Political Theory*, edited by Romand Coles, Mark Reinhardt, and George Shulman, 113–48. Lexington: University Press of Kentucky.
Marres, Noortje. 2012. *Material Participation: Technology, the Environment and Everyday Publics*. Basingstoke: Palgrave Macmillan.
McCallum, E. L., and Mikko Tuhkanen. 2011. "Introduction." In *Queer Times, Queer Becomings*, edited by E. L. McCallum and Mikko Tuhkanen, 1–24. Albany: State University of New York Press.
McDermott, Lydia. 2016. *Liminal Bodies, Reproductive Health, and Feminist Rhetoric*. Lanham, MD: Lexington Books.
McGowan, Mary Kate. 2009. "Oppressive Speech." *Australasian Journal of Philosophy* 87:389–407.
———. 2014. "Sincerity Silencing." *Hypatia* 29:458–73.
———. 2019. *Just Words: On Speech and Hidden Harm*. Oxford: Oxford University Press.
McKim, Joel. 2008. "Agamben at Ground Zero: A Memorial Without Content." *Theory, Culture and Society* 25:83–103.
McNay, Lois. 2012. "Suffering, Silence, and Social Weightlessness." In *Embodied Selves*, edited by Stella Gonzalez-Arnal, Gill Jagger, and Kathleen Lennon, 230–49. Basingstoke: Palgrave.
Medina, José. 2012. *The Epistemology of Resistance: Gender and Racial Oppression, Epistemic Injustice, and the Social Imagination*. Oxford: Oxford University Press.
———. 2023. *The Epistemology of Protest: Epistemic Activism and the Communicative Life of Resistance*. Oxford: Oxford University Press.
Menely, Tobias. 2015. *The Animal Claim: Sensibility and the Creaturely Voice*. Chicago: University of Chicago Press.
Mercer, Kobena. 1994. *Welcome to the Jungle*. New York & London: Routledge.
Merleau-Ponty, Maurice. 1962. *The Phenomenology of Perception*. Translated by Colin Smith. London: Routledge and Kegan Paul. Orig. pub. 1945.
———. 1973. *The Prose of the World*. Translated by John O'Neill. Evanston, IL: Northwestern University Press. Orig. pub. 1969.
Mignolo, Walter D. 2009. "Epistemic Disobedience, Independent Thought and Decolonial Freedom." *Theory, Culture and Society* 26:159–81.
Mill, John Stuart. 1989. "On Liberty." In *"On Liberty" and Other Writings*, edited by Stefan Collini, 1–116. Cambridge: Cambridge University Press.
Mills, Charles W. 1999. *The Racial Contract*. Ithaca, NY: Cornell University Press.
———. 2007. "White Ignorance." In *Race and Epistemologies of Ignorance*, edited by Shannon Sullivan and Nancy Tuana, 26–31. Albany: State University of New York Press.
———. 2017. *Black Rights/White Wrongs: The Critique of Racial Liberalism*. Oxford: Oxford University Press.
Mitchell, Timothy. 2002. *Rule of Experts: Egypt, Techno-Politics, Modernity*. Berkeley, CA: University of California Press.
Mitchell, W. J. T. 1986. "Visible Language: Blake's Wond'rous Art of Writing." In *Romanticism and Contemporary Criticism*, edited by Morris Eaves and Michael R. Fischer, 46–96. Ithaca, NY: Cornell University Press.
Montanaro, Laura. 2012. "The Democratic Legitimacy of Self-Appointed Representatives." *Journal of Politics* 74:1094–107.
Mudde, Cas, and Cristóbal Kaltwasser. 2017. *Populism*. Oxford: Oxford University Press.
Muers, Rachel. 2004. *Keeping God's Silence: Towards a Theological Ethics of Communication*. Oxford: Blackwell.

———. 2015a. "Why Silence Isn't 'Doing Nothing,' and Why It Might Be All Right to Do Nothing: Spiritual Challenges from Silent Worship to Contemporary Culture." *Modern Belief* 56 (3): 333–41.

———. 2015b. *Testimony: Quakerism and Theological Ethics*. London: SCM Press.

Myers, Ella. 2013. *Worldly Ethics: Democratic Politics and Care for the World*. Durham, NC: Duke University Press.

Nancy, Jean-Luc. 1997. *The Gravity of Thought*. Atlantic Highlands, NJ: Humanities Press.

Noelle-Neumann, Elisabeth. 1974. "The Spiral of Silence: A Theory of Public Opinion." *Journal of Communication* 24:43–51.

———. 1993. *The Spiral of Silence*. Chicago: University of Chicago Press.

Norgaard, Kari Marie. 2011. *Living in Denial: Climate Change, Emotions, and Everyday Life*. Cambridge, MA: MIT Press.

Nyhan, Brendan, and Jason Reifler. 2010. "When Corrections Fail: The Persistence of Political Misperceptions." *Political Behavior* 32:303–30.

Ohmer, Sarah S. 2019. "'In the Beginning Was Body Language': Clowning and Krump as Spiritual Healing and Resistance." *Evoke: Crossing Borders* 1:14–29.

Olson, Kevin. 2006. *Reflexive Democracy*. Cambridge, MA: MIT Press.

Panagia, David. 2009. *The Political Life of Sensation*. Durham, NC: Duke University Press.

Peirce, Charles Sanders. 1955. *Philosophical Writings of Peirce*. Edited by Justus Buchler. New York: Dover Publications.

Pettit, Philip. 1994. "Enfranchising Silence: An Argument for Freedom of Speech." In *Freedom of Communication*, edited by Tom Campbell and Wojciech Sadurski, 45–56. Aldershot: Dartmouth.

———. 2011. "The Instability of Freedom as Noninterference: The Case of Isaiah Berlin." *Ethics* 121:693–716.

———. 2018. "Two Concepts of Free Speech." In *Academic Freedom*, edited by Jennifer Lackey, 61–82. Oxford: Oxford University Press.

Petty, Sheila. 1998. "Silence and Its Opposite: Expressions of Race in *Tongues Untied*." In *Documenting the Documentary*, edited by Barry K. Grant and Jeannette Sloniowski, 416–28. Detroit: Wayne State University Press.

Philips, S. U. 1985. "Interaction Structured Through Talk and Interaction Structured Through 'Silence.'" In *Perspectives on Silence*, edited by Muriel Saville-Troike and Deborah Tannen, 205–16. Norwood, NJ: Ablex Publishing.

Picard, Max. 1952. *The World of Silence*. Chicago: Henry Regnery.

Pitkin, Hannah. 1967. *The Concept of Representation*. Berkeley: University of California Press.

Plumwood, Val. 1993. *Feminism and the Mastery of Nature*. London: Routledge.

———. 1995. "Has Democracy Failed Ecology? An Ecofeminist Perspective." *Environmental Politics* 4:134–68.

Polanyi, Michael. 1969. *Knowing and Being*. Chicago: University of Chicago Press.

———. 2009. *The Tacit Dimension*. Chicago: University of Chicago Press.

Polsby, Nelson. 1963. *Community Power and Political Theory*. New Haven, CT: Yale University Press.

Posner, Richard A. 1973. "An Economic Approach to Legal Procedure and Judicial Administration." *Journal of Legal Studies* 2:399–459.

Purdy, Jedediah. 2015. *After Nature: A Politics of the Anthropocene*. Cambridge, MA: Harvard University Press.

Rancière, Jacques. 2004. *The Politics of Aesthetics: The Distribution of the Sensible*. Edited and translated by Gabriel Rockhill. London: Continuum.

Ratcliffe, Krista. 2005. *Rhetorical Listening: Identifications, Gender, Whiteness*. Carbondale: Southern Illinois University Press.

Rawls, John. 1996. *Political Liberalism*. Cambridge, MA: Harvard University Press.
Resina, Joan Ramon. 2021. *Dismembering the Dictatorship: The Politics of Memory in the Spanish Transition to Democracy*. Leiden: Brill.
Rich, Adrienne. 1979. *On Lies, Secrets, and Silence*. New York: W. W. Norton.
———. 2013. *The Dream of a Common Language: Poems, 1974–1977*. New York: W. W. Norton. Orig. pub. 1978.
Riggs, Marlon T. 1991. "Black Macho Revisited: Reflections of a Snap! Queen." *Black American Literature Forum* 25:389–94.
———. 1996. "Tongues Re-tied." In *Resolutions: Contemporary Video Practices*, edited by Michael Renov and Erika Suderburg, 185–88. Minneapolis: University of Minnesota Press.
Roberts, Andrew. 2008. "Pre-Trial Defense Rights and the Fair Use of Defense Witness Identification Procedures." *Modern Law Review* 71:331–57.
Rollo, Toby. 2017. "Everyday Deeds: Enactive Protest, Exit, and Silence in Deliberative Systems." *Political Theory* 45:587–609.
———. 2019. "Two Political Ontologies and Three Models of Silence: Voice, Signal, and Action." *Contemporary Political Theory* 18:435–41.
Romero, Javier, and John Dryzek. 2021. "Semiotics and the Communicative Networks of Nature." *Environmental Values* 30:407–29.
Rosenblum, Nancy. 2008. *On the Side of Angels*. Princeton, NJ: Princeton University Press.
Runciman, David. 2007. "The Paradox of Political Representation." *Journal of Political Philosophy* 15:93–114.
Sabl, Andrew. 2015. "The Two Cultures of Democratic Theory: Responsiveness, Democratic Quality, and the Empirical-Normative Divide." *Perspectives on Politics* 13:345–65.
Saldaña-Portillo, María. 2003. *The Revolutionary Imagination in the Americas and the Age of Development*. Durham, NC: Duke University Press.
Santino, Jack. 2006. "Performative Commemoratives: Spontaneous Shrines and the Public Memorialization of Death." In *Spontaneous Shrines and the Public Memorialization of Death*, edited by Jack Santino, 5–16. New York: Palgrave Macmillan.
Saw, C. L. 2005. "Protecting the Sound of Silence in 4'33'': A Timely Revisit of Basic Principles in Copyright Law." *European Intellectual Property Review* 27:467–76.
Saward, Michael. 2006. "The Representative Claim." *Contemporary Political Theory* 5:297–318.
———. 2010. *The Representative Claim*. Oxford: Oxford University Press.
Schaap, Andrew. 2008. "Book Review: Marianne Constable, *Just Silences*." *Social and Legal Studies* 17:290–92.
———. 2020. "Do You Not See the Reason for Yourself? Political Withdrawal and the Experience of Epistemic Friction." *Political Studies* 68:565–81.
Schlosberg, David. 2007. *Defining Environmental Justice: Theories, Movements, and Nature*. Oxford: Oxford University Press.
Schlozman, Kay, Sidney Verba, and Henry E. Brady. 2010. "Weapon of the Strong?" *Perspectives on Politics* 8:487–509.
Schröter, Melani. 2013. *Silence and Concealment in Political Discourse*. Amsterdam: John Benjamins.
Schwartzberg, Melissa. 2010. "Shouts, Murmurs and Votes." *Journal of Political Philosophy* 18:448–68.
Schweber, Howard. 2016. "The Limits of Representation." *American Political Science Review* 110:382–96.
Sciacca, Michele Frederico. 1957. "Meaningful Silence." *Philosophy Today* 1:250–54.
———. 1963. *Come si vince a Waterloo*. Milano: Marzorati.

Scott, James C. 1985. *Weapons of the Weak: Everyday Forms of Resistance*. New Haven, CT: Yale University Press.

———. 1990. *Domination and the Arts of Resistance: Hidden Transcripts*. New Haven, CT: Yale University Press.

Scott, Susie. 2018. "A Sociology of Nothing: Understanding the Unmarked." *Sociology* 52:3–19.

Scudder, Mary. 2020a. *Beyond Empathy and Inclusion: The Challenge of Listening in Democratic Deliberation*. Oxford: Oxford University Press.

———. 2020b. "The Ideal of Uptake in Democratic Deliberation." *Political Studies* 68:504–22.

Sedgwick, Eve. 1990. *Epistemology of the Closet*. Berkeley: University of California Press.

———. 1993. *Tendencies*. Durham, NC: Duke University Press.

Sells, Michael A. 1994. *Mystical Languages of Unsaying*. Chicago: University of Chicago Press.

Seymour, David M. 2013. "This Is the Piece that Everyone Here Has Come to Experience: The Challenges to Copyright of John Cage's 4'33''." *Legal Studies* 33:532–48.

Shotwell, Alexis. 2016. *Living Ethically in Compromised Times*. Minneapolis: University of Minnesota Press.

Simmel, Georg. 1906. "The Sociology of Secrecy and Secret Societies." *American Journal of Sociology* 11:441–98.

———. 1950. *The Sociology of Georg Simmel*. Translated and edited by Kurt H. Wolff. Glencoe: Free Press.

Simpson, Robert. 2013. "Un-Ringing the Bell: McGowan on Oppressive Speech and the Asymmetric Pliability of Conversations." *Australasian Journal of Philosophy* 91:555–75.

Singh, Shane P. 2019. "Compulsory Voting and Parties' Vote-Seeking Strategies." *American Journal of Political Science* 63:37–52.

Skerker, Michael. 2010. *An Ethics of Interrogation*. Chicago: University of Chicago Press.

Sontag, Susan. 2009. "The Aesthetics of Silence." In *Styles of Radical Will*, 3–34. London: Penguin Classics.

Southard, Belinda A. Stillion. 2007. "Militancy, Power, and Identity: The Silent Sentinels as Women Fighting for Political Voice." *Rhetoric and Public Affairs* 10:399–417.

———. 2011. *Militant Citizenship: Rhetorical Strategies of the National Woman's Party*. College Station: Texas A&M University Press.

Spivak, Gayatri. 1988. "Can the Subaltern Speak?" In *Marxism and the Interpretation of Culture*, edited by Cary Nelson and Lawrence Grossberg, 271–313. Basingstoke: Macmillan.

Stevens, Doris. 1995. *Jailed for Freedom: American Women Win the Vote*. Edited by C. O'Hare. Troutdale, OR: New Sage. Orig. pub. 1920.

Stone, Christopher. 1972. "Should Trees Have Standing? Toward Legal Rights for Natural Objects." *Southern California Law Review* 45:450–501.

Stow, Simon. 2017. *American Mourning: Tragedy, Democracy, Resilience*. Cambridge: Cambridge University Press.

Strauss, Mary. 2008–9. "The Sounds of Silence: Reconsidering the Invocation of the Right to Remain Silent Under Miranda." *William and Mary Bill of Rights Journal* 17:773–829.

Suisman, David. 2009. *Selling Sounds: The Commercial Revolution in American Music*. Cambridge, MA: Harvard University Press.

Sunstein, Cass. 1996. "Social Norms and Social Roles." *Columbia Law Review* 903:903–68.

———. 2001. *Designing Democracy: What Constitutions Do*. Oxford: Oxford University Press.

Superti, Chiara. 2015. "Vanguard of Discontent." Semantic Scholar. Accessed March 11, 2019. https://www.semanticscholar.org/paper/Vanguard-of-Discontent-%3A-Comparing-Individual-Blank-Superti/539a07f56a8f4660053102e9703ebad8012714fe.
Sussman, A. 1917. "The Silent Sentinels." *The Suffragist*, October 27, 5. Orig. pub. in *Philadelphia Jewish World*.
Tanasoca, Ana. 2020. *Deliberation Naturalized: Improving Real Existing Deliberative Democracy*. Oxford: Oxford University Press.
Thaler, Mathias. 2022. *No Other Planet: Utopian Visions for a Climate-Changed World*. Cambridge: Cambridge University Press.
Thompson, Dennis. 2005. "Democracy in Time: Popular Sovereignty and Temporal Representation." *Constellations* 12:241–58.
Tocqueville, Alexis de. 2011. *Democracy in America*. Translated by Arthur Goldhammer. New York: Library of America.
Toop, David. 2011. *Sinister Resonance: The Mediumship of the Listener*. London: Bloomsbury.
Tribe, Laurence H. 2018. "Soundings and Silences." In *The Invisible Constitution in Comparative Perspective*, edited by Rosalind Dix and Adrienne Stone, 21–60. Cambridge: Cambridge University Press.
Trinh, T. Minh-ha. 1988. "Not You/Like You: Post-Colonial Women and the Interlocking Questions of Identity and Difference." *Inscriptions* 3–4:71–77.
Tulis, Jeffrey K. 1987. *The Rhetorical Presidency*. Princeton, NJ: Princeton University Press.
Tushnet, Mark V., Alan K. Chen, and Joseph Blocher. 2017. *Free Speech Beyond Words: The Surprising Reach of the First Amendment*. New York: New York University Press.
Véliz, Carissa. 2020. *Privacy Is Power: Why and How You Should Take Back Control of Your Data*. London: Bantam Press.
Verba, Sidney, Kay L. Schlozman, and Henry E. Brady. 1995. *Voice and Equality*. Cambridge, MA: Harvard University Press.
Versteeg, Mila, and Emily Zackin. 2016. "Constitutions Unentrenched: Toward an Alternative Theory of Constitutional Design." *American Political Science Review* 110:657–74.
Villiers, Nicholas de. 2012. *Opacity of the Closet: Queer Tactics in Foucault, Barthes, and Warhol*. Minneapolis: University of Minnesota Press.
Vogel, Steven. 2006. "The Silence of Nature." *Environmental Values* 15:145–71.
———. 2015. *Thinking Like a Mall: Environmental Philosophy After the End of Nature*. Cambridge MA: MIT Press.
Wagner, Roi. 2012. "Silence as Resistance Before the Subject, or Could the Subaltern Remain Silent?" *Theory, Culture and Society* 29:99–124.
Warren, Mark. 2011. "Voting with Your Feet: Exit-Based Empowerment in Democratic Theory." *American Political Science Review* 105:683–701.
Weber, Max. 1978. *Weber: Selections in Translation*. Edited by W. G. Runciman. Translated by E. Matthews. New York: Cambridge University Press.
Weis, Lael K. 2018. "Environmental Constitutionalism: Aspiration or Transformation?" *International Journal of Constitutional Law* 16:836–70.
West, Caroline. 2012. "Words that Silence? Freedom of Expression and Racist Hate Speech." In *Speech and Harm: Controversies over Free Speech*, edited by Ishani Maitra and Mary Kate McGowan, 222–48. Oxford: Oxford University Press.
Whitehouse, Andrew. 2015. "Listening to Birds in the Anthropocene: The Anxious Semiotics of Sound in a Human-Dominated World Environmental Humanities." *Environmental Humanities* 6:53–71.
Wicomb, Zoë. 1998. "Shame and Identity: The Case of the Coloured in South Africa." In *Writing South Africa: Literature, Apartheid, and Democracy, 1970–1995*, edited

by Derek Attridge and Rosemary Jolly, 91–107. Cambridge: Cambridge University Press.
Wilson, Woodrow. 2017. *Constitutional Government in the United States.* New York: Routledge. Orig. pub. 1908.
Wolfson, Elliot R. 2005. *Language, Eros, Being: Kabbalistic Hermeneutics and Poetic Imagination.* New York: Fordham University Press.
Young, Harvey. 2000. "Memorializing Memory: Marlon Riggs and Life Writing in *Tongues Untied* and *Black Is Black Ain't*." *a/b: Auto/Biography Studies* 15:248–60.
Young, Iris Marion. 1990. *Justice and the Politics of Difference.* Princeton, NJ: Princeton University Press.
———. 1996. "Communication and the Other: Beyond Deliberative Democracy." In *Democracy and Difference*, edited by Seyla Benhabib, 120–37. Princeton, NJ: Princeton University Press.
———. 1997. *Intersecting Voices: Dilemmas of Gender, Political Philosophy, and Policy.* Princeton, NJ: Princeton University Press.
———. 2001. "Activist Challenges to Deliberative Democracy." *Political Theory* 29:670–90.
———. 2002. *Inclusion and Democracy.* Oxford: Oxford University Press.
———. 2011. *Responsibility for Justice.* New York: Oxford University Press.
Zerilli, Linda. 2014. "Against Civility: A Feminist Perspective." In *Civility, Legality, and Justice in America*, edited by Austin Sarat, 107–31. Cambridge: Cambridge University Press.
Zerubavel, Eviatar. 2006. *The Elephant in the Room: Silence and Denial in Everyday Life.* Oxford: Oxford University Press.
———. 2019. "Listening to the Sound of Silence: Methodological Reflections on Studying the Unsaid." In *Qualitative Studies of Silence: The Unsaid as Social Action*, edited by Amy Jo Murray and Kevin Durrheim, 59–70. Cambridge: Cambridge University Press.

# INDEX

ableism, 4
Achen, Christopher, 184
Acheson, Kris, 4, 17, 52, 101, 111, 114, 141
ACT UP, 30
Adams, Tony, 31
affect, 18–19, 84, 106, 114, 199n2 (chap. 7)
Agamben, Giorgio, 19, 111–12, 115
agency
  autonomous, 61
  collective, 62–63, 85, 87, 186
  of deaf people, 4
  deliberative, 139
  and democracy, 5, 11, 17, 60, 94, 97, 187
  discursive, 74–76, 78
  erased, 15
  individual, 40, 45, 60, 62–63, 74
  material, 172, 175
  nonhuman, 172–73, 175
  narrow understanding of, 29
  participatory, 139
  political, 5, 11, 17, 19, 59, 89–90, 98, 112–14, 165–68, 174–75, 192–93
  and power, 19
  and racist oppression, 72
  relational, 160
  and representation, 160
  and sexuality, 87
  as truth and emancipation, 23
  as unfreedom and outness, 32
  as voice, 187, 192
agency-less, 22, 172
Alcoff, Linda, 67, 98, 154–55, 161–62
Alexander, Larry, 196n18
ambiguity, 29, 33, 50, 53, 64, 115, 120, 129, 131–34, 141, 147, 152–53, 158, 160, 192
amendment, constitutional, 133, 135
  first, 44–45, 52, 59, 196n3
  fifth, 49, 196n3
  ninth, 198n6 (chap. 5)
  nineteenth, 90
Anderson, José F., 49
Anker, Elisabeth, 173
apathy, political, 12, 141, 184, 188

apophasis, 34–36, 195n5 (chap. 1)
appropriated voice, 154
Arendt, Hannah, 1, 115–16, 119–20, 198n2 (chap. 5)
Aristotle, 1
Armijo, Enrique, 40, 59
Asenbaum, Hans, 33
Athanasiou, Athena, 2, 88, 95, 103–4, 110, 115, 155–56
Austin, J. L., 15
authorization, passive, 79, 131, 155, 158, 161
Ayala, Saray, 79–80

Bachrach, Peter, 19, 125
bad speech, 5, 80–81
Baratz, Morton, 19, 125
Bargu, Banu, 13, 17–18, 20, 111, 115
Barry, Brian, 2
Bartels, Larry, 184
Barthes, Roland, 16, 33, 192, 195n4 (chap. 1)
Bataille, George, 66
Batiste, Stephanie L,. 17
Batman, Michael E., 19
Beaumont, Peter, 197n1 (chap. 4)
Beausoleil, Emily, 60, 75, 115
Beck, Ulrich,183
Bejan, Teresa, M. 34, 70–71
Bell, Catherine, 94
Bennett, Jane, 173
Berger, John, 38
Bernal, Angélica Maria, 117
Bhaduri, Bhubaneswari, 14
Bickford, Susan, 21, 70, 75, 189
Big Mijo, 17, 195n6
Bindeman, Steven, 17
Black Lives Matter, 17, 68, 108–9, 117
blank vote. *See* vote, blank
Blasi, Vincent, 46, 48
Blocher, Joseph, 49, 52, 54, 57
Block de Behar, Lisa, 13
Bond, H. Lawrence, 196n6
Braaten, Carl A., 35
Brady, Henry E., 146
Brekhus, Wayne, 189

Brendese, P. J., 128–29
Brennan, Jason, 149–50
Brito Vieira, Mónica, 4, 141, 146, 153, 155, 173, 176, 178–80, 182–83
Brooks, Peter, 41
Brown, Mark, 199n4 (chap. 7)
Brown, Michael Jr., 108–9
Brown, Wendy, 5, 15, 20, 23–24, 26, 28–30, 32–33, 36–37
Brummett, Barry, 6
Butler, Judith, 17, 84, 104, 109, 114, 197n2 (chap. 3)

Cage, John, 54–59, 197n21
capacity, communicative, 7, 16, 18, 28, 37, 50–57, 65–67, 70, 84, 137–39, 145–48, 171–79
Carreras, Miguel, 151
Carson, Anne, 198n7 (chap. 4)
Carson, Rachel, 169–71, 184
Cavarero, Adriana, 92, 95, 140
Ceccarelli, Leah, 169
censorship, 25
    self-, 61–65
Chapman, Mary, 92, 95–96, 98
Chen, Alan K., 52, 54, 57
Chicot v. Canada, 49, 196n15
choice, 32, 34, 40, 62, 123, 125, 187–88
    democratic, 128
    electoral, 140, 147–52
    expressive, 45, 59
    free, 18, 42–43, 46
    lifestyle, 79
    and Miranda opinion, 40
    political, 3, 37, 67, 135, 142, 147–52
civility, 70, 73–74
claims-making, 155–56, 160, 162–64, 167–68, 171, 176–78, 183–84, 199n3 (chap. 6)
Clair, Robin, 15
clauses
    by law, 133, 181
    by sunset, 133, 198n7 (chap. 5)
Clinton, Hillary, 109
Cobussen, Marcel, 36, 38
Cochrane, Alasdair, 166
Cohen, Leonard, 137
Cohen, Stanley, 185
Coleman, Stephen, 147
Colley, Linda, 118
coming out, 20, 30–32
Connor, Steven, 11
Constable, Marianne, 42–43
Constant, Benjamin, 124

constituency, silent, 160
constructivism, and political representation, 22, 138, 153, 155, 160–64
Cook, Fay L., 145
counter-diction, 116
counter publics, 20
counter-subjectification, 20
counter-tales, 23
Cusa, Nicholas of, 196n6 (chap. 1)

Dahl, Robert A., 3, 138, 154
Dassonneville, Ruth, 151
Dauenhauer, Bernard, 6, 56, 120–21, 194
Davies, Stephen, 197n23
Davis, Anthony, 38–39
Davis, Ryan, 76
Decena, Carlos Ulises, 7, 31–32
denial, ecological, 182–86
Derrida, Jacques, 15, 122
Devenney, Mark, 162
Dewey, John, 17, 59
Dhawan, Nikita, 24
DiAngelo, Robin, 76–77
Dienstag, Joshua Foa, 166–67, 170
Disch, Lisa, 138, 146, 152–53, 162, 168–69, 173, 184, 199n5 (chap. 6)
disempowerment, 7, 18, 32
    See also empowerment
dissenters
    silent, 84
    vocal, 63
Dixon, Rosalind, 123–25, 129, 133–34
Dobson, Andrew, 166, 173
Dodd, Julian, 197n23
Dolar, Mladen, 92–93
Dolgert, Stefan, 165
domination, 15, 18, 29, 40–43, 47, 61, 71, 104
    and communicative capacity, 66
    and democracy, 47
    and empowerment, 20
    empowerment against, 20
    and exit, 71
    as imposition of will, 51, 104
    by others, 36
    and power, 42, 51, 104
    risk of, 15
    safeguard against, 41
    social, 14, 36, 51, 66
    structural, 51
    of women, 87
    See also non-domination; oppression; power

## INDEX

domination/resistance binary, 29
Donaldson, Sue, 167, 199n1 (chap. 7)
Donoso, Alfonso, 166–67, 173
Dovi, Suzanne, 16, 144
Doyle, Oran, 130, 198n3 (chap. 5)
Driscoll, Amanda, 150
Dryzek, John S., 167, 183
Du Bois, W. E. B., 99
Dufourmantelle, Anne, 36–37
Duncan, Patti, 34

Eckersley, Robyn, 166
Eddo-Lodge, Renni, 71–72, 75–76, 81, 197n1
Eisgruber, Christopher L., 134
Eliasoph, Nina, 6, 12
Elster, Jon, 63
Ely, John Hart, 135
emancipation, 18, 23, 26, 30, 32, 103
Emerson, Ralph Waldo, 97
empowerment, 5, 7, 12, 30, 40, 163
  citizen, 2, 40, 44
  against domination, 20
  and power, 193
  and silence, 5, 32, 113
  voice, 26, 30, 32, 139
  women's, 89
  *See also* disempowerment
Enroth, Henrik, 160
Esposito, Roberto, 181
exit, discursive, 51–52, 71–72, 81, 140, 147–48, 150–52

femininity, 91, 195n3 (chap. 1)
feminism, 87, 88–89
  silent protest tradition, 85
Ferguson, Kennan, 4–5, 93, 198n11
Ferguson, Michaele, 132
Ferguson protests, 67, 108–9
Festenstein, Matthew, 61, 70
Finnegan, Margaret, 92
Fiumara, Gemma Corradi, 68, 74–77, 189
Fleming, Sean, 176, 199n4 (chap. 7)
Foley, Michael, 134–35
Ford, Linda, 95
Fortner, Michael, 157
Fossen, Thomas, 146, 154–55
Foucault, Michel, 140
Frank, Jason, 21, 123
Franke, William, 35
Freeden, Michael, 4–5, 10–11, 15, 18, 124
freedom
  from, 5, 24, 33–34, 44, 46, 50, 152
  to, 5, 20, 24, 34, 40, 46, 48, 50–51, 62, 152, 192

Fricker, Miranda, 68–69
Friskics, Scott, 166–68
Fumagalli, Corrado, 78–79, 81
Fung, Archon, 12

gag rules, 120, 123, 125–26, 128–29
Garner, Robert, 166
Gauthier, X., 89
Gaventa, John, 125
Gerber, Megan, 108
Ginsburg, Tom, 123–25, 129, 133–34
Glenn, Cheryl, 6–7, 15
Glennon, Lynda, 15
Goffman, Erving, 61
Gonzales, X., 108
Goodin, Robert, 83, 178
Gray, Sean, 4–5, 16, 18, 52, 60, 113, 141–43, 193, 199nn1–2 (chap. 6)
Green, Jeffrey Edward, 2
Griffiths, Paul, 57
Guillaume, Xavier, 4, 6, 15, 43
Gündoğdu, Ayten, 182
Guzmán, Joshua Javier, 31

Haines, Christian, 103
Hall, Robert L., 45
Halley, Janet, 48
Hamilton, Lawrence, 34
Haraway, Donna, 172
Hardon, Anita, 8
Harris, Randy, 169
Havel, Václav, 47
Hawhee, Debra, 7, 171–72
Higginbotham, Evelyn Brooks, 100
Hill, Lisa, 149–50
Hill, Shonagh, 92, 149–50
Hirschman, Albert O., 71
Hobbes, Thomas, 69–70, 158, 173–76, 180–82, 199nn3–4 (chap. 7)
Hoekstra, Kinch, 71
Holmes, Stephen, 124, 126
Holpuch, Amanda, 197n1 (chap. 4)
homophobia, 25, 33
Honig, Bonnie, 72, 81, 120
hooks, bell, 32, 84, 88–89, 195n3 (chap. 1)
Hornsby, Jennifer, 67, 198n2 (chap. 4)
Horton, John, 61–62
Horwitz, Paul, 46
HUAC, 49
Huntington, Samuel, 3
Huxley, Aldous, 17

ignorance, pluralistic, 64
Ikuta, Jennie, C. 63

# INDEX

Inness, Julie, 196n8 (chap. 1)
involvement, displaced, 15, 138, 146, 153–54, 160, 164
Irigaray, Luce, 19
Irwin, Inez Haynes, 97

Jackson, John, 44
Jackson, Vicki C,. 130
Jakee, Keith, 151
Jaworski, Adam, 6–7, 140
Jefferson, Mark, 106
Johnson, Bobbie, 196n7 (chap. 1)
Johnson, Grace Nail, 99
Johnson, James Weldon, 99–102
Jung, Carl, 54
Jung, Theo, 3–4, 6, 13
Jungkunz, Vincent, 4–5, 34, 73, 76, 93

Ka'a'gee Tu First Nation, 49
Kahn, Douglas, 55–56
Kalamaras, George, 6
Kalin, Alan, 48
Kaltwasser, Cristóbal, 157
Kaminsky, Ilya, 4, 8–9, 195n4 (intro.)
Katz, Daniel, 64
Keenan, Alan, 131, 135
Keller, Catherine, 27, 35–36
Khatchadourian, Haig, 4
Kirkpatrick, Jennet, 81
Kostelanetz, Richard, 197n22
Kramer, Elizabeth, 38
Krause, Sharon, 18, 74, 78, 177
Kukla, Rebecca, 66–67
Kurzon, Dennis, 6, 66
Kymlicka, Will, 167

Laclau, Ernesto, 159
Langton, Rae, 67
Latour, Bruno, 172
Lawrence, Charles R., III, 80
Lear, Lea, 170
Leiter, Brian, 65, 80.81
Lepora, Chiara, 83
Lepoutre, Maxime, 82
LGBTQ, 31
LGBTQIA+, 36
Lichau, Karsten, 107
List, Christian, 176
Loevlie, Elisabeth, 159
logos, 92, 137, 139, 171
    devocalized, 92 (*see also* speech: unvocalized)
Loraux, Nicole, 105
Lorde, Audre, 88
Loughlin, Martin, 121, 124, 198n1 (chap. 5)

Luckyj, Christina, 93
Lukes, Steven, 19, 124

MacKenzie, Michael, 4, 19, 43, 76, 84, 189
Maitra, Ishani, 78–79, 89
majority, silent, 22, 82,107, 138 157–63, 199n4 (chap. 6)
Manza, Jeff, 145
Marcuse, Herbert, 64–65
Marjory Stoneman Douglas High School massacre, 108
Marion, Jean-Luc, 196n5 (chap. 10)
Markell, Patchen, 20, 113, 117, 146
Marres, Noortje, 173
masculinity, 29, 32
McCallum, E. L., 20
McDermott, Lydia, 95
McGowan, Mary Kate, 67, 81
McKim, Joel, 112
McNay, Lois, 12, 141, 161–62
Medina, José, 67–68, 73
Menely, Tobias, 7, 171–72, 199n2 (chap. 7)
Mercer, Kobena, 27
Merleau-Ponty, Maurice, 15, 17
Mill, John Stuart, 62–64, 70
Mills, Charles W., 72
minority, vocal, 82
Mitchell, Timothy, 173
Mitchell, W. J. T., 118
Montanaro, Laura, 153
mourning silence *See* silence: mourning
Mudde, Cas, 157
Muers, Rachel, 55, 103, 110–12, 114–16, 135, 159, 162
Myers, Ella, 59, 116–17, 191

NAACP (National Association for the Advancement of Colored People), 99–100, 103, 157
NAWSA (National American Woman Suffrage Association), 93, 99–100
Nancy, Jean-Luc, 17
Noelle-Neumann, Elisabeth, 64, 159
Nelson, Michael J., 150
neutrality, counterfeit, 128
Nixon, Richard, 157
non-domination, 5, 40, 50–51, 146
    *See also* domination; oppression; power
nonhuman constituencies, 165, 172–79, 181–87, 199n3 (chap. 7)
Norgaard, Kari Marie, 12, 185
NWP (National Woman's Party), 90, 93–94, 96
Nyhan, Brendan, 82

Ohmer, Sarah S., 17
Olson, Kevin, 139
opinion, legal
   Berghuis v. Thompkins, 196n6 (chap. 2)
   Chicot v. Canada, 49, 196n15
   Miranda v. Arizona, 21, 39–43, 196nn1–2 (chap. 2)
   Moran v. Burbine, 196n5 (chap. 2)
   Salinas v. Texas, 196n6 (chap. 2)
   Spence v. Washington, 53–54, 57, 197n19
   West Virginia State Board of Education v. Barnette, 44–48, 196nn9–14
   Wooley v. Maynard, 44, 196n9
oppression, 23–24, 26–27, 32, 66, 72, 88–89, 104, 144, 164, 187, 196n1 (chap. 2)
   *See also* domination; non-domination; power
ostracism, 63, 110

Pact of forgetting (Pacto del Olvido), 126–29
Panagia, David, 60
Pankhurst, Emmeline, 91
parrhesia, 17
pathology, 4, 74
Peirce, Charles Sanders, 170
personhood (legal), 31, 69, 99, 126, 175–76, 179, 181, 199n4 (chap. 7)
Pettit, Philip, 46, 50–51, 140, 176, 196n16
Petty, Sheila, 29
Philips, S. U., 16
Picard, Max, 1, 6, 16
Pitkin, Hannah, 22, 155, 160, 167
Plumwood, Val, 175, 181–83
pluralism, 138–39, 146, 161
pluralistic ignorance, 64
Plutarch, 198n7 (chap. 4)
Polanyi, Michael, 6–7
Polsby, Nelson, 138
Posel, Deborah, 8
Posner, Richard A. 123
power
   to act, 40, 64, 180–81
   and agency, 19
   among,, 114
   to do, 18, 20, 37, 72, 180–81
   of expression, 59
   to hold back, 187
   to influence, 193
   of interruption, 73
   to make claims, 176
   to make silence, 117
   negative, 11, 19, 42, 60, 126
   not to say, 42
   over, 18–20, 112–13, 117, 126, 136, 155, 177, 193
   of the political scene, 117
   positive, 60
   to say, 42, 66
   of silencing, 128
   of the speaker, 78
   of speech (*see* speech: power of)
   to, 112–14, 117, 155
   of tradition, 121
   of voice, 19, 91
   of voting, 137
   to with/hold, 19
   of the word, 118
   *See also* domination; non-domination; oppression
Purdy, Jedediah, 182

Quakerism and silence, 93–94, 116, 198n11

Rancière, Jacques, 27, 100
Ratcliffe, Krista, 6–7
Rawls, John, 70
Reifler, Jason, 82
Resina, Joan Ramon, 126
responsibility, 15, 77–80, 94, 105, 164, 175, 185, 188, 199n5 (chap. 6)
   *See also* silence: responsibility for
responsiveness, 19, 60, 72, 76, 137–38, 145–46, 148, 151–52, 154–55, 157, 160, 162–64, 172
Retallack, Joan, 59
Rich, Adrienne, 21, 86–88, 103, 162
Riggs, Marlon T., 23–27, 29–30, 195n1 (chap. 1)
right, 4, 14
   to anonymity, 33
   to association, 49
   to conscience, 47
   constitutional, 179, 198n6 (chap. 5)
   to exist, 181
   to exit, 152 (*see also* exit: discursive)
   to flourish, 176, 181
   and interests, 181
   to know, 169
   and nature, 181
   to opinion, 47
   to privacy, 33
   to religion, 47
   to secede, 130
   to silence (*see* silence: right to)
   to speech (*see* speech: right to)
   to thought, 47
   to vote, 90–91, 93, 96, 114, 140, 150, 158
   women's reproductive, 86

Roberts, Andrew, 44
Rollo, Toby, 4, 15–16, 49, 114, 139, 195n1 (intro.)
Romero, Javier, 167
Rosenblum, Nancy, 158
Runciman, David, 153, 161, 173, 178–80, 199n5 (chap. 7)

Sabl, Andrew, 154
Saldaña-Portillo, María, 159
Santino, Jack, 107
Saw, C. L., 57–58, 197n23
Saward, Michael, 153, 155, 160–61, 169, 173, 199n3 (chap. 6)
Schaap, Andrew, 43, 72
Schlosberg, David, 183
Schlozman, Kay, 146
Schröter, Melani, 2
Schwartzberg, Melissa, 160
Schweber, Howard, 154
Schweiger, Elisabeth, 15
Sciacca, Michele Frederico, 8, 76–77
Scott, James, C. 5
Scott, Susie, 10–12, 33, 187
Scudder, Mary, 72, 75
secession, 13, 130–31
Sedgwick, Eve, 31, 33
self-censorship, 61–65
Sells, Michael A., 35
Seymour, David M., 57–58, 197n23
Shiffrin, Seana, 46, 48
Shotwell, Alexis, 154
silence
    as absence, 1–3, 15–16, 34, 51, 54–57, 59, 83, 89, 92, 98, 101, 106, 114, 120–23, 133, 138–41, 145, 158, 162–63, 189, 191
    and abstention, 10, 11, 15, 140–43, 147–52
    accommodating, 79, 152
    and agency, 10, 12, 18–19, 116, 156, 160–61
    agentic, 5, 10–11, 18–19
    and anti-politics, 2, 3, 88, 139, 190–91
    as authorization, 79, 131, 161
    breaking, 20, 23–24, 33, 169
    and choice, 40–41, 51, 53, 60, 77, 84–85, 193, 196n4
    closeted, 31–33
    commissive, 10–13, 142, 150, 163, 191
    and conversation, 70–82, 91, 109, 125–26, 185, 189, 196n16
    deaf, deafblind, deafdisabled, 4
    and deafness, 4, 8–9, 195n3
    as deferral, 120, 123–29
    as democratic right, 143
    democracy-hindering, 3, 189
    democracy-making, 117, 119, 123–25
    and denial, 12, 20, 31, 35–36, 58, 63, 77, 93, 109, 128, 135, 143, 145
    and difference, 24, 30, 33, 60, 75, 87, 112, 146, 159, 175, 189
    and domination, 39–40, 43
    enacting, 153–57
    enfranchising, 147–52
    and empowerment, 5, 32, 113
    and equality, 2, 5, 21, 60, 69–70, 74–75, 190
    as expression, 6–7, 10, 13, 15, 17–18, 24, 32–37, 39, 41, 44–47, 57–59, 61, 64, 69, 71, 140, 145, 147, 150, 158, 163, 189
    as expressive freedom, 52–60
    and freedom: from, 5, 24, 33–34, 44, 46, 50, 152; to, 5, 20, 24, 34, 40, 46, 48, 50, 152
    as gesture, 17–18, 24, 35, 45, 74, 111, 114–15
    and inclusion, 4–5, 21, 54, 60, 166
    and inequality, 69, 75–76, 138
    insubordinate, 5
    as mediality, 112, 120–21
    mourning, 90, 100, 103–8, 110, 112, 197n2, 198n7 (chap. 4)
    and mutuality, 69, 75
    non-agentic, 10
    and non-domination, 5, 146
    as not saying, 16, 24, 34, 36–37, 45, 120, 131–33, 156
    omissive, 10–13, 29, 62, 118, 142, 150–52, 163, 188, 191
    and participation, 2–3, 43, 60, 71, 84, 138, 191, 196n16
    as participation, 2–4, 11, 43–44, 48, 60, 71, 84, 91, 138–39, 152, 191, 196n16
    as permission, 130–31
    as presence, 11, 15, 22, 39, 50, 55–56, 58, 83, 92, 101, 103–8, 111–12, 115, 139–41, 144, 152, 154, 156, 158–59, 162–63, 174, 191, 195n1 (intro.), 196n16
    and privacy, 37, 47, 48
    productive, 5, 20, 43, 112, 127
    reactive,, 5
    and reciprocity, 5, 19, 69–71, 74, 76, 111, 193
    as reflective nonparticipation, 43, 84, 152
    and representation, 4, 15, 22, 66, 96, 98, 101, 137–68, 170–72, 175–80

responsibility for, 15, 77–80, 94, 127–28, 139, 162, 188
right to, 20–21, 37, 39–50, 60–61, 63, 73, 77, 85, 143, 189, 196n3, 7, 8 (chap. 2)
as saying, 34–36, 76, 109, 111, 120, 133
as saying anew, 36
as saying away, 34–35
and secrecy, 3, 37
as signal, 7–8, 13–16, 18, 43, 53, 103, 137, 141–48, 156, 158, 163, 168–71, 192
spiral of, 63, 159
and sublime, democratic, 99–102
and truth, 62–63, 65, 116, 143
uncivil, 70–73
and unrepresentability, 135
as unsaying, 24, 34–37, 109, 191, 193
and voice, 92–93, 95–98, 146–48, 158–59, 192
'white,' 76–78, 109
as withdrawal, 11, 46–49, 63, 69, 71–73, 75, 77, 120, 188, 191
world-building, 116
world-making, 3, 89
*See also* silencing; speech; voice
silencing
power of, 128
self-silencing, 19–21, 63–64, 69–71, 74–76, 126
as speech effect, 4, 28, 34, 64–66, 96–97, 101, 108–10, 115, 140–41, 153, 159–63, 187
as structural injustice, 65–69, 188
systemic, 10, 21, 66–69, 77, 119
tactical, 7, 21, 78
*See also* silence; speech; voice
silent constituency, 160
silent dissenters, 84
silent majority. *See* majority: silent
silent Parade, 89–90, 99, 101–4, 114, 117
Silent Sentinels, 91, 93–98, 100, 113–14, 98n3 (chap. 4)
*Silent Spring*. *See* Carson, Rachel
silent vigils. *See* vigils, silent
Simmel, Georg, 37, 48
Simpson, Robert, 82
Singh, Shane P., 150–51
Skerker, Michael, 39
snapping (Snap Rap) as unsaying, 29
Solon, 198n7 (chap. 4)
Sontag, Susan, 159
Southard, Belinda A. Stillion, 94, 198n3 (chap. 4)
speech
and agency, 10, 69, 162

bad, 5, 80–81
counter, 23, 80–83
power of, 4, 19, 21, 70, 77–78, 118, 192–93
and responsibility, 15
right to, 2, 21, 25, 39–51, 60–61, 67–69, 73–74, 85, 93, 140
unvocalized, 101
*See also* silence; silencing; voice
spiral of silence, 63, 159
Spivak, Gayatri, 14, 162
Stevens, Doris, 91
Stone, Christopher, 170, 176, 181
Stow, Simon, 105
Strauss, Mary, 42, 196n8
subjectification. *See* counter-subjectification
Suisman, David, 101
Sun, Guang-Zhen, 151
Sunstein, Cass, 85, 118, 124, 130, 132
Superti, Chiara, 149
Sussman, A., 93

tactical silencing, 7, 21, 78
Tanasoca, Ana, 85
Thaler, Mathias, 182–84
Thompson, Dennis, 194
three-fifths compromise, 126, 198n4 (chap. 5)
Tocqueville, Alexis de, 63–64, 79, 158, 161
toleration, indiscriminate, 65
Toop, David, 56
Tribe, Laurence H., 111, 119, 135, 198n1
Trinh, T. Minh-ha, 33
truth, 40, 102
Tuhkanen, Mikko, 20
Tulis, Jeffrey K., 96–97
Tushnet, Mark V., 52, 54, 57

uncivility. *See* civility
unresponsiveness, 72, 76
unvocalized speech. *See* logos: devocalized; speech: unvocalized
unvoicing, 109, 137, 187

Vasilyeva, Nadya, 79–80
Véliz, Carissa, 36–37
ventriloquism, of nature, 105, 167–68, 176, 181
Verba, Sidney, 146
Versteeg, Mila, 135
victimhood, 18
vigils, silent, 89, 96, 102–4, 106, 110, 114–15
Villiers, Nicholas de, 32–33

vocal dissenters, 63
vocal minority, 82
vocalization, 2, 12, 17, 28, 45, 63, 73–74, 88, 91–92, 99, 101, 116, 139–40, 145–47, 159, 163, 171, 199n2 (chap. 7)
Vogel, Steven, 166–67,
voice, 3–5, 15–16, 19, 22, 28, 68, 73, 79, 106, 163–64, 171, 191–93
   appropriated, 154
   authorial, 58
   of Black gay community, 25–26
   and democracy, 95–101, 137, 144–46, 161, 187–88
   empowering, 26
   equal, 69
   and feminism, 88–89
   and free speech, 50, 62, 66, 88–89, 109, 113
   and listening, 116
   marginalized, 74
   and non-human creatures, 171–72
   nonverbal, 29
   political, 3, 22, 47, 50–51, 67, 88–92, 95–100, 138–40, 190
   and power, 125, 138–39
   and representation, 137, 144–46, 150, 153–54, 156, 178
   and social hierarchy, 66

*See also* silence; silencing; speech
voiceless, 4, 22, 88, 92, 139
vote, blank, 138, 140, 143, 147–50, 152
voting, compulsory, 138, 150–52, 199n1

Wagner, Roi, 66
Warren, Mark, 40–41, 71, 139, 152
Warren Court, 40–41
Weber, Max, 193
Weis, Lael K., 179
West, Caroline, 27
West Virginia State Board of Education v. Barnette, 44–48, 196nn9–14
'white silence,' 76–78, 109
Whitehouse, Andrew, 171
Wicomb, Zoë, 28
Wilson, Woodrow, 91, 94–98, 198n3 (chap. 4)
Wolfson, Elliot R,. 34
Women in Black, 89–90, 102–7, 110–12, 114, 156, 198nn4–6, 198n8 (chap. 4)
womanness, 195n3 (chap. 1)

Young, Iris Marion, 53, 66, 71, 74, 76, 162, 172, 199n1 (conclusion)

Zerilli, Linda, 70
Zerubavel, Eviatar, 2, 12, 83

Other books in the series:

Karen Tracy, *Challenges of Ordinary Democracy: A Case Study in Deliberation and Dissent* / Volume 1

Samuel McCormick, *Letters to Power: Public Advocacy Without Public Intellectuals* /Volume 2

Christian Kock and Lisa S. Villadsen, eds., *Rhetorical Citizenship and Public Deliberation* / Volume 3

Jay P. Childers, *The Evolving Citizen: American Youth and the Changing Norms of Democratic Engagement* / Volume 4

Dave Tell, *Confessional Crises and Cultural Politics in Twentieth-Century America* / Volume 5

David Boromisza-Habashi, *Speaking Hatefully: Culture, Communication, and Political Action in Hungary* / Volume 6

Arabella Lyon, *Deliberative Acts: Democracy, Rhetoric, and Rights* / Volume 7

Lyn Carson, John Gastil, Janette Hartz-Karp, and Ron Lubensky, eds., *The Australian Citizens' Parliament and the Future of Deliberative Democracy* / Volume 8

Christa J. Olson, *Constitutive Visions: Indigeneity and Commonplaces of National Identity in Republican Ecuador* / Volume 9

Damien Smith Pfister, *Networked Media, Networked Rhetorics: Attention and Deliberation in the Early Blogosphere* / Volume 10

Katherine Elizabeth Mack, *From Apartheid to Democracy: Deliberating Truth and Reconciliation in South Africa* / Volume 11

Mary E. Stuckey, *Voting Deliberatively: FDR and the 1936 Presidential Campaign* / Volume 12

Robert Asen, *Democracy, Deliberation, and Education* / Volume 13

Shawn J. Parry-Giles and David S. Kaufer, *Memories of Lincoln and the Splintering of American Political Thought* / Volume 14

J. Michael Hogan, Jessica A. Kurr, Michael J. Bergmaier, and Jeremy D. Johnson, eds., *Speech and Debate as Civic Education* / Volume 15

Angela G. Ray and Paul Stob, eds., *Thinking Together: Lecturing, Learning, and Difference in the Long Nineteenth Century* / Volume 16

Sharon E. Jarvis and Soo-Hye Han, *Votes That Count and Voters Who Don't: How Journalists Sideline Electoral Participation (Without Even Knowing It)* / Volume 17

Belinda Stillion Southard, *How to Belong: Women's Agency in a Transnational World* / Volume 18

Melanie Loehwing, *Homeless Advocacy and the Rhetorical Construction of the Civic Home* / Volume 19

Kristy Maddux, *Practicing Citizenship: Women's Rhetoric at the 1893 Chicago World's Fair* / Volume 20

Craig Rood, *After Gun Violence: Deliberation and Memory in an Age of Political Gridlock* / Volume 21

Nathan Crick, *Dewey for a New Age of Fascism: Teaching Democratic Habits* / Volume 22

William Keith and Robert Danisch, *Beyond Civility: The Competing Obligations of Citizenship* / Volume 23

Lisa A. Flores, *Deportable and Disposable: Public Rhetoric and the Making of the "Illegal" Immigrant* / Volume 24

Adriana Angel, Michael L. Butterworth, and Nancy R. Gómez, eds., *Rhetorics of Democracy in the Americas* / Volume 25

Robert Asen, *School Choice and the Betrayal of Democracy: How Market-Based Education Reform Fails Our Communities* / Volume 26

Stephanie R. Larson, *What It Feels Like: Visceral Rhetoric and the Politics of Rape Culture* / Volume 27

Billie Murray, *Combating Hate: A Framework for Direct Action* / Volume 28

David A. Frank and Franics J. Mootz III, eds., *The Rhetoric of Judging Well: The Conflicted Legacy of Justice Anthony M. Kennedy* / Volume 29

Kristian Bjørkdahl, ed., *The Problematic Public: Lippman, Dewey, and Democracy in the Twenty-First Century* / Volume 30

Ekaterina V. Haskins, *Remembering the War, Forgetting the Terror: Appeals to Family Memory in Putin's Russia* / Volume 31

Carolyn D. Commer, *Championing a Public Good: A Call to Advocate for Higher Education* / Volume 32

Derek G. Handley, *Struggle for the City: Citizenship and Resistance in the Black Freedom Movement* / Volume 33

José G. Izaguirre III, *Becoming La Raza: Negotiating Race in the Chican@ Movement(s)* / Volume 34